D0241432

Published in 2002 by
Laurence King Publishing Ltd
71 Great Russell Street
London WC1B 3BP
Tel: + 44 20 7430 8850
Fax: + 44 20 7430 8880
enquiries@laurenceking.co.uk
www.laurenceking.co.uk



A catalogue record for this book is available from the British Library.

ISBN 1 85669 305 8

Printed in China

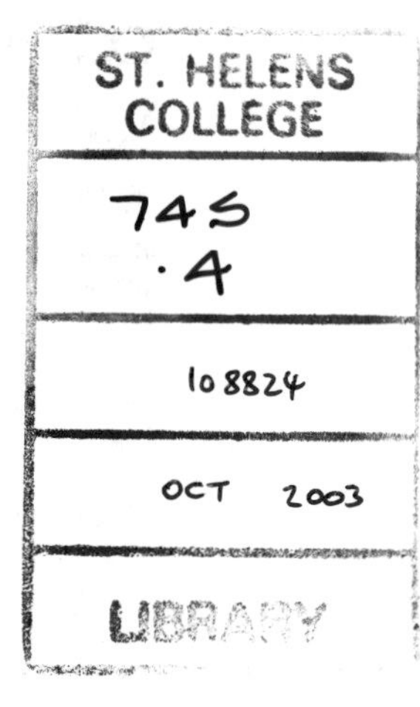

# CREATIVE ISLAND

## INSPIRED DESIGN FROM GREAT BRITAIN

JOHN SORRELL

**Acknowledgements**

Special thanks to Adriana Paice for project management and research; Nick Skeens for the interviews; Quentin Newark at Atelier Works and Glenn Howard at Untitled for design; Philippa Richards and Hannah Ford for research; Frances Sorrell for her ideas, advice, support and encouragement; and all the designers who created the work shown in this book.

**To Frances**

# CREATIVE ISLAND

**John Sorrell:** "The designers who work within the shores of this island come not just from the UK but from all over the world. They thrive in a creative climate that has been described as 'the design studio of the world'. What makes it such a fertile environment for creativity? Why is it that such great work is produced across not just one or two design disciplines but right across all of them, from architecture to fashion, graphics to furniture, interior to products, engineering to new media, and many more?

"This book began in my head when I was chairman of the UK Design Council and was continually asked to explain the answers to these questions as well as to give examples of what I was talking about. This book is packed full of such examples. Some of the work has won awards, some has had little exposure, some is brand new. I like all of it and admire the people who did it. They are, of course, very different as individuals but, I believe, remarkably similar in the way they think when creating new ideas and solving problems.

"I believe that the strength of design here grows from the way in which one discipline informs another. It's a kind of 'Greenhouse Effect', that doesn't just propagate one particular breed of creativity – it cross-fertilizes. It starts in our great design colleges and continues in design businesses that range from one person to hundreds in size.

"A new wave of design innovation is fuelling a creative renaissance in the UK. We talk about creativity now in every aspect of life. Businesses large and small are actively embracing creativity and seeking creative people. Design is at the forefront of that creative renaissance, partly because, of course, it is a perfect marriage of creative thinking applied to business problems.

"I've gathered the examples of work in this book in a series of themes. It starts with *Reflections* – which is about how people are developing great work from a heritage of design tradition. For example, how Aston Martin is still creating wonderful new cars by drawing on its rich tradition of design, and Burberry is reinventing itself by design. At the other end of the book – *Projections* – I look at work that hasn't happened yet. Designers' ideas. Visionary ideas for new buildings, products and interactivity. These two contrasting themes – one area seeking inspiration from heritage, the other looking forward – provide the two ends of the UK design spectrum.

"In between I've explored another eight themes, each of which highlights a specific aspect of British design. They give it its subtle identity and flavour. For example, *Renewal*, exemplified by the Eden Project or the Tate's new identity. And just in case we take ourselves too seriously, it's no accident that this theme sits just before *Subversion*. For me, subversion is quintessentially British. It's all about our island's sense of humour, about making fun of ourselves and the system. Take a look at Paul Smith's navy-blue suit with a difference or TBWA's ads for Sony Playstation.

"This book presents and explores the relationships between what on the surface seem to be completely different things. It tries to indicate the extraordinary diversity that exists across the design disciplines, and the connections between them: how the minds of our cutting edge designers seem to be in tune. Some might say: ''twas ever thus'. Britain has always been incredibly inventive. But like all things, genius comes in phases, in waves. And the evidence is that those waves are crashing on Britain's shores once more.

"Creativity has never been more important to a nation. It is the key to economic and social survival and prosperity in this rapidly changing world. It inspires and changes things for the better and improves quality of life. This book of inspired design from Great Britain aims to give us a glance inside the mind of this creative island".

**118**
liquescence, liquifaction, flux, fusion, wet, deliquescence, thaw, molten, runny, flow, curvaceous

# FLUIDITY

**138**
accuracy, truth, rightness, exactitude, meticulous, rigour, finite, hi-fi, dead-on, unerring, punctual, right, infallible, fastidious, fair dinkum

# PRECISION

**158**
translucent, hyaline, crystalline, see-through, pellucid, transpicuous, diaphanous, revealing, naked, sheer, nude, exposed, honest

# TRANSPARENCY

**178**
symbol, myth, statement, big, enormous, grand, great, vast, gigantic, immensity, magnificent, majestic, spacious, mighty, eminent, abundance

# MONUMENTALITY

**200**
predictions, casting, forecasting, overhang, jut, forewarning, prophecy, prognosis, foresight, prospectus, prospect, protrusion, future projects

# PROJECTIONS

# REFLECTIONS

# ASTON MARTIN V12 VANQUISH

*Ian Callum was born in Scotland in 1954. He studied industrial design at the Glasgow School of Art, and automobile design at the Royal College of Art. Ford recruited him in 1978. He has worked on interior and exterior design for the Fiesta, the Mondeo, the Ford RS200 mid-engined sports car, and the Escort RS Cosworth. He designed the award-winning DB7, the most popular and successful Aston Martin model of all time. He is now Jaguar's director of design. Inspired by his predecessors, his work is an inspiration to future generations.*

**Ian Callum:** "Is it beautiful? Well, it's certainly got a lot of presence. It's got an edge of agitation about it and that was all quite deliberate. It has gravitas and energy. The way it sits solid to the road and looks like it's going to leap forward at any moment. It's got momentum tied up in the tensions of its design.

"That design was intuitive. We only had one sketch before we started, and I figured if I could capture the sketch's momentum in the final design, then I knew it would work. The whole project was about realizing that early sketch.

"There's a line that comes from the very tip of the grille – the Aston line – and runs right up to the A pillar [the windscreen front pillar]. The line moves from negative into a positive and back into a negative. It kisses the bumper on the front wing and then spins back over the surface to create the bonnet's structure before reaching the A pillar. The highlights on that line were immaculately executed and it took a long time to get that right. It started to develop when I realized I had to run the fender into the bonnet. I then knew I had to get that line to run from the front to the back, over the whole bonnet. But it was defining the translation on the way that fascinated me most.

"The overall effect is that you know there's something there, but it's just not that apparent. The car is full of things like that, actually. For example, at the rear, the way the line snaps up, coming vertically up the car and whooshing back in a pretty determined manner – it creates movement and threat. And the 'surface tension' of the bonnet – it's like skin under the pressure of powerful muscle. It gives a feeling of controlled, sensual power. And if you look at the bonnet's 'power bulge', you can see the way the main surface of the bonnet runs through a slight negative curve and up onto the bulge itself. Now that's very hard to make out of aluminium. But it's worth it, because in certain lights you get a slight shadowing that emulates the nostrils of the old Aston – a hint of a hard-breathing, muscular powerful animal.

"Form follows function – hmmm! In the case of sports cars, sometimes the form *is* the function. How it looks is part of what it does and what it's about. It's an exotic car, and how do you make something exotic? You compromise in some areas so that you can have excess in others. The most difficult problem was fitting in the driver and passengers and making room for the engine. Large engines mean large emissions and large catalysts. But the engineers were absolutely superb. It's all very tight.

"I was right on the edge of reason and sometimes I had to push hard to convince the engineers that what I was suggesting was a) possible and b) worth doing. But I'm quite pragmatic. If an engineer I respect says: 'Listen, mate: this isn't going to work!' I'll find an alternative. But they were a good team and they didn't really flinch – too much.

"I think the Vanquish is a lot more aggressive than the famous 'James Bond' car, the DB5. It's probably more suited to the harsher modern world than the more genteel and debonair world of the '60s. Probably better for the modern James Bond. But the clearest reflection of the old car is in the grille – it has a sort of contented, knowing, slightly arrogant grin.

"The Vanquish is the best thing I've ever done. And I suspect it will always be my favourite."

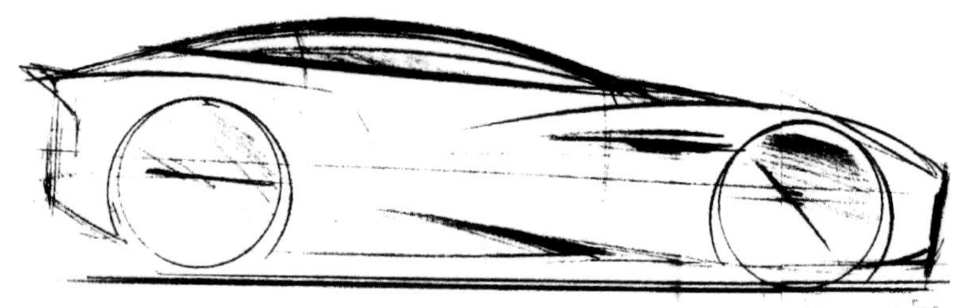

# CONNOLLY TOOL-KIT

*Connolly is famous for its car leather. The idea was to branch out into top-quality leather products that were more than just expensive motoring accessories. And the firm chose top designers to help it do just that. Sebastian Conran is creative director of Conran & Partners, a 70-strong design and architecture practice responsible for providing the creative vision for Conran Group. This also includes Conran Shops and Conran Restaurants. Sebastian trained at Central School of Design in 1974 and has gained a reputation for simplicity and mechanical ingenuity. The man who gave the Sex Pistols their first booking and designed The Clash's "corporate" identity (e.g. their record covers and posters) then went on to do design work for a whole host of companies and products, ranging from Bodum kettles to Concorde interiors.*

Sebastian Conran:

"Some 40 years ago, when my dad was still with my mother, we had a leaky pipe at home and the plumber came. No big deal, except, like Mary Poppins, he had a magic bag. He carried it in and laid it open on the floor. It wasn't a bag anymore; it was a circle of leather, with a couple of handles on each side. And on it, neatly laid out, were all his tools. I can't have been more than four at the time, but it really stuck with me.

"After that I developed a bit of a love affair with tools. Especially the French Facom tools. Top quality – joi d'artisan! The lovely slanting red handles on the hammers. Tools with style. I also had a love affair with cars. I knew all about Connolly leather. Then I heard about the Connolly shop. It's the most fantastic shop. I went in to buy something – I came out with a £40 knitted tie – the cheapest thing there. The man said: 'We could trim your car out in leather.' 'What, my little Fiat?' '£800.' 'Fair enough.' After that they came back to me, asking: 'Would you like to design us some motor accessories?' 'Yes please!' I went to their factory. It was decorated with the original illustrations by William Heath Robinson – another passion of mine. It was all a perfect fit.

"I don't own a kit myself. I think the design fee was less than the cost of the product! Well, we've just done the interior of Concorde, and I don't have one of them, either..."

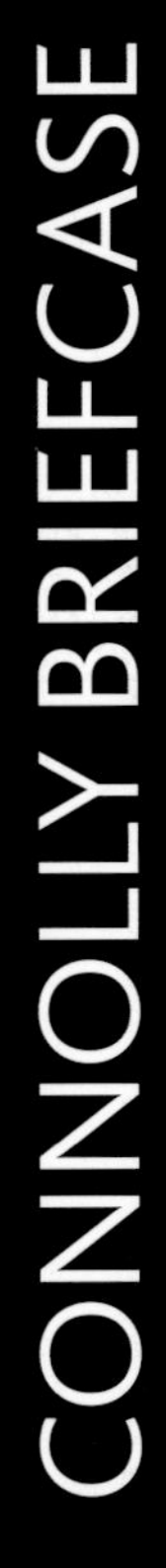


*Richard Seymour and Dick Powell of Seymour Powell are famous for taking products that have been designed to death and then reinventing them. They achieved this in a simple, beautiful and practical way with the Connolly briefcase. Famous now for their* Designs on Your… *Channel 4 TV series, in which they redesigned the loo, car and bra, their clients include Nokia, Dell, Yamaha, Casio, Jaguar and BMW. Famous products include Casio 'Baby G' Watches, the Tefal 'Classic' Toaster, and the first-ever cordless kettle, the Tefal Freeline.*

Richard Seymour:
"Connolly wanted to create some high notes, goods that were beautiful quality, but that were also actually affordable. Something that you or I could say: 'Yes, that is beautiful and practical, and if I really want it, I can afford it.'

"We took a practical approach. We'd not done a briefcase before. We wanted to make something expressively beautiful but which really worked. We looked at leather from new angles, and we began to see it as a fantastic engineering material. It's strong, it's supple, it's flexible, it gets better the more you use it, it smells wonderful…"

Dick Powell:
"And then we thought about the user. When you buy an attaché case, you want the thing you see in the shop – you don't want some bulging monstrosity. So we asked: how best can you keep the shape as it fills? And then we thought of Wheatstone, famous for developing the concertina, for producing all those wonderful billows. We now had a solution that was slim and beautiful and which would, however much you put in it, always be the minimum size it could possibly be. As soon as you removed bulky contents, it would revert to its original shape. We introduced magnetic catches into the base. You're never aware of them, of course, but they hold the bottom of the case together. They part as the case fills up, but attract back to each other as soon as the case is emptier.

"And I love the handle – it has the most divine handshake…"

# BURBERRY PRORSUM COLLECTION

*Thomas Burberry's 19th-century tale of the invention of waterproof gabardine reflects many stories within this book – most from more than a century later. The story goes: he met a shepherd near Basingstoke, Hampshire, and remarked on the way his smock threw off the rain. The shepherd reckoned it was down to picking his sheep up to put them in the dip – he thought the smock had absorbed some oily substance from the wool. Burberry thought about this idea and finally came up with a method of waterproofing that he could apply to yarn – it became famous as gabardine. Now a new design revolution is happening at Burberry, under the direction of Christopher Bailey.*

**Christopher Bailey:** "Thomas Burberry used to say: 'Burberry clothing is a cover as nature intended.' Even now, natural feel and flow are a vital part of the dynamics in our clothes. Burberry also said: 'Freedom is found in subtle ways without altering the appearance or character of the garment'.

"These two statements were foremost as we sought to reinvigorate this great British brand. Over the last three years, our design team has embraced our predecessor's ethos with an approach that unites functionality with an aesthetic that is clean and modern. By returning to the Burberry archives for inspiration, we have reinterpreted the classics with ingenious cuts and exclusive fabrics.

"This whole endeavour has been to show a new generation what this classic brand is all about. And with the emphasis on quality of luxury in high fashion, a new generation is now discovering Burberry as they seek out the authentics, the brands with a serious track record.

"Freedom is core to our designs – a sense of space and sophistication. It goes naturally with the outdoor image. There's a finely cut ruggedness, fabric innovation and strength in the designs that harks back to the Antarctic exhibitions Burberry clothed, but sits well in the brimming style of the city. It was at the heart of Burberry's philosophy. Tough but stylish exteriors, concealing a beautiful, almost secret complexity."

THE TIELOCKEN
"This coat is so comfortable that I shall be sorry when it is worn out. It is the best protection against wind, snow and rain that I have ever met."—H.S.
Illustrated Naval or Military Catalogues Post Free
Officers' Complete Kits in 2 to 4 Days or Ready for Use
The Severest Test
that a Weatherproof can undergo is a campaign, involving exposure to every kind of weather for months on end, and it is under such conditions that THE TIELOCKEN BURBERRY proves itself "the most effectual safeguard ever invented."
BURBERRYS Haymarket LONDON
8 & 10 Boul. Malesherbes PARIS; and Provincial Agents

# BURBERRY LAUNCH PARTY INVITATION

*What's an invitation card doing in this book? Hardly a serious example of design! But this is more than just an award-winning visual trick. Andy Bone's idea, drawing on our familiarity with the topological layout of underground maps, provided an unlooked-for but most welcome resolution to Burberry's re-branding exercise. The card captured the company's modernity while reflecting its traditions through the use of the check grid.*

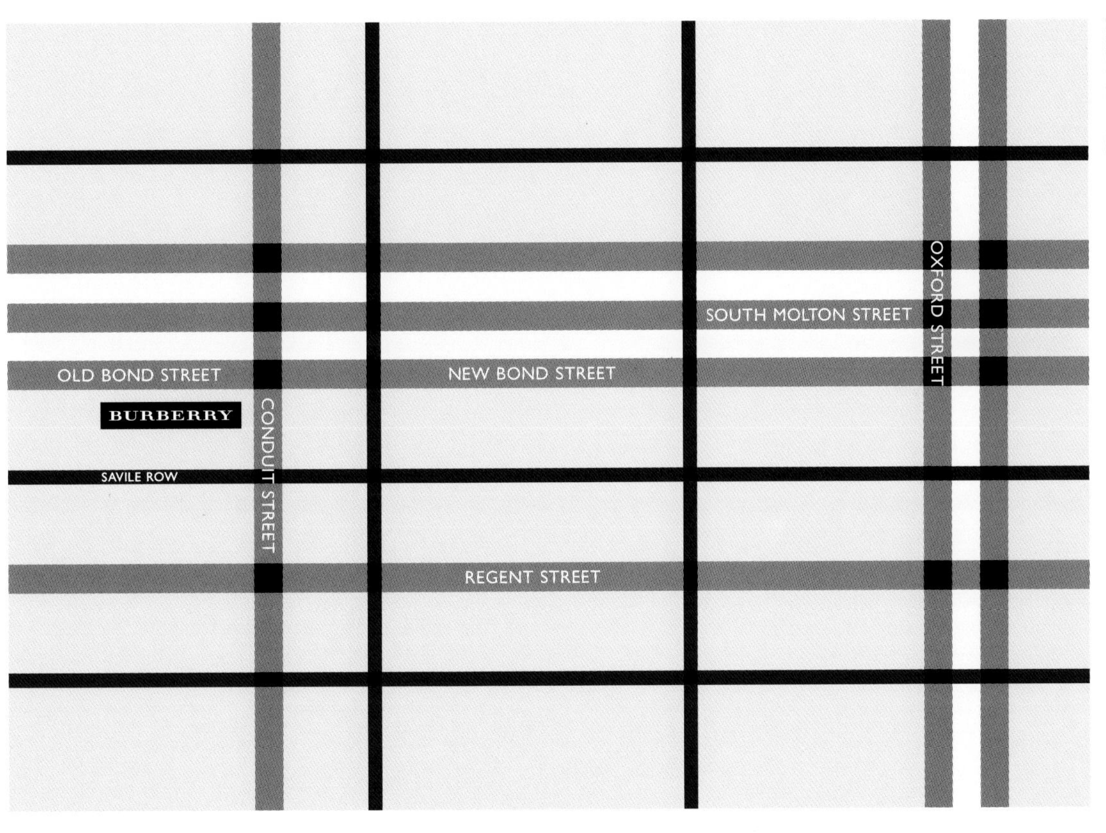


**Andy Bone:** "This is a good example of an idea that just arrived and clicked. It came to me in a London taxi-cab on the way back from a Burberry meeting. We'd been discussing the relaunch brochure. Burberry was moving to a store in New Bond Street. That in itself was a statement of Burberry's move towards embracing a contemporary image. The traditional image of outdoor-quality raincoats, typified by the supply of weatherproof clothing to Scott's tragic Antarctic expedition, was in need of modernization. Now it was going for a younger, hipper market, and the advertising revolved around young partying aristocrats. We had created the 'checkbook' – a brochure, the title of which was a pun on the famous Burberry check, illustrated with images of London.

"It suddenly occurred to me that the 'check' pun could work visually. We could use it to represent a street map, illustrating Burberry's literal repositioning. I thought: 'This would make a great invitation and postcard. A street map, made up of the Burberry check, showing how the company had moved into the intersection of traditional and contemporary fashion, on the crossroads around Old Bond Street, New Bond Street, Conduit Street and Savile Row. A visual representation of the move. A working map, and a symbol! Everybody in the industry knows the names – they are all redolent of the fashion industry. A relocation. A new grid reference.'

"Well, it wasn't an answer to a brief, it was just my idea, wonderfully executed by my team. You have to have a very good relationship with the client to push through an idea like this. The idea was also used on letterhead and press material."

*The current* Economist *advertising campaign has been running since October 1988. Now it's the job at Abbott Mead Vickers BBDO that everyone wants a part of. David Abbott and graphic artist Ron Brown created the first executions.*

**David Abbott:** "When we were first offered the business, we actually contemplated turning it down. Media accounts can be troublesome. So we nearly turned down a prize. But it was difficult in the early days. I was writing long copy ads and they had to be cleared by a list of about 20 journalists, all of whom understandably considered themselves good copy writers themselves. It could take ages to get clearance.

"Thinking about this problem, I noticed that the magazine's masthead logo was shaped roughly in the same proportions as a 48-sheet poster. I said to Ron: 'Why don't we recommend going outdoors, onto posters?' Everything flowed from that.

"The new campaign was conceived back in the thrusting, ambitious '80s. Our research said people read *The Economist* to give them an advantage over non-readers. It was a pretty simplistic proposition: 'read this and be successful'. We had to find a way to say that laterally rather than literally.

"The first one read: 'I never read *The Economist*.' This I qualified with the byline: 'Management Trainee, aged 42'. Well, of course, the point was this character was training for a management position at 42 precisely because he hadn't been reading *The Economist* regularly.

"By the time we got to the more caring '90s the message became less about securing the corner office. It was more 'read it and be informed; don't get embarrassed by your ignorance.' One line I remember was: 'Would you like to sit next to you at dinner?'

"We weren't always politically correct. I remember one which went something like: 'If you're a reader, ask your chauffeur to hoot your horn as you pass this poster.' And once we put a poster on the roof of some London buses. It read: 'To all our readers in high office.'

"The one I liked best? 'It's lonely at the top, but at least there's something to read.' The beauty of it now is that we don't even have to name the magazine. We've claimed red. You can recognise an *Economist* ad long before you can read it."

**Ron Brown:** "Everyone at the agency wants to work on it, to get at least one or two of the executions onto their CVs.

"When Richard Foster and John Horton took over the job they broke all the rules. They came up with a simple graphic idea. It was the title of the magazine in a red square and just a keyhole in the middle of the page. As if somehow the magazine gave you a secret advantage, like you could see things you shouldn't and hear things you mustn't. It was an award-winning execution.

"And it was liberating. Now we could use visual jokes. The campaign seemed to be getting simpler and smarter. Until it arrived at the piece you see here – the red poster with a bit of jigsaw missing. The idea being '*The Economist* will provide the missing piece.'

"But it can cause embarrassment when people don't get the jokes. I remember one which read:

'Could you be
be more alert?'

"Well, that was shown to a senior partner (who shall remain nameless) and he said: 'Yes, not bad...' But we knew he didn't get it. It was quite embarrassing..."

Would you like to sit
next to you at dinner?

The Economist

*The Great Court at the heart of the British Museum was one of London's long-lost spaces. The centrally located British Library round reading room began to be surrounded by buildings to house the ever-increasing collection of books. The reading room has been the inspiration to some of the world's greatest writers and thinkers – Marx, Lenin, Trotsky, Kipling, Forster, Woolf, Wilde, Yeats, Hardy, Shaw and Mahatma Gandhi among them. But with the British Library moving to a new site, Foster and Partners had a sacred task: to create a modern place that paid homage to the old.*

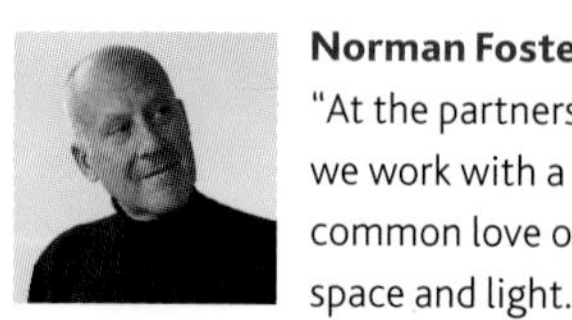

**Norman Foster:** "At the partnership we work with a common love of space and light. We believe in transparency and accessibility, in breaking down the social barriers. The roof of the Great Court at the British Museum is about just that. It's now a meeting place in a wonderful outside space. It exists, in its own right, independent of the museum's opening hours.

"Any space can be tuned in a variety of ways. Our starting-point is often accessibility and openness, and from that liberating launch pad, we love to push the boundaries. If there is a Foster personality in the buildings and projects we create, it arises from these passions."

**Spencer de Grey:** "We've also developed a philosophy for intervention in historic buildings. We aim to create a balanced contrast between the existing historical building and new interventions in a contemporary architectural idiom. In short, to make the new reflect the old to best advantage. There's a strong rectilinear geometry in the original façade, and we wanted to create a complete contrast with the new roof, but a contrast that showed respect for the old.

"We demolished the bookstores that surrounded the round reading room and revealed a wonderful courtyard. Above, we wanted to do something visual that was completely different. It had to be as delicate as possible. We conceived a glass roof that literally floats above you like a veil, so that when you sit in the courtyard you feel like you are outside, but yet you are warm – as if you were in a Mediterranean piazza.

"We were always very anxious to avoid any visible means of vertical support for the roof. It was a huge technical challenge. The existing façade was strong enough to take the pure vertical load, but it couldn't take any horizontal load. This was because the Egyptian Galleries run the full length of the façade without a single cross-wall, so there was no lateral resistance. We solved this with a sliding joint between the roof and the façade which translated horizontal load into vertical. It is about working *with* the building, not against it.

"One of the most stimulating moments was when we took away the 600 props supporting the roof while we built it. It dropped 150mm in height, and spread 90mm laterally as it settled on the sliding bearings. The sliding joints allow the roof to move naturally, responding to changes in temperature and, say, the weight of snow.

"What am I most proud of? Well, the whole thing. The delicacy of the roof, and the quality of the natural light, the space being so uncluttered. The quality, the space and the light give me huge pleasure. I'm rather glad it's something I'll leave behind me.

"To me, a public historic building hasn't succeeded unless it excites people. It should have an impact. It should make them say: 'wow!'"

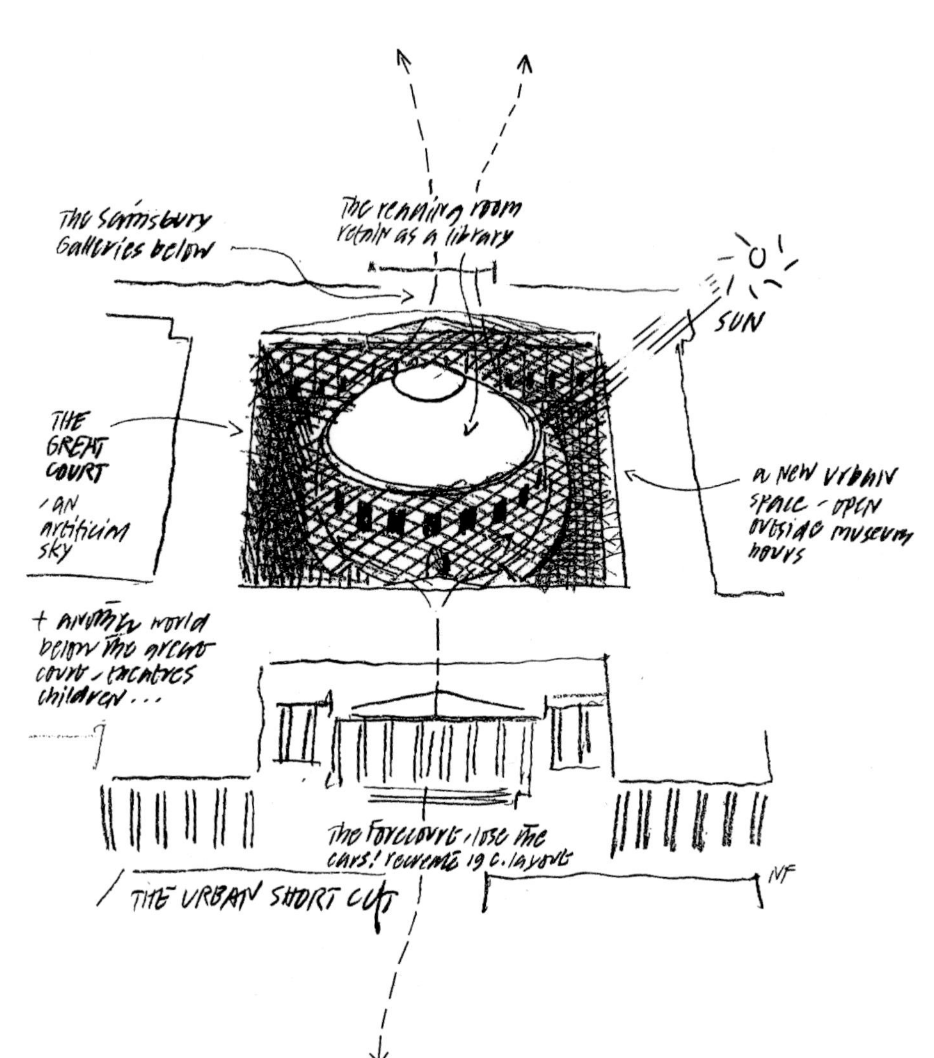

and let thy feet
millenniums hence
be set in midst of knowledge

# POLYPROPYLENE CHAIR

*This must surely be the most successful and ubiquitous modern chair design in the world. It has become an icon of contemporary furniture. Made and marketed by Hille, this simple, smart, comfortable, tough, good-looking chair has penetrated every country in the world, turning up in village halls, schools and meeting rooms from Armenia to Zimbabwe. It was born in the 1950s and first hit the market in 1962. It was an instant hit for Hille. Its secret lay in its ease of manufacture, its comfort, its range of colours and its stackability. It was given a second coming over the millennium by Tom Dixon at Habitat, in the company's 20th Century Legends range, illustrating the furniture pieces that "will take us from this century into the next". And it was created by one of the world's greatest furniture designers: the modest, gentlemanly and supremely talented Robin Day – truly a legend in his own lifetime.*

**Robin Day:** "I was interested at the time, and still am, in designing good but low-cost furniture accessible to many people. I had just done stacking chairs in moulded plywood for Hille, which were proving pretty accessible in themselves.

"When polypropylene was invented by an Italian, Professor Nata, in the early '60s, Shell bought the licence to manufacture it here. In order to familiarize designers, the firm ran a design competition for artefacts of any sort using the new material, and asked me to be a judge. Well, how could I be a judge of a material about which I knew nothing? So I asked for samples of sheet and rod, and started heating it up and bending it in my workshop to get some feeling for it. Nothing much came of the competition, but it was dawning on me this was the material I had been waiting for – the very stuff with which to make a low-cost, overtly good-looking, ergonomically OK chair!

"It so happened that Leslie Julius, who owned Hille, had had a similar response to the material, and was very open to my enthusiasm. Tooling up for the project was a very big and costly gamble. Hille might have gone bankrupt if it had failed.

"What inspired me? The material. The chair derives its ergonomics from the polypropylene. And its final form was linked to production methods. Of course, I had my own feeling for what the shape should be, but materials, construction limitations, manufacturing considerations, economy and ergonomics all dictated the final product.

"It sold very well. Other manufacturers saw it was a success, jumped on the bandwagon and started making copies – some were almost identical. Hille spent a lot of time trying to sue people. Sometimes it was successful, but it was an expensive course to pursue.

"How do I feel now? Well, to walk into a school in a poor African village and see the chair there, it gives me a great deal of pleasure! They're everywhere and look like they could last for ever!

"I've been freelance-designing for 60 years. I think, yes, there is a renaissance in British design. We've just been through a period of 'newness for its own sake' – not necessarily good design. Often fairly trivial and sometimes sensational. Perhaps it was necessary. Yes, something is happening now, something more serious – if only in reaction against the recent triviality."

*Leading designers recently paid tribute, creating designs based on Robin's chairs. In cooperation with Habitat, the show was called 'Mode – The Contemporary Home Show 2001' "My Chair Project", raising awareness and funds for Gilda's Club London. Nick Crosbie produced 'Robin Da-lmation' for Inflate, Matthew Williamson created the 'Fluro Blossom Chair' and Julia Barfield made 'Julia's Savage Rocker' (see above right).*

*The Church of England, ever aware of the problem of the faithful straying from the paths of righteousness, is keen to remove all barriers to worship. Which is one reason why it decided to redesign the* Book of Common Worship, *which contains the liturgy (words and ritual used in the Sunday service), the Psalms, and prayers for various feasts, plus various events, occasions and circumstances. So if you want to offer up a word for those engaged in Commerce and Industry, for Justice, or for the Peace of the World, pages 104 and 105 will help you find the right words. The other reason for the redesign was the millennium. The Church turned to the extraordinary Derek Birdsall at Omnific to do the job.*

**Derek Birdsall:** "This book is all about comfort. It's comfortable to read, comfortable to worship by and comfortable to hold. The Church of England appointed a design panel (very smart of them) headed by Professor Chris Frayling and two members of the clergy. Plus two lay people, another from publishing, and so on. They invited 20 design groups to express interest, one of which was ours. To my astonishment, only eight responded – extraordinary. Anyway, we and two others were asked to do three or four specimen spreads and present them in person in, of all places, the Jerusalem Chamber in Westminster Abbey, where, as Chris Frayling pointed out, *The Book of Common Worship* was first authorized.

"My assistant designer at Omnific, John Morgan, and I made a little book, a kind of Chinese fold of the spreads. We wanted to make it the right size. Size and shapes are important in terms of the typography and holding it in your hand – well, it's the whole point of a prayer book. The Church was very taken by the freshness of it and my constant emphasis on comfort. The other thing that took them was my decision to use solid red at the start – a left-hand page. It just seemed to me a rather appropriate start. It was comforting, it was rather joyful, actually, and became a useful device for separating sections. Chris Frayling described our work as 'creativity married to precise process'. Which was nice.

"Clarity was paramount. It had to be easy to read in dimly lit churches by an elderly-readership. We did a lot of tests. It was self-evident that Gill Sans was by far the clearest type. And the most readable. And Eric Gill was English, and very religious, of course, so he was a perfect fit. We used 9 on 12 point. But the italic instructions, when printed in red, looked smaller than in black. So we enlarged it by a tenth of a point. You'd be amazed – it made an enormous difference.

"We wanted to highlight the Eucharist section and might have been tempted to use a red bar bleeding off the bottom of the page, as others have done. But we achieved more clarity by simply making the footer and page number red – as distinct from black in other parts of the book. Little devices like these made all the difference. And the end papers are a sort of ecclesiastical purple. I actually got the colour off a napkin in a Turkish restaurant!

"The original copy contained bullet points. I have a horror of bullet points. But I suddenly realized if I used the old paragraph signs, the pilcrows, it would be almost traditional and they could work as bullet points. It made the appearance of the pages less spare; somehow it made them richer.

"It's easy to find your way around this book. All the side headings are over to the right – easy to spot above the 'cloud' of prayer. Wherever possible we avoided the need for the congregation to have to turn over a page during a prayer. And I suggested ivory-coloured paper. It seemed to me not only to work well with the black and red text, and in itself communicate the sense of an ancient, sacred text, but it made it easier on the eye. There's less show-through on the 55 gram paper than there would have been with white.

"I'm not religious. I went to chapel when I was a kid, and apart from weddings and funerals that was the only time I went to church. The panel never asked about our religious views, which I was quite taken by, really. Some have said that there's so much love and care gone into this design, they figured I was religious. But it's all really about respect and care for the text. In their curious ideas of modern layout, the committee said you don't need to use prompting words in the margin like 'All'. On the contrary, I said, they are most important. People are not used to going to church. They need all the help they can get!"

¶ *Christmas*

*25 December* **Christmas Night** *Principal Feast*

*Collect*

Eternal God,
who made this most holy night
to shine with the brightness of your one true light:
bring us, who have known the revelation of that light on earth,
to see the radiance of your heavenly glory;
through Jesus Christ your Son our Lord,
who is alive and reigns with you,
in the unity of the Holy Spirit,
one God, now and for ever.

*Post Communion*

God our Father,
in this night you have made known to us again
the coming of our Lord Jesus Christ:
confirm our faith and fix our eyes on him
until the day dawns
and Christ the Morning Star rises in our hearts.
To him be glory both now and for ever.

**380** *Collects and Post Communions*

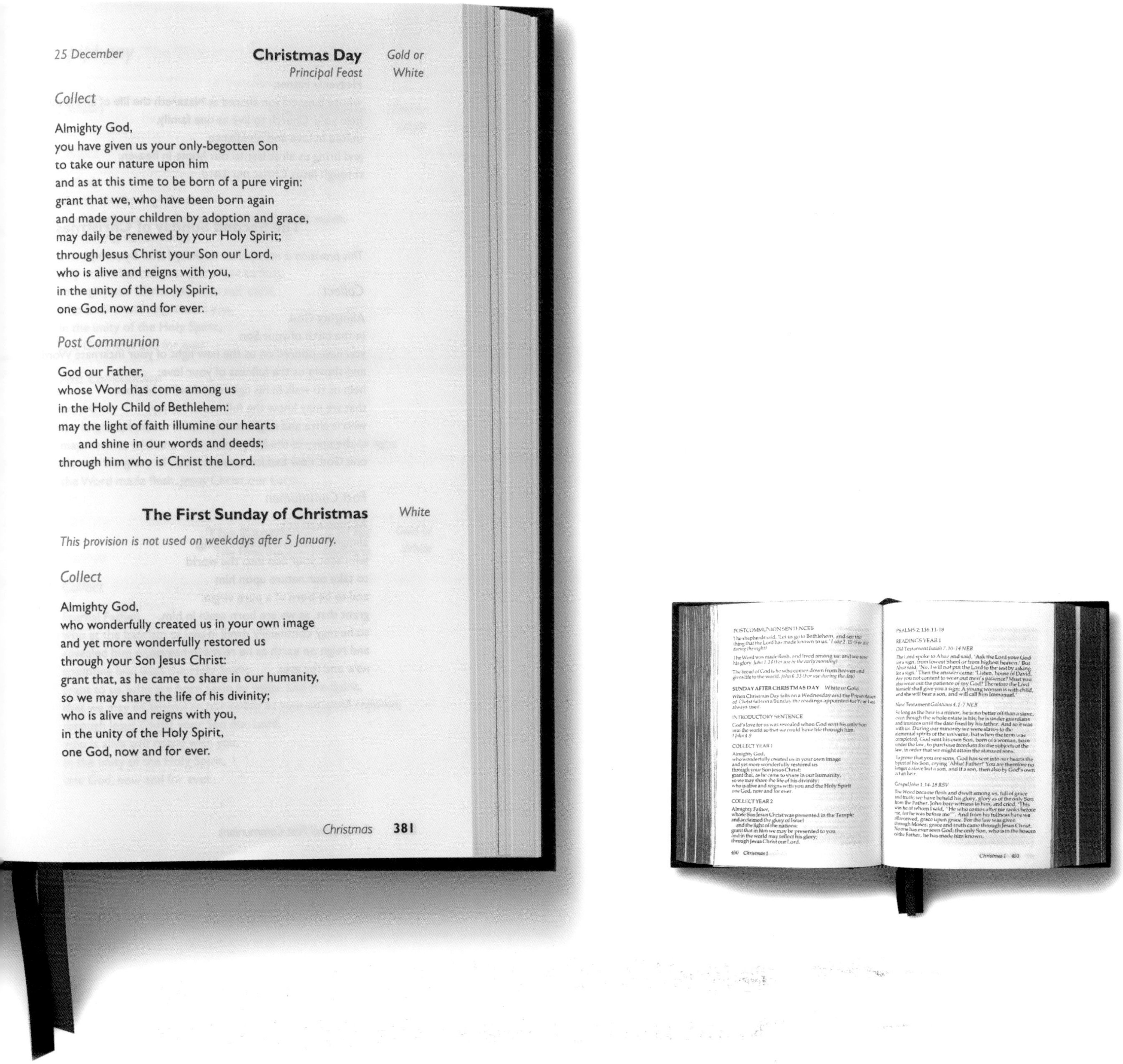

*25 December* **Christmas Day** *Gold or White*

*Principal Feast*

*Collect*

Almighty God,
you have given us your only-begotten Son
to take our nature upon him
and as at this time to be born of a pure virgin:
grant that we, who have been born again
and made your children by adoption and grace,
may daily be renewed by your Holy Spirit;
through Jesus Christ your Son our Lord,
who is alive and reigns with you,
in the unity of the Holy Spirit,
one God, now and for ever.

*Post Communion*

God our Father,
whose Word has come among us
in the Holy Child of Bethlehem:
may the light of faith illumine our hearts
  and shine in our words and deeds;
through him who is Christ the Lord.

**The First Sunday of Christmas** *White*

*This provision is not used on weekdays after 5 January.*

*Collect*

Almighty God,
who wonderfully created us in your own image
and yet more wonderfully restored us
through your Son Jesus Christ:
grant that, as he came to share in our humanity,
so we may share the life of his divinity;
who is alive and reigns with you,
in the unity of the Holy Spirit,
one God, now and for ever.

*Christmas* **381**

POSTCOMMUNION SENTENCES

The shepherds said, 'Let us go to Bethlehem, and see the thing that the Lord has made known to us.' *Luke 2.15 (For use during the night)*

The Word was made flesh, and lived among us; and we saw his glory. *John 1.14 (For use in the early morning)*

The bread of God is he who comes down from heaven and gives life to the world. *John 6.33 (For use during the day)*

SUNDAY AFTER CHRISTMAS DAY White or Gold

When Christmas Day falls on a Wednesday and the Presentation of Christ falls on a Sunday the readings appointed for Year I are always used.

INTRODUCTORY SENTENCE

God's love for us was revealed when God sent his only Son into the world so that we could have life through him. *1 John 4.9*

COLLECT YEAR 1

Almighty God,
who wonderfully created us in your own image
and yet more wonderfully restored us
through your Son Jesus Christ:
grant that, as he came to share in our humanity,
so we may share the life of his divinity;
who is alive and reigns with you and the Holy Spirit
one God, now and for ever.

COLLECT YEAR 2

Almighty Father,
whose Son Jesus Christ was presented in the Temple
and acclaimed the glory of Israel
  and the light of the nations:
grant that in him we may be presented to you
and in the world may reflect his glory;
through Jesus Christ our Lord.

450 *Christmas 1*

PSALMS 2; 116.11-18

READINGS YEAR 1

*Old Testament Isaiah 7.10-14 NEB*

The Lord spoke to Ahaz and said, 'Ask the Lord your God for a sign, from lowest Sheol or from highest heaven.' But Ahaz said, 'No, I will not put the Lord to the test by asking for a sign.' Then the answer came: 'Listen, house of David. Are you not content to wear out men's patience? Must you also wear out the patience of my God? Therefore the Lord himself shall give you a sign: A young woman is with child, and she will bear a son, and will call him Immanuel.'

*New Testament Galatians 4.1-7 NEB*

So long as the heir is a minor, he is no better off than a slave, even though the whole estate is his; he is under guardians and trustees until the date fixed by his father. And so it was with us. During our minority we were slaves to the elemental spirits of the universe, but when the term was completed, God sent his own Son, born of a woman, born under the law, to purchase freedom for the subjects of the law, in order that we might attain the status of sons.

To prove that you are sons, God has sent into our hearts the Spirit of his Son, crying 'Abba! Father!' You are therefore no longer a slave but a son, and if a son, then also by God's own act an heir.

*Gospel John 1.14-18 RSV*

The Word became flesh and dwelt among us, full of grace and truth; we have beheld his glory, glory as of the only Son from the Father. John bore witness to him, and cried, 'This was he of whom I said, "He who comes after me ranks before me, for he was before me"'. And from his fullness have we all received, grace upon grace. For the law was given through Moses; grace and truth came through Jesus Christ. No one has ever seen God; the only Son, who is in the bosom of the Father, he has made him known.

*Christmas 1* 451

# SELFRIDGES EXTERIOR LIGHTING

*Selfridges in London's Oxford Street has long been one of the world's most famous stores. But with increasing competition, it became clear to the management it was time to reinvent itself. But how do you renew interest in a store that has been famous for so long and which has begun to develop a reputation for being, frankly, a bit old-fashioned? A redesign is the obvious answer. But it's got to be subtle. It's easy to throw the baby out with the bath-water. So Selfridges turned to Isometrix and used the lighting expertise of Arnold Chan, both inside and out. Arnold trained in architecture at Central London Polytechnic, and his company has blue-chip clients across the world. The exterior solution at Selfridges contained a magic paradox...*

Arnold Chan:

"The brief was to re-establish Selfridges' street presence. The truth is it had been there for so long people didn't really notice it anymore. But with such a beautiful old façade, it was going to be tricky. We needed to be subtle. We wanted to highlight the beauty of the original architecture without making the lighting too obvious. In short, we had to give it a powerful street presence in the most discreet way possible – something of a contradiction in terms!

"When you have such an intricate classical façade you need to be very careful where you place the lights. They can really be an eyesore. So we built models to test our ideas. And then we used very small exterior spots at the base of each column to wash light up each column. We wanted to produce a very even effect. We coloured the lights to match the tone of the stone work. Now it wasn't that long ago that the façade was black from pollution. But Selfridges had just spent a good deal of time and money on cleaning the exterior, revealing a stone colour that was off-white.

"The hardest part was unifying the lighting on the columns with the massive cornice above them. So we hid lights behind the upper mouldings and created the impression that the light was flowing up the building and continuing through to the top. Of course, this is impossible to do with one light source without the most dreadful shadows, but it had to look as if it were unified. We were very careful to match the tone of two light areas, the upper and the lower. We used metal halide lights for the pillars – the sort of light used in some street lights, though a more sophisticated version, much warmer. Higher up we used cold cathode – like a white neon.

"This may have been a coincidence, but when we first switched the lights on – without any ceremony or publicity – the effect was impressive, because the following day Selfridges experienced a 25% increase in customers. Of course it's true to say, and has been long established, that a shop with good lighting will pull in more people than its poorly lit neighbour, but this was spectacular.

"If I were to pick a building where the lighting hasn't worked, it would probably be the river façade of the Savoy. You will notice the scheme highlights the columns on the façade. But the material of the column itself has been made uneven by age and weathering. A very strong, narrow spotlight rises up the column and only works to pick out the pitmarks and flaws. It gives it a rather ghostly effect. I would have used a softer light and, if possible, used lighting in the garden in front of the façade to get a softer angle.

"It seems to me more and more industries are using creative expertise from other industries to bring new ideas into their arena. Car manufacturers are bringing in furniture designers to create concept cars, for example. We find this very stimulating. We have a philosophy of securing diverse projects, just to keep us creative and help us maintain freshness. Things are changing and design is to the fore. When I started this company 14 years ago, no one thought about lighting. Now you can read articles solely about lighting effects for the home in consumer magazines. Designers used to be the back-room boys. Not any more. Journalists ring me up for my opinion! That never used to happen."

# OYSTER DAYBED FOR LLOYD LOOM

*In 1922, a new type of furniture appeared in Britain with the legend: "Neither cane nor wicker – superior to either!" This magic material, already famous in America, was "impervious to damp and dirt!", "didn't warp!" and was "unaffected by heat!" It was Lloyd Loom, invented by Marshall B Lloyd, made out of "paper with a twist", and made into an enormous range of easy chairs, sofas, daybeds and prams. In the UK they were designed and manufactured by William Kennard Lusty & Sons. His model No 32 was one of his largest armchairs and gained fame on the airfields of the RAF, where fighter pilots would sit out on the grass in their Lusty chairs, dressed in full flying garb, nervously smoking their pipes and waiting for the telephone call that would send them scrambling for the Spitfires. But the London factory was destroyed in the war, and finally the company collapsed in 1968. In 1986, Lloyd Loom of Spalding emerged as a cottage industry. It grew quickly, creating a new paper weave called Loomtex, used for carpets and rugs. Then it commissioned top designers like Nigel Coates to create a new furniture range with the new material…*

**Nigel Coates:** "How would I describe the Daybed? I guess when you're designing these things, you don't really understand what you've done until you've done it. The idea was to make a horizontal plane and then cut it so that the central section became a tongue – a wave-like shape that fits your body. The surrounding frame is sort of like a table, but the centre of it 'waves' to make the body shape which extends to lip over the frame. It's a materialization of the contest between the body and the ground. It is, if you will, all about the relationship between geometric form and sensual form.

"I guess I wanted the object to have a simplicity on the one hand and complexity on the other. A sort of contradiction; an enigma. It's a characteristic of a lot of the furniture I make. I do love those qualities. Basically it's a plywood frame on steel legs. The fabric is Loomtex, a mixture of paper and linen. It has a fine weave and a lovely softness to the touch, and you can paint it in any colour. It's deceptively strong. There's no need for metal rods.

"Oh, I think it's very comfortable. I feel I could float off in it, like a magic carpet. It's certainly one of my favourite pieces. I guess what I like most about it is that you can look at it from the side, when it's not being used, and still see a human in it. It seems to anticipate you sitting in it. I think it's going to be around for a while!

"I'm really an architect. I trained as an architect and that's how I think. I've done all these other things but it all stems from a spatial and architectural way of working. I love working with ideas. If there's not an idea, a sensibility about something, I'm not really interested in doing it. That underlies all of my work. That's why I like teaching: I really love ideas.

"There is a flourishing of British design, though of course, design is coming to prominence globally as well. British design has a kind of wit which points up the connection between the everyday and the dreamy. Linking those two is something that has made British design communicate and travel very well, as Italian furniture manufacturers will be only too keen to tell you. Many of their products are by British designers.

"But design equals money, and sometimes there's too much design in Britain. You can't go to a restaurant that hasn't been designed! I'm not too sure about this statistic, but it certainly seems that there is a greater concentration of creative industry in London than anywhere else in the world."

# RENEWAL

*There were many Millennium Projects around the country designed to illustrate rebirth and renewal at the turn of the century. But none was more successful, or more powerful, than the Eden Project, the £86 million showcase for global diversity. Sir Nicholas Grimshaw is famous for a wide range of work, specialising in covering vast spaces in gravity-defying structures – the International Terminal at Waterloo Station being one of his most high-profile projects. His geodesic domes, or biomes, at their quarry site in Cornwall have already become international icons, representing the desperate need to take care of this planet.*

**Nicholas Grimshaw:** "It was incredibly exciting looking for the site for this grand project. We searched all over Cornwall, and when we found Bodelva Quarry it was like discovering a lost world. We climbed to the top of a hill, pushed through thick bushes and stumbled to the edge of a 300-foot-deep (100-metre) bowl in the ground. We could see wonderful south-facing white cliffs soaring up away to our left, the clefts rich in vegetation, like some Chinese painting. The potential for solar gain was immense!

"We quickly decided to build against the cliffs. Our first idea was to have a series of huge structural members, similar to the trusses at Waterloo, spanning between the cliff face and quarry floor and glazed in between. But the immediate problem with this plan was the uneven terrain: the ground rose up and down, and the cliff swept in and out. We realized that we needed a more universal, organic structure that could be adapted to suit the ground profile. It was then that the hexagonal geometry was born.

"We also had to consider the lightness of the structure. The lighter we could make the biomes, the more economical they would become, both in transport and material costs.

"We turned to spherical geometry and the present-day capabilities for building geodesic structures that were so famously pioneered by Buckminster Fuller immediately after the Second World War.

"Using glass to enclose the structure would have compromised the design because it is relatively heavy and has a limited span. So we went for ETFE (Ethylene Tetra Fluoro Ethylene) – a thin but immensely strong membrane that is transparent to a wide spectrum of light.

"We used it in a triple layer for insulation, infilling the hexagonal structure with inflated pillows. The pillows gain strength from being constantly pressurized.

"ETFE is an amazing material, self-cleaning and resilient. Because it weighs a fraction of the glass equivalent, the whole structure actually weighs little more than the air it contains. This certainly solved the problem of huge foundations – in fact, we were more concerned that the structure might blow away!

"The Eden Project is about a sustainable future, demonstrating that if we lost all the vegetation in the world, then life could not exist. That's a pretty clear message.

"Right at the moment I think that there is a great renaissance in British design. In architecture, for example, many of us are successfully exporting our skills, and this strikes me as very significant. You cannot win commissions overseas unless you are generating creative heat at home. It is a wonderful time for the creative professions in this country."

THE EDEN PROJECT

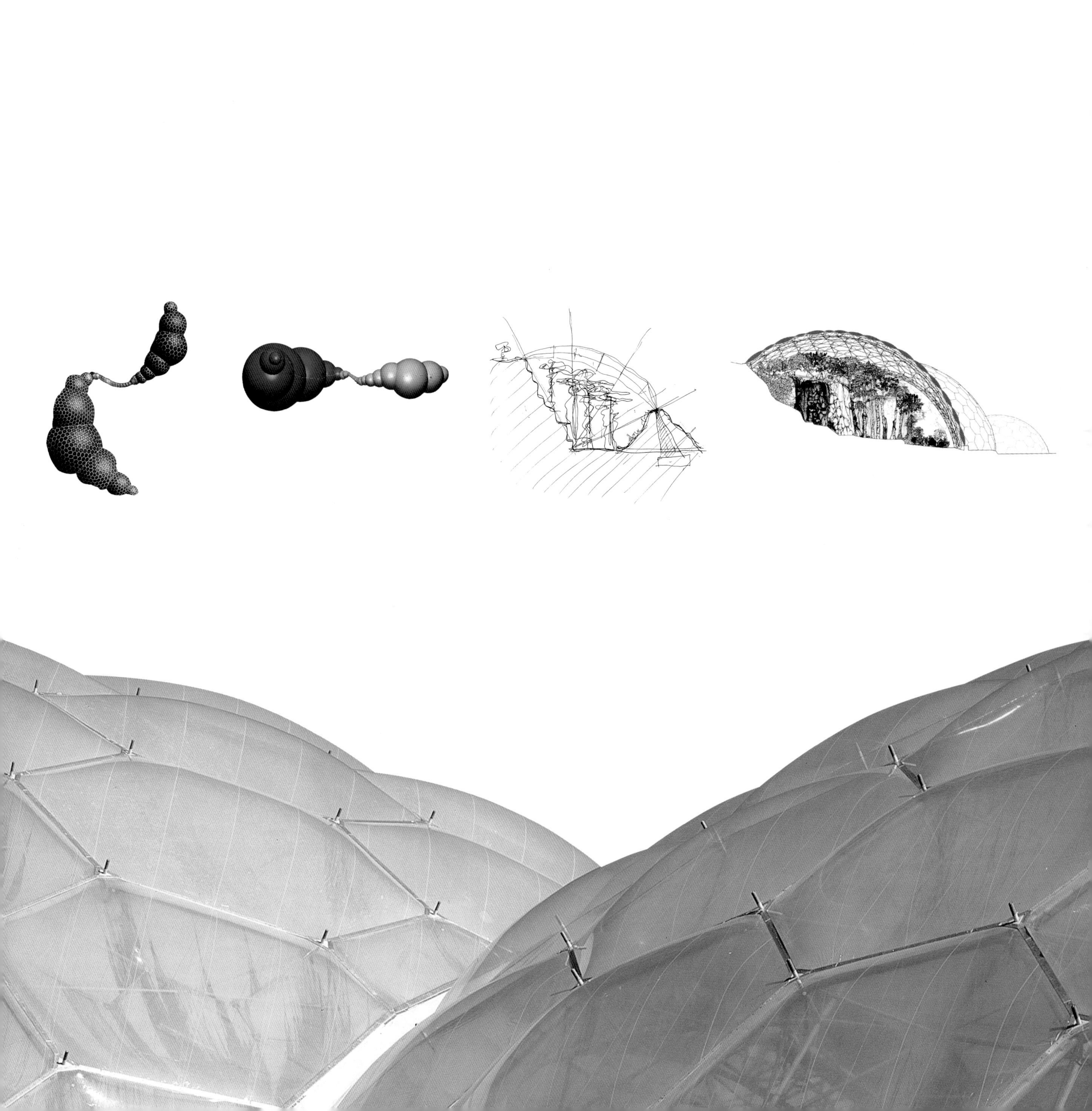

# OZWALD BOATENG SUIT

*It's Ozwald Boateng's self-belief, as well as his consummate skill as a Savile Row tailor, that has got him where he is. Born in London's Muswell Hill of Ghanaian parents, he's fought a long, hard battle to get to the top of the design hierarchy. He has learnt a lot about renewal as his business has been through a lot of up and down cycles. But now business is booming and Ozwald's instinctive approach to creativity and passion for the perfect cut will take him wherever he wants to go.*

**Ozwald Boateng:** "This is a beautiful turquoise. It's like a classic take on my pinstripe. It's colourizing formality. Colour is really important in my work, but my real skill lies in my attention to detail and the way I cut.

"I use a lot of hidden detail – like the jackets are open at the cuff, and there's always a contrasting fabric there. You don't actually see it – only if you choose to open the cuff button. It's hard to pin down what my hallmark is; it's all down to the cut. I enhance shape by angling the pockets, my jackets are usually high-closing, the trousers generally taper, and the suits feature concealed buttons and vivid linings. It makes for a lively and self-confident suit.

"Of course I can't tell you how I make my cut! That's a trade secret! But the key is balance: where I position the waistline. That's the art. You cut well and you can create illusions. Get it right and your man will look slimmer, taller. And he'll feel better than he ever has. I've spent many years perfecting that cut. I can create illusions.

"I did an orange suit in a collection for Milan three seasons ago. The whole show was inspired by the birth of my child, Emelia, because the ultimate creative statement is having a child. I called the show 'Creativity' and it was a celebration of all types of creativity using powerful, vivid colours to express it. There were three focal colours in the exhibition: orange, turquoise and cream.

"I like the orange suit because it was such a challenge to make a suit of such vivid colour actually wearable. People often say: 'Oh, such colours look good, but you can't wear them.' Well, this one you can. Somehow it looks warm and fun, assured and relaxed. And yet it's orange.

"My work is always based on the way I feel. This is very conscious. My feelings and moods change, so my work changes; it keeps it dynamic. I've been developing techniques over the years for translating mood into work. My mood is influenced by many things, of course. From the birth of Emelia to a violent storm to a video game. The birth of my daughter spoke to me. I thought: 'Oh, she's beautiful. She looks like her mother...' This is difficult to express, but somehow, that moment, that feeling, inspired me to do the show.

"Something is definitely happening in this industry. There's space now for new British creators. At the moment there aren't very many well-known British designers. But there's going to be an opportunity for many more British players on the world stage. Big companies are embracing individual talent and we're going to see the emergence of British superbrands – the British equivalents of Gucci."

*Fred Scott was one of the world's leading office furniture designers. His genius for design didn't save him from the pain of rejection. The good news is that before he died on 13 January 2001, he saw some of his greatest work being recreated by the Keen Group. The tragic news is he didn't live to see the final success.*

**Fred Scott by Charles Keen:** "Fred Scott's death was a tragedy. He never really received the recognition he should have done. Happily, we were able to begin to redress that balance a little towards the end of his life. But let's start at the beginning.

"His father was a boilerman, his mother worked as an administrator. In 1964 he got his big break. He was discovered by the Hille sisters, and so, like Robin Day, became a designer at Hille. His first work for them included sofas and stacking chairs. By the mid-'70s he was well established there. He then left after a row but returned in 1976 with his plans for the Supporto Chair. After a series of ups and downs, during which Hille was sold, the Supporto was produced and sold well, becoming a classic in office chairs.

"But then Hille's direction changed and Fred became disillusioned. His depression fed the illness that finally killed him. He was also under serious financial pressure. Then his wife died in a car accident. It rolled him over the edge. He became very paranoid about people around him.

"But he was most at home when we spoke about the technology behind his work. When we started Keen we negotiated with him for the rights to produce the whole Supporto range, the chairs and the table ideas he had. He showed me some wonderful drawings of his cast-aluminium tables. When we acquired the Supporto business, he could see we were serious. I told him: 'We'll do all these elements, Fred.' He became more and more excited. Now he had the opportunity to finish his life's work.

"So we funded the engineering and the drawings. Over Christmas 2000 he led a seminar for us in the showroom about the table designs, which featured some strip cartoons about the system. Thank the Lord he did that for us, because it gave us a clear picture of his vision and the design envelope he had conceived. He died a few weeks later.

"The system was launched over a series of exhibitions in the following months. At 'Workplace 2001' Fred received a special award for flexible furniture. It was a fabulous accolade because it's not a style award; it's about functionality and technology. The challenge was to reconfigure an office space with the computer systems intact inside 10 minutes. The Supporto system did it in 30 seconds. The judges were hardy facility managers.

"The hallmark of his work is simplicity, high functionality, minimum materials, low weight and a pleasing aesthetic. He was really one of these natural engineers, an industrial designer who believed in integral design. It wasn't a linear process – it wasn't step-by-step, because that approach so often leads to an add-on mentality: 'Oh, let's tack this on, let's enhance this with that.' Fred's integral design resolves all the issues with a wholeness. They have a name for his approach in the automotive industry now. It's called 'simultaneous engineering.' The idea is you get everyone round the table at the concept stage: production engineers, precision toolmakers, marketing, sales. A very joined-up approach. Fred was a master of it. He had worked on production lines and in machine shops, and he'd lectured a lot at the RSA. His friends were on the shop floor. He was very much against all the fancy doohda stuff. He was a man of the material, a man of the product. He figured products that are all style fall by the wayside. Designers who understand the whole process, and design with it in mind – they are the ones that will last. Scott, Eames, Corbusier...

"The process of diecasting aluminium had been done in small sections, but not on the huge shells required for a chair. But Fred was doing it. It really was a breakthrough; it enabled him to resolve all the shape and posture problems, and provide slim cushions and a slim shell without it being hard and heavy. And it was designed for comfort, whether you were leaning back or perched forward to type.

"The chair is so simple. It consists of a five-star base with a gas strut, the shell, a seat pad, a back and a cushion on it. That's it. Assembly and repair were very, very simple. We are often asked to service chairs over 20 years old."

STORY BOARD. SUPPORTO CHAIRS ADITIONS.



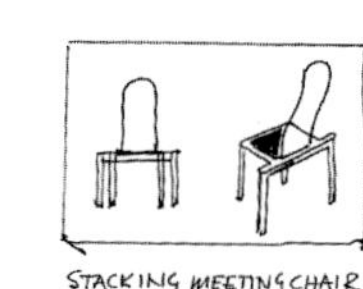

STACKING MEETING CHAIR.
-DINING CHAIR.
STEEL WITH LAMINATED BACK.

SUPPORTO 4 LEG CASTING
MEETING CHAIR. BOARDROOM
CHAIR.


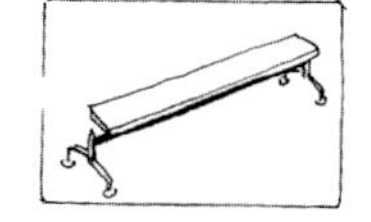
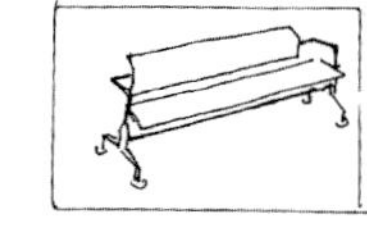
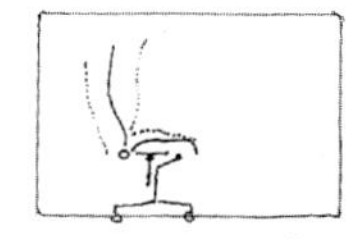
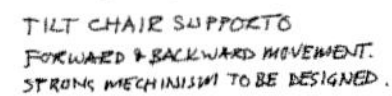

SUPPORTO 4 LEG CHAIR
WITH WRITING, MOUSE TABLE
ASSEMBLY AREAS.
SUPPORTO BENCH SEATING
ALSO LONG TABLE. PRESS STUD
UPHOLSTERED SEAT
SUPPORTO BENCH SEATING
WITH BACK 2, 3, 4 SEATER
INTRICAL SKIN SEAT & BACK FOR
WEATHER CONDITIONS.
TILT CHAIR SUPPORTO
FORWARD & BACKWARD MOVEMENT.
STRONG MECHANISM TO BE DESIGNED.

BEAM AND BENCH SEATING.
RESTRANT AND PUBLIC AREAS.
FLOOR FIXED.
HIGH TABLES ITERNET CAFES.
ALTERNATIVE DESKING
SOCIAL AREAS.
FLOOR FIXED.
SUPPORTO CHAIR
NEW SHORT ARM TO BE
DESIGNED. FOR VDU WORK.

STOREY BOARD. SUPPORTO FOLDING TABLE. STACKING MEETING CHAIR.

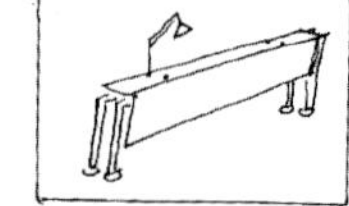

TABLE 2400 x 1200
WIRE MANAGMENT.
TABLE ONE FLAP CLOSED
CAN BE OPEN FOR MEETINGS
TABLE CLOSED. FOR STORAGE
OR PLACED ON OUTER AREAS
FOR DIFFERENT ROOM FOTION.


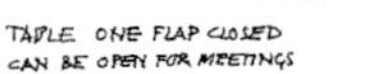
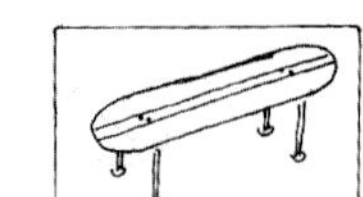
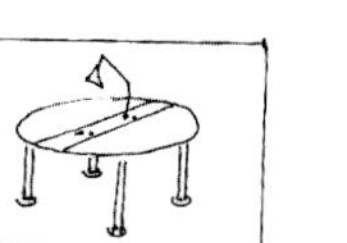

D END TABLE. MEETINGS.
ROUND TABLE
ROUND TABLE.
1/2 FOLDED.


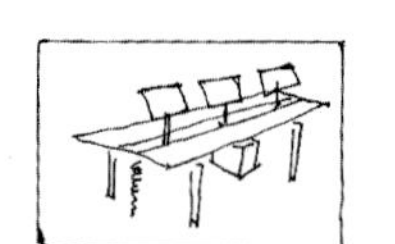
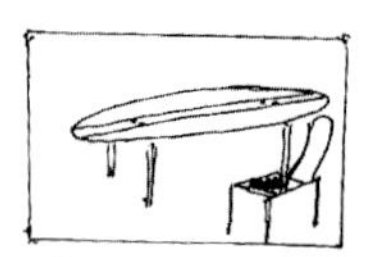

TABLE WITH WIRE MANAGMENT
AND FLAT SCREENS
PIVOTING CPU BOX SO IT CAN FOLD.
OVAL MEETING TABLE 3000 x 1500
STACKING MEETING CHAIR.
TABLE WITH SCREEN
SYSTEM AND SHELVES.

# YELLOW PAGES TYPEFACE

*When BT decided to revamp its Yellow Pages, it turned to Michael Johnson at Johnson Banks. In turn, he sought out Freda Sack at The Foundry to generate a typeface which could include more information on a page and yet be easy to read. The Yellow Pages is a phenomenon in itself. Every household and every business has one, and consequently the directory is used 40 times every second. If you laid them all end to end they'd stretch from London to Beijing. Follow the yellow-book road...*

**Freda Sack:** "The challenge was to create a typeface that took up less space than the previous one and yet was easier to read. The print-runs are absolutely massive: millions upon millions of copies of multiple versions with each copy around 1,500 pages long. So if you can reduce the type size and yet increase legibility, you save enormous amounts on space, ink, paper, metal for plates, distribution costs, etc.

"Inspiration comes more easily if I have tight restrictions to work with. They make you think and function in different ways. The typeface had to work well in two weights, bold and regular, so you can show a hierarchy of information. (The names are in bold, the addresses are in regular, the numbers are in bold.)

"Bold creates the biggest problems in volume high-speed printing, because the ink can bleed and fill in the letters. So we condensed the letter form and kept the lowercase x-height as large as possible, which allowed us to have more counter space (the space enclosed inside the letters). If you look closely, you'll see the line thicknesses change in the bold form. This takes less ink and is much easier to read. We also chiselled off the stroke endings to a taper, to allow for some ink spread (e.g. the e, c and t).

"It was a fine balance between legibility and saving space. We condensed the letters. It takes up less room, and looks smart and modern, but if you go too narrow it's less easy to read. We solved a lot of problems by using shorter ascenders and descenders. This allowed the lines to be closer together – what we call 'negative leading.'

"People appreciate design more now. And graphic artists often look to other disciplines for inspiration. There's a lot more crossover."

**Bennett R.M**, 54 Drumalig Rd ............ **Carryduff 812278**
**Benson S.S**, 96 Thornhill Rd,Rock ............ **Pomeroy 758257**
**Benson T**, 19 Cannagola Rd,Portadown ........ **Annaghmore 851435**
**Berry J.D**, 41 Brootally Rd,Lisagally ............ **Armagh 522355**
**Berry N.D. & Sons**, 41 Tullyraine Rd ............ **Banbridge 62767**
**Berry W**, 20 Chapelhill Rd,Tynan ............ **Caledon 568384**
**Best R.D**, The Cairn,14 Brankinstown Rd ............ **Aghalee 651222**
**Bethel W**, 36 Point Rd ............ **Banbridge 62455**
**Bethel Wm**, 6 Island Rd ............ **Newtownhamilton 878345**
**Biggerstaff Norman**, 84 Diamond Rd ...... **Dromore(Dn) 692555**
**Biggerstaff R.S**,
57 Upper Quilly Rd,Banbridge ............ **Dromore(Dn) 692419**
**Bill John**, 802 Antrim Rd ............ **Templepatrick 432673**
**Bingham Barney**, 28 Carnew Rd ............ **Katesbridge 71329**
**Bingham D.W**,
68 Ballymartin Rd,Templepatrick ............ **Ballyclare 352272**
**Bingham Edward**,
65 Annaghilla Rd,Auger ............ **Ballygawley 68287**
**Bingham Jsph**, 14 Lackan Rd,Ballyroney ........ **Rathfriland 30364**
**Bingham Noel**, Ballinsaggart Rd ............ **Ballygawley 68444**
**Bingham R**,
203 Sevenmile Straight,Crumlin ............ **Templepatrick 432236**
**Bingham S**, 38 Tullycorker Rd,Auger ............ **Clogher 48353**
**Birch J.A**,
Mill View Farm,8 Abbacy Rd,Ardkeen ............ **Portaferry 28030**
**Birch S**, 1 Keadybeg Rd,Mountnorris ............ **Glenanne 507314**
**Birney F**, Tullanaglare ............ **Irvinestown 21480**
**Birt E**, 137 Mullaghboy Rd ............ **Bellaghy 386738**
**Birt Michl.E**, 10 Bogashen Rd ............ **Portglenone 821354**

**GalfraSemiBold** GalfraLightCond **GalfraSemiBold**

| | | |
|---|---|---|
| **Bennett R.M**, 54 Drumalig Rd | **Carryduff** | **812278** |
| **Benson S.S**, 96 Thornhill Rd,Rock | **Pomeroy** | **758257** |
| **Benson T**, 19 Cannagola Rd,Portadown | **Annaghmore** | **851435** |
| **Berry J.D**, 41 Brootally Rd,Lisagally | **Armagh** | **522355** |
| **Berry N.D.& Sons**, 41 Tullyraine Rd | **Banbridge** | **62767** |
| **Berry W**, 20 Chapelhill Rd,Tynan | **Caledon** | **568384** |
| **Best R.D**, The Cairn,14 Brankinstown Rd | **Aghalee** | **651222** |
| **Bethel W**, 36 Point Rd | **Banbridge** | **62455** |
| **Bethel Wm**, 6 Island Rd | **Newtownhamilton** | **878345** |
| **Biggerstaff Norman**, 84 Diamond Rd | **Dromore(Dn)** | **692555** |
| **Biggerstaff R.S**, 57 Upper Quilly Rd,Banbridge | **Dromore(Dn)** | **692419** |
| **Bill John**, 802 Antrim Rd | **Templepatrick** | **432673** |
| **Bingham Barney**, 28 Carnew Rd | **Katesbridge** | **71329** |
| **Bingham D.W**, 68 Ballymartin Rd,Templepatrick | **Ballyclare** | **352272** |
| **Bingham Edward**, 65 Annaghilla Rd,Auger | **Ballygawley** | **68287** |
| **Bingham Jsph**, 14 Lackan Rd,Ballyroney | **Rathfriland** | **30364** |
| **Bingham Noel**, Ballinsaggart Rd | **Ballygawley** | **68444** |
| **Bingham R**, 203 Sevenmile Straight,Crumlin | **Templepatrick** | **432236** |
| **Bingham S**, 38 Tullycorker Rd,Auger | **Clogher** | **48353** |
| **Birch J.A**, Mill View Farm,8 Abbacy Rd,Ardkeen | **Portaferry** | **28030** |
| **Birch S**, 1 Keadybeg Rd,Mountnorris | **Glenanne** | **507314** |
| **Birney F**, Tullanaglare | **Irvinestown** | **21480** |
| **Birt E**, 137 Mullaghboy Rd | **Bellaghy** | **386738** |
| **Birt Michl.E**, 10 Bogashen Rd | **Portglenone** | **821354** |

**Yellow-Bold** Yellow-Regular **Yellow-Bold**

# WESTMINSTER & NORTH GREENWICH STATIONS

*The new Westminster Underground Station became part and parcel of Portcullis House – the new office accommodation for MPs. The site threw up enormous complications, with roof beams so corroded they threatened to sag onto the trains beneath. But with the decision to appoint Michael Hopkins and Partners to build both construction projects, it was possible to create a more unified solution, as David Selby, director explains...*

**David Selby:** "Working on both station and building gave us a wonderful opportunity to weave the two together. By incorporating huge arches we were able to take structural support up into the building above and sandwich in the new ticket hall.

"Complications arose from the existing tracks that cross the station diagonally. But we turned it into a virtue, creating a diagonal structure that resulted in the unique spatial quality of the ticket hall level connecting, by a series of subway fingers, to adjacent streets.

"We stacked the subways vertically rather than side-by-side. We had to be careful not to undermine Big Ben, which is on timber piles. By putting the tunnels on top of each other we minimized the disturbed ground. They connect in the Escalator Hall, perhaps the most striking feature of the project, with its wonderfully intricate views.

"The perimeter diaphragm is a buttress against the earth and the clay. A wide grid of beams is strutted by solid steel. With the suspended walkways weaving this way and that, the space has a Piranesian feel (Piranesi was famous for his drawing of underground structures.)

"The approach was to take advantage of the bones of this structure and reveal it rather than cover it up. It has the feel of a huge engine room.

"The whole thing is an essay in civil engineering and architecture married into one."

*This nine-year project began before there was any talk of the Millennium Dome, but when there were plenty of plans to regenerate East London. The development was aimed at servicing new housing and offices. Things changed when it became clear the station was going to serve a new purpose as the Dome station. Alsop & Störmer were on the case from the outset.*

**Will Alsop:** "The usual method for building an underground station is 'cut and cover'. You dig a big hole, in this case one that was 400 metres long, 20 metres wide and 35 metres deep. You line it out, put a lid on it and cover it with earth. I tried hard to persuade London Underground and the Jubilee Line Extension people not to cover it. I said: 'Imagine a razor-sharp edge to a beautiful rectangular hole. People will feel safer being in touch with the surface, people can shout up from the bottom... You won't have to burn so much electricity for light; smoke extraction is easier. You'd buy a ticket on the surface of the earth and descend through hanging gardens...'

"In the end, of course, we had to put the top on – the new Transport and Works Act saw to that. But the idea still resonates in my mind, and the station still works as we had intended. We kept the open feel.

"There are two things I am particularly proud of. One is the proportion of the Y-shaped columns: I think they've worked extremely well. Their oval form, oriented in the direction of the trains, gives a dynamic to the length of the station.

"And the length itself provides a perspective so that when you stand at the bottom, the columns seem to taper to the top. The proportions are good.

"I also like the large, blue-glass wall with the working lights behind. It all hides a multitude of sins, of course, but I think it works well. It gives a non-defined edge to the box."

Way out
PLEASE KEEP YOUR LUGGAGE WITH YOU
AT ALL TIMES
DANGER NO ENTRY
Way out

NORTH GREENWICH
first train

# MILLENNIUM DOME

*Although the Millennium Dome at Greenwich received a massive thumbs up from its six million visitors, and its creation played a crucial role in the regeneration of a derelict area, it became a focal point for media cynicism. Few, however, argued with the brilliance of the extraordinary building designed by the Richard Rogers Partnership, with Mike Davies as project director.*

**Mike Davies:** "Contrary to popular belief, the Dome itself was delivered on time and under budget. At £43 million it cost less than £500 per square metre – that's less than a supermarket 'shed'.

"We decided fairly early on that what we needed was a universal cover. It allowed us to start on site early. It freed us up to move forward with the infrastructure whilst the NMEC thought through what was going to go inside. And the Dome was superb at responding to the changing content proposals.

"Early solutions ranged from inflatable buildings to tensioned structures. In the end we plumped for the latter – we and our engineers Buro Happold are very experienced in tensioned structures.

"The design also had to be iconic, and the Dome achieved that. It quickly stuck in people's minds, all over the world – there has never been a structure like it anywhere. Symbolically, it represented the dawn of the new millennium. In practice it was a great response to the old British Gasworks site.

"We also managed to make the Dome non-referential and yet stand out in the mind. That is not easy to achieve. We made it round because the site demanded it and because roundness creates a sense of focus and unity, and this project was all about unifying the country in celebration. And it was about openness and transparency and freedom to move around – a sort of loose-fit, non-constraining, friendly overcoat.

"What went wrong? Nothing went wrong with the Dome itself. It fulfilled its purpose admirably. One of the major issues was that, despite the phenomenal dedication of its staff, NMEC failed to communicate the project content and spirit. And I never felt the content was either good enough or adventurous enough. Some aspects were very good, of course, but some were absolutely appalling. The Dome was always too close to government – it should have been artistically driven rather than message-managed. The project always needed an artistic ringmaster, or group of ringmasters, since no one person I can think of could have handled that much responsibility.

"A small group of theatre directors, designers, artists, poets, scientists and teachers working together to create something special: this would have delivered a more challenging, aspirational and magical experience."

# MILLENNIUM MEDAL

*As part of the UK's millennium celebrations, a special range of millennium medals was commissioned for the public, staff who worked at the Dome, and VIPs. Ten artists, medallists and graphic artists were invited to present ideas for three different kinds of medal. Wendy Ramshaw won the commission, which included making a special medal for the Queen, with copies to go to the British Museum and Greenwich Museum.*

**Wendy Ramshaw:** "I really wanted this commission. As a child I went to the 1951 Festival of Britain. I was entranced and amazed.

"For the Queen's medal, pictured here, my inspiration was the architecture of the dome itself and, of course, navigation through time. The webs are based on architectural drawings. One is of the dome's skin, the other the tensioning wires. They are effectively simplified architectural drawings.

"The glass box symbolizes the world, the two webs symbolize the dome, and within them lies the medal. The medal spins when you pick it up, each ring spinning round like an astrolabe – a representation of the universe.

"The central sphere is made of zeradour, a transparent ceramic. Totally inert, it's used in the new generation of telescopes currently scanning our universe.

"This zeradour sphere has another, much smaller web inside, representing the central part of the Dome's architecture.

"The disc inside is stainless steel and is covered in a blue iridescent coating of nano-crystalline diamond. This is so thin the increase in thickness is imperceptible. Diamond materials are expected to be the technology of the new millennium.

"One application is in replacement hip joints. Current ones wear away, but if you coat them in nano-crystalline diamond, they could last forever."

"A lot of my work contains symbols of navigation. My father was a ship's navigator. Well, Greenwich is about navigation, is it not?"

TATE

*It was over a century since the last London river crossing was built, so competition was hot for the commission to build the Millennium Bridge. Foster and Partners, sculptor Anthony Caro, and Arup (represented here by project director Roger Ridsdill Smith) won the competition and worked together to realize the dream. It was a design process fraught with difficulties, but the result has been a bridge that changes all the rules, and is an object-lesson in what happens when you push the boundaries and take risks. And now, as the dust settles, most designers agree the bridge, for all its early problems, is a triumph of design.*

**Norman Foster:** "The Millennium Bridge is on the very frontier of technology, and on the frontier there will always be teething problems. We regret the inconvenience the problems caused, but we still feel the approach was right. We challenge conventions, and go where others, frankly, are reluctant to go. The bridge has had a tremendously warm public response.

"The key to all our work is to get under the skin of the project. To try and understand the inner realities and practicalities. It's not just about understanding the hard-edged, measurable world of materials; it's about the human stuff that's so difficult to quantify. We make a great effort to really get to know why people are going to use a building or a bridge. We want to know what they want out of it, and we want to know it better than the client. This process is a major source of inspiration.

"It's a great buzz. In fact, the way we compile a team of creative, expert individuals who spark off each other is something we've pioneered, and it's wonderful to be part of this process. There is an art to bringing a wealth of various and specialized talent together in a single-minded quest. We have developed a self-confidence tempered by humility that questions and challenges all the time.

"Design and architecture has undergone dramatic growth in the UK. It's possible to read about design-thinking in the national media on a daily basis. Such a thing was unthinkable back in the early days of the practice. There has been a long period of slow, but steady change, and now we are in a shorter period of more significant change.

"We have some new materials with which we're working on projects in Asia. I can't really talk about it yet, but the prospects are incredibly exciting. There's wonderful scope for a greater integration between the structure that holds the building up and the services that supply heating and cooling. It's going to take architecture in some fantastic new directions."

**Roger Ridsdill Smith:** "What we were looking for in this bridge was a really minimal statement of what a bridge crossing was. What got us going was the reduction of the bridge to just a line between two banks. Chris Wise and I brainstormed with Foster and Partners. As we talked, we sketched this line, this blade of light, stretching across the river.

"It was flat, with as little curve as possible, because we didn't want to impede views of St Paul's or Tate Modern at either end. We sat down with Foster and Partners and thought long and hard about the way people would use it. And we realised that the bridge would be a great opportunity to view the London skyline from new perspectives. The bridge is all about views: views from either end, views from the middle, views of it and from it.

"We all decided to keep all the supporting structure as low as possible. From that arose the way we arranged the cables – and so discovered that the arrangement we designed has all sorts of advantages. The cables, positioned so well outside the width of the deck, give considerable stability in the wind. It allowed us to simplify the deck's structure, creating a very shallow elevation. It's 320 metres long and the cables dip just 2.3 metres from the top of the river supports to their lowest points at midspan. We wanted it to look, literally, like a thin, illuminated blade of light by night, a ribbon of steel by day.

"When I first noticed the wobble, I thought: 'That's interesting...' Over 100,000 people used the bridge that weekend. We started to watch the way people were moving more closely, with growing concern. And then we went to work to find a solution.

"Once news spread of the problem, we began getting some interesting feedback: that this had happened before. An 85-year-old engineer wrote to us telling us that Auckland Harbour roadbridge had moved sideways in a similar way after they closed two lanes to allow a pedestrian protest march across it. And we also read eyewitness accounts of that San Francisco's Golden Gate showing the same sideways sway when 200,000 people crossed it on the bridge's 50th anniversary.

"One alternative was to restrict numbers on the bridge, but it was not the right solution; the bridge is about accessibility. We worked long hours in the glare of the media spotlight to find an elegant solution.

"It's been a tough project. It was tight in terms of timing and budget, and the politics of central London are quite complex. But the bridge brought together an incredible team who demonstrated huge commitment and dealt with intense stress.

"Well, now there's a damping system that dissipates the sideways movement by transferring the energy into shock absorbers – not unlike a car's piston shock absorbers. The bridge still looks like a blade – the system is pretty discreet, given the amount of damping we've decided to add.

"It's a watershed in bridge design. In future all bridges used by pedestrians will have to take into account the results of our research."

*As part of the renewal of the Thames's South Bank, and part, indeed, of the renewal of the Tate, the Tate Modern was constructed next to the Millennium Bridge. Wolff Olins got the job of generating a new brand identity, as designer Adam Throup explains...*

**Adam Throup:** "What we had was a well-established institution keen to present a new, modern identity. So we wanted something that wasn't institutional. We wanted something dynamic and alive, something that challenges preconceptions of what a gallery is and can be.

"Colour was important. We created a 10-colour palette, with five quite acidic, and another five more earthy. We wanted the image to be soft – not hard as big institutions can be. Softness was important. The mark had to be able to sit in the background, out of the way. It had to be seen, but not overwhelm.

"We wanted it to act as an invitation. We wanted it to say: 'This organization is continually fresh, accessible and always stimulating and exciting.' It had to feel open to the public.

"But mostly we just wanted to create something that felt a lot more exciting, and something that suggested the different types of art in the different buildings around the country.

"There is something electric about the mark. It's partly because the London site was built on a power station, and also because this pulsing Tate identity is, by its nature, animated. It gives a sensation of something alive. It suggests neon – something that is usually associated with places where you have fun and which are welcoming.

"Well, I don't know whether 'proud' is the right word, but I am happy with the way it all came together to create a fresh and clear idea. And it makes me smile to see the number of purple Tate bags wandering around London."

# SUBVERSION

# PAUL SMITH SUIT

*Paul Smith is one of Britain's best- known designers, creating collections for men and women sold through his many shops, most of which are outside the UK. His suits are famous for their beautiful, classic tailoring and their subtle subversion of that tailoring. They are top- quality suits with a sense of humour. Or, as the commentators would have it: 'classic with a twist'. Here, Paul Smith talks about the thinking behind them, why his work is so popular in Japan, and design trends in Britain.*

**Paul Smith:** "My background, and what I really love, is tradition and craftsmanship. I really value and enjoy high-quality work. But I also enjoy surprises.

"This suit is a classic, navyblue, three-button suit, made of a beautiful fabric. But what amuses me is the lining, the union jack flag on a pale blue background. Now you can't see this, of course, in the normal course of events. But as you walk down the street, someone might say: 'What a classic suit – how quintessentially British!' But they wouldn't know just how British it really was. It's a suit with a sense of humour. It contains a double-take. It's one thing outside and something slightly subversive inside.

"Where the idea came from, I've absolutely no idea, but then I never can explain where the ideas come from; they just leap into my head for some reason. You get all sorts of cuts on suits. This is an undercut – undercutting the convention!

"The suit I'm wearing today is a navy blue suit, very, very classic outside, but if you look under the lapel you'll see bright purple stitching which only the wearer knows about. If you look inside you see a purple piping and little pocket jets in a lilac colour. And the shirt I've got on today is a classic blue-and-white striped shirt, but underneath the cuff is a bright-coloured print which has no relevance to the shirt at all!

"It's the sort of stuff that has been my handwriting for years.

"There are a number of reasons why the Japanese go for my stuff. One is the fact that I've been to Japan over 50 times. I like the place, I've got to know the people, and have built a great relationship with the country. And I think the Japanese like me. When I'm interviewed I don't just bang on about my suits, but I talk about graphic design, or the arts, or architecture, or even life itself! I'm very straightforward in interviews and they seem to like that.

"The other factor? Well, hopefully the clothes come into it as well... It's back to that dreaded expression again: 'classic with a twist'. I think it's because the clothes are essentially easy to wear, and are very acceptable in most situations. And they've always got that little something unexpected which makes you smile or makes you feel special. It's a talking point.

"So many clothes around the world are either very extreme (which means they are very difficult to wear unless you are quite an eccentric person) or they are very, very classic – which is fine, but there's a lot of it about.

"These suits are about allowing you to be a bit of both. I think it's just the fact that they've got that little edge which appeals.

"A lot of creative industries run in parallel without the creatives realizing it. There might be a trend towards black-and-white photography – and that might also coincide with a trend for very minimal monochrome interiors, which itself might coincide with a simplicity of graphic design...

"Certainly with interior design right now there's a movement away from the minimalist interior. People are starting to add some colour, some more ethnic ingredients. And that happens with fashion as well – so you might get a classic suit with a shirt or a blouse that's got a ethnic influence with embroidery or with the strong colours from the orient.

"I don't think it's a conscious thing at all; just that most creative people are interested in all aspects of creativity and soak it up from all different types of design. I think it all just flops along in parallel.

"Hopefully at Paul Smith there is still a tremendous amount of individuality. And that's because we're not locked into the pressure of shareholders wanting more and more and more. We are interested in expanding our business, but we still want to do it with a heart, and with individuality. And that's becoming more and more rare because shareholders want people to perform better and better for them. We're lucky!"

WWW.SKOOLRUSH.COM

*How do you engage children at school? How do you make them want to be involved? The key is to speak to them in their own language. As part of the Joinedupdesignforschools pilot project, Deepend designers Simon Waterfall, Peter Everett and David 'Gravy' Streek worked with Swanlea School in East London and, with the pupils as their clients, came up with an online computer game that was informative about the school, educational and fun.*

**David Streek** (shown left, along with Peter Everett, Nick Holmes and Simon Waterfall)**:** "The kids wanted the game to represent their school as accurately as possible. There were people from a wide variety of ethnic backgrounds. The boys wanted it to be action-based. The girls wanted it to be more challenging to the mind – they didn't want something that was just a beat-'em-up. The boys were keen to give the teachers a good kicking in the game; that was a bit too subversive! We compromised accordingly and went for an adventure game.

"We took lots of pictures of the kids, and the layout and the teachers. We wanted to reproduce the school in the game. We asked the kids to identify things about specific areas that stood out. Their preconception was that all the places were pretty similar – noisy, with kids screaming and teachers shouting. But they learnt it was all more subtle than that. It was a good process for them – they learnt to see their space in different light.

"The children were heavily involved in generating ideas for the game. Our job was to develop and execute their ideas.

"And so the game became a mission – a challenge. It's designed to help newcomers get to know the school and encourage current pupils to explore through the game. In the game, the head teacher sets the players a task. For example – fetch this biology encyclopedia from the Science Block. To complete the mission the players have to answer curriculum-based questions along the way, and have to avoid various obstacles. They are in a race against the clock.

"If they find they're running low on energy, they go to the canteen. If they stock up on junk food, of course, they don't get much joy. But if they go for the healthier food, they are given more energy because it's better for them. If they pick up litter on their way they get bonus points. If they crash into people in their rush to complete their mission, they lose energy, so it doesn't pay to run too fast.

"You can choose your character from a large variety of choices. You can choose different skin colour or hair colour. You can wear different ethnic dress. If you are playing a disabled character, in a wheelchair, you get to move faster, but you have fewer points of access, having to move to lifts rather than taking the stairs. It all balances out.

"I think it is very positive. Usually computer games are discouraged at school; here the kids were being encouraged to play, and playing actually worked educationally. We did this as a charity project for the joinedupdesign pilot project, but we were caught up in the children's enthusiasm and really poured a lot of effort into it. And we learnt a lot technically from trying to achieve what they wanted us to do. The Department of Education has shown a keen interest in the game. It seems they think there's a lot of potential for development."

# JACK LIGHT AND STOOL

*Tom Dixon started work doing graphic designs for a video nasties firm. He became a party organizer, putting together warehouse raves. Then he collaborated to form Creative Salvage – a company dedicated to making new stuff from old. During this period his attention changed to electric lighting design, and he set up Eurolounge to industrialize and wholesale the Jack Light. He recently became Habitat's UK head of design.*

Tom Dixon: "Geometry: I've been fascinated with it since childhood. Mathematical beauty. Wonderful. When I started to get interested in lighting and lamps, I was trying to think of making lamps in a more industrial way. I wanted to do as good a job as the Italians.

"So I set about trying to find an inexpensive plastic-moulding technique. I was looking at street bollards, thinking: 'Maybe that's the way ahead'.

"I looked at the way these plastics could diffuse light. I began to learn about rotational moulding, how it was used rarely for domestic products, except for a few large garden toys. So I borrowed 20 grand and set to work.

"I wanted to create a new type of lighting: exciting, versatile, different. I wanted lighting to be a feature of different types of furniture.

"I wanted there to be lighting in a chair, lighting in a table, as well as lighting where it is more traditionally found – in a lamp. I wanted the lighting to be multifunctional, too. And I wanted the furniture that contained it to be multi-functional too.

"I came up with a dodecahedron shape before settling on the six protrusions. The six-pointed version is the minimum that doesn't compromise the design. It effectively consists of two tripods, so it can remain steady as a seat, it can stack, and it has three upper legs that can support a glass tabletop.

"If you stack four on top of each other, they can generate a lovely, warm, low-level light.

"Reactions to it have been interesting. People say the six protrusions, rounded and warm, are phallic. Others see the split lines of the mould running between the protrusions as a female crotch.

"The Japanese see it as a sea creature found on their shores. Others see fertility symbolism in it, like it is echoing primitive art. Still others see it as a molecular structure.

"Well, those responses are beyond design. It's great to see it working beyond the original concept."

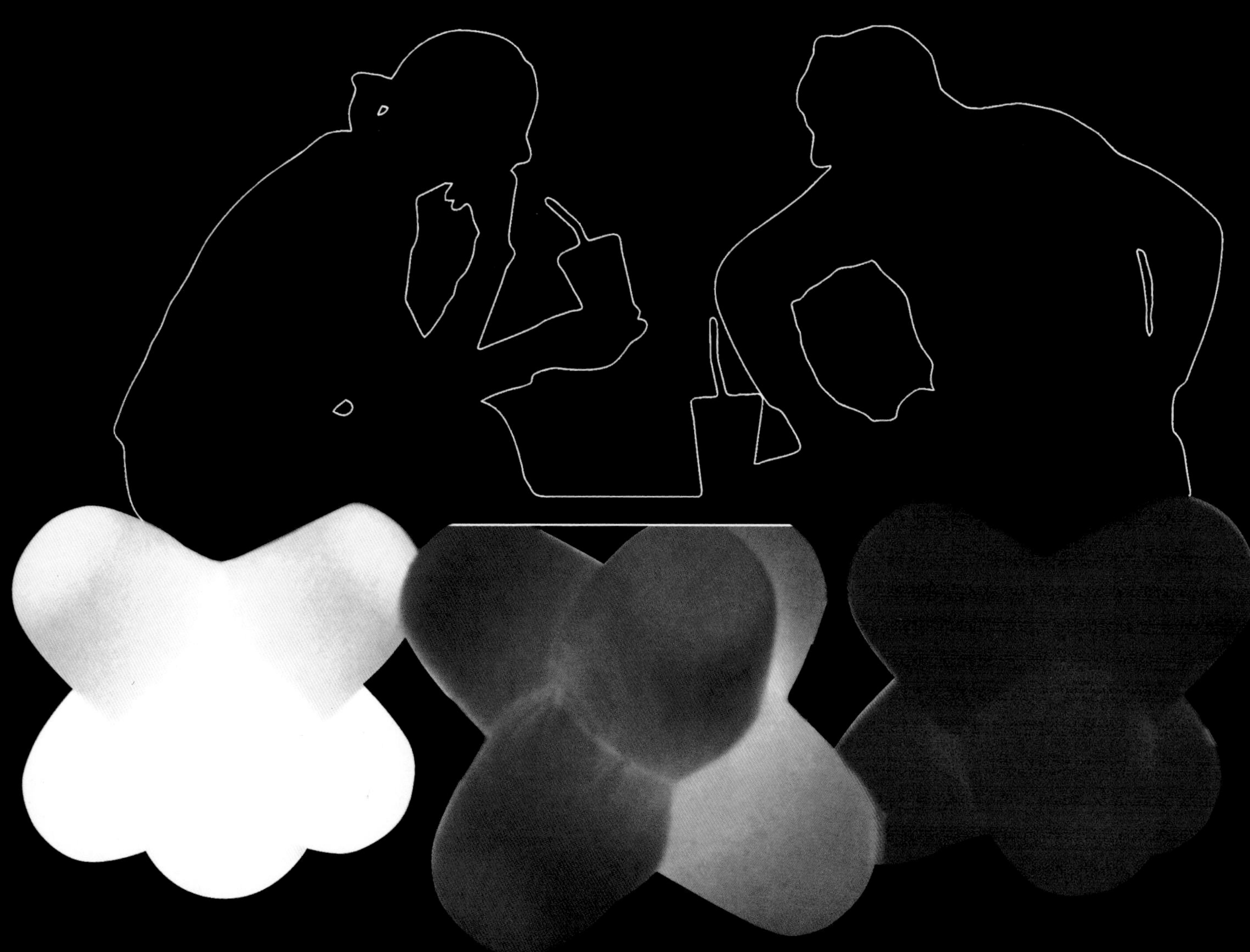

# NOVA STENCIL CAMPAIGN

*Illustrator Bernie Reid and fashion and print designer Beca Lipscombe came up with a highly original approach to a fashion shoot. Take some up-and-coming people from the fashion industry, dress them, photograph them, and then stencil their images all over the docks in Leith. The idea secured a 12-page spread in* Nova *and work from Chloé and Stella McCartney.*

**Bernie Reid:** "Basically Beca was the one who came up with the idea. I'd been mucking about with some other stencil stuff, all inspired by some stencil art I'd seen in Paris, and Beca said: 'why don't we do a fashion story in the same style?'

"She presented the idea to *Nova*, and they absolutely loved it. They gave us 12 pages. So then the photographer Andy Shaw came down and Beca contacted people she knew in the fashion industry, people who are well-known if you move in those circles. We went out onto the street, found some good locations and created the artwork. We weren't supposed to, but we didn't harm anyone and no one really complained.

"The technique is pretty straight-forward. You spray colours on top of other colours through a stencil, a little bit like printing.

"We were just trying to do something different, and we thought we could mix both our interests.

"So we got a fashion story that wasn't just photographic. Often in a fashion shoot you just see a bit of clothing and the model's face."

**Beca Lipscombe:** "Bernie and I are partners in real life. I give him ideas and he gives me ideas.

"What was refreshing was the fact that we picked people we liked. We knew them all and admired them all.

"We didn't choose models – we chose people like you and me who work hard in an aesthetic business. We mixed high and low fashion – Top Shop here, one-off designers there…

"I really like the diamond socks. They were from a collection I'd done prior to doing the shoot. Bernie sprayed in the diamonds – his medium mixed into my medium. It was a bit of a *trompe l'oeil*".

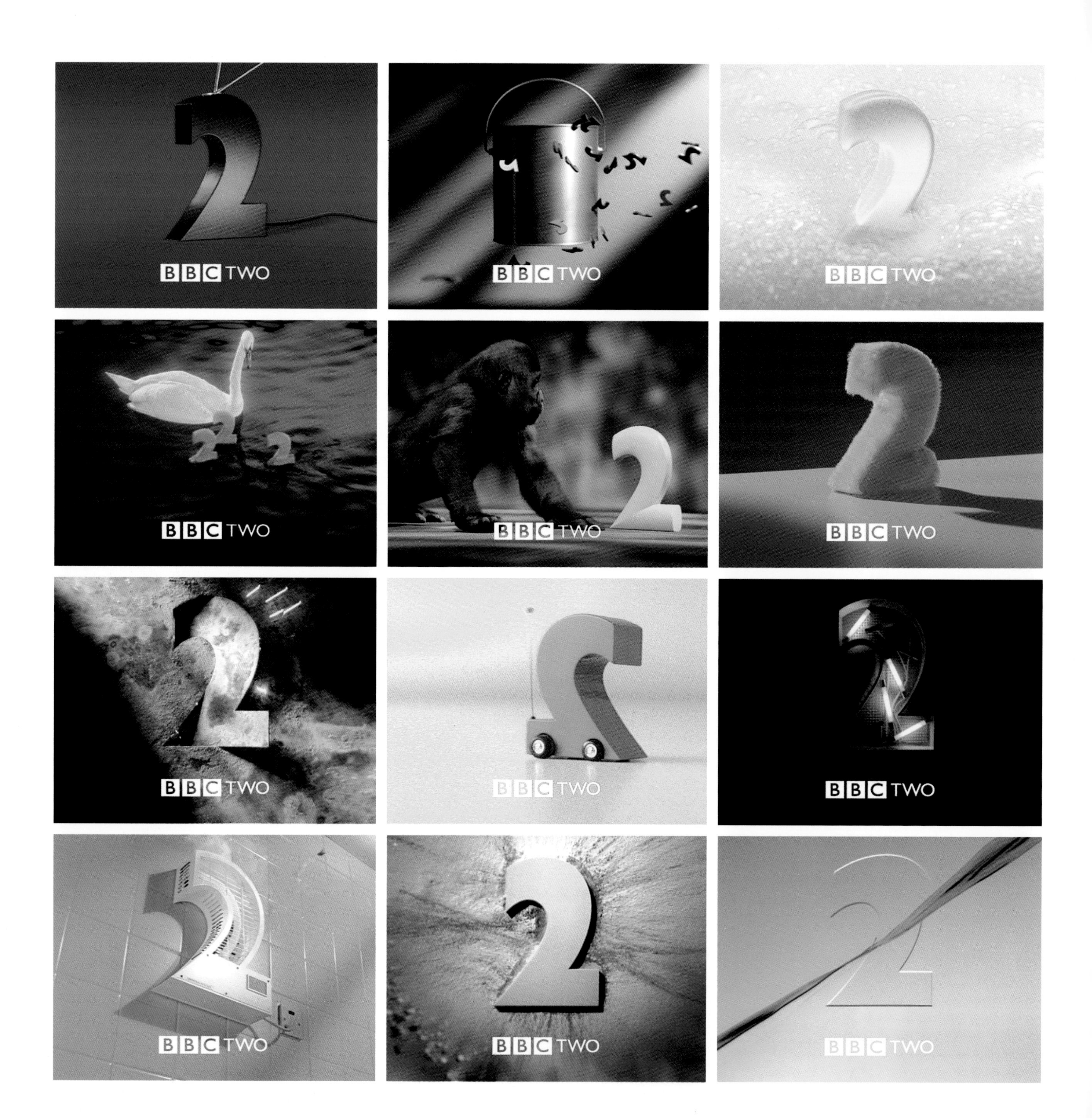
BBC TWO
BBC TWO
BBC TWO
BBC TWO
BBC TWO
BBC TWO
BBC TWO
BBC TWO
BBC TWO
BBC TWO
BBC TWO
BBC TWO

*BBC2 caught the attention of television viewers with their brilliant revolutionary identity, which saw paint splashing over a 3D number 2, among many other incarnations. The message being skilfully communicated by Lambie-Nairn was that BBC2 was unusual, clever, surprising and entertaining. The BBC launched new designs over Christmas 2001, reflecting a shift in the station's positioning.*

**Martin Lambie-Nairn:** "The animated 2 was pretty revolutionary for its time. And the inspiration came from advertising. Remember the Silk Cut sardine can that unrolled to reveal cigarettes? That tone appealed to us. So it became a case of devising a form of the number 2 that would allow us to do lots of different things. We decided the 2 should be solid.

"The reference points came from the world of art, say, Dadaism. But not always art – sometimes they'd reflect the social context. Remember the fluffy dog that roamed all over the screen and then stopped and did a back flip? That came out when those toys were being bought by everyone.

"Eventually the campaign began to use itself as a reference point, such as the shot of the paint hitting the 2 in that dramatic splurge, and then later, the tiny 2s cascading onto the paint tin. My favourite is 'Fly Zapper', when the fly blows up the insect-frying machine, and gets away singed. And I still love the back-flip dog, and the 2 as a radio-controlled car. They still make me smile.

"The new idents reflect BBC2's lighter tone. It's also easier to use in print for advertising and the below-the-line stuff. So we went for yellow, with a purple logo type. The original has no particular colour theme. There are more gags in the new ones. The reference points are no longer art, but, say, popular animation. They are familiar to a broader audience.

"Now the 2 works like a character. It can have arms. It can do things to other things – things don't just happen to it. In the design business you know when something's working when you can have five or six ideas in 10 minutes. That's an idea starting to roll."

September / October

30
1
2
3
4
5
6

*One of the primary functions of design is communication. Graphic art, product design, fashion and architecture are all eloquent. They say things like: 'This is how you use me. Isn't this amazing? Doesn't this make you feel great?' But design can also make you laugh. Wolff Olins, co-founder, Michael Wolff, believes corporations need to find a way to present a more human face. So he created the 3i cartoon calendar.*

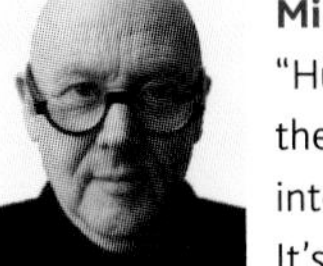

**Michael Wolff:** "Humour is one of the reasons we get into relationships. It's the fun side of business. You get close to someone when you laugh together.

"Investors In Industry (3i) pride themselves in building long-term relationships with businesses, and I remember saying to them back in 1985 that you must do something to show your human face. It didn't have to be a big deal, just a promotional gift, something showing how we can laugh at ourselves and celebrate what's funny in the business world. I persuaded them without much difficulty to give people a cartoon a week.

"Well, we had this meeting to discuss the content. I laid out 70 cartoons on this enormous table on the main boardroom floor. Nigel, responsible for the project, walked silently around the display. He picked up six cartoons and took them off the table. I said: 'That's no problem, Nigel, we can get rid of those.' 'No, Michael,' he said. 'Those are the only ones that are funny.'

"Anyway, I eventually persuaded them that this couldn't be edited by vote or committee, so I got the job of editor. And apart from a few conflicts over some of the raunchier jokes and one about alcoholism, it's been a very, very pleasant project. Over the years there've been a few moves to say: 'Isn't it time we did something else?' But so far the cartoon calendar has survived. It is, happily, still enormously popular. I have to say that's pretty rare among corporate communications! It goes to show that communicating humanity actually works.

"I did two issues based on *Punch*, but then turned to cartoonists drawing for the *New Yorker* through their Cartoon Bank. They are just wonderful. Who says Americans don't have a sense of irony?

"Cartoons can make points about human relations that novelists take whole books to make. And they record such wonderful moments. I remember one, a Charles Barsotti cartoon, which featured a panicky-looking man with two speech bubbles. The first says: 'What's next?' and the other right next to it: 'Don't tell me!' It sort of sums up the human condition!

"This is a Mick Stevens cartoon, the cat sitting outside the hole, hopelessly disguised as a mouse. Why does it work? God knows. For some people it doesn't, of course, but for others it resonates with personal experience – perhaps some forlorn attempt by someone in business to copy the competition and so destroy them. Who knows? Some people just crack up at that cartoon. They're very personal.

"I remember another Mick Stevens cartoon: 'The Ladder of Success.' It was a hamster wheel. And another I remember by him: a group of people are walking the corporate walk down the road with fishing rods coming out of their collars. The rods dangle a carrot ahead of each of them. And driving by is Mr Success in his sports car – which is, of course, a carrot. Such a wonderful sense a humour. It makes you say: 'Why are we running around after this stuff? Are we stupid?!'

"Communication at this level is so important in the corporate world, and it would benefit personally and financially if it learnt to be more human. But the corporate world is so obsessed by the perfect answer, so wrapped up with appearances, with 'looking good' and 'being right'. With being 'corporate', to me, looking good and being right are the two deadly sins."

*The Design Council has undergone a major turnaround in recent years. In 1994 it stood on the edge of being axed. But after a review which gave it new purpose and direction, followed by a period of transformation, it's now re-established as the leading voice on design in the country, and is influential around the world. David Stuart, one of the founding member of The Partners, was brought in to show that the new Design Council knew a thing or two about communication. They came up with a marvellous and, given the audience, subversive way of showing how the organization was changing and what it was trying to do.*

**David Stuart:** "The Design Council was suddenly preparing itself to talk to a wider audience. Our job was to tell people what the new Design Council was doing and what it was going to do.

"Everything the council did became a statement. Every time you got a letter from them, we included a quote explaining what it was about. Every communication included a means for the council to bang its own drum.

"We also wanted to demonstrate that this was no longer an ivory-tower quango. This one was in touch. One day, a few weeks before Christmas, they said they wanted to send something out which would make people really think about good design.

"Well, that concentrated our minds. And so we came up with this cup, with the handle on, upside down. We found a potter and got him to make them very quickly indeed. The cup bore the slogan: 'The new Design Council believes that bad design can be upsetting.'

"It was certainly unusual in a corporate communication. Normally such freebies are positive. But this one was negative. The advertising industry understands the power of the negative. It's much more effective to show someone slopping tea all over themselves before announcing that 'Wizz-off washes whiter' than only showing a white shirt that is so white because of Wizz-off's wonderful powers. This had the same message: 'Pay attention to design. It may seem trivial, but really it's very important.' Everyone was amused by it – that is, everyone who noticed the handle was upside down.

"It was quite subversive for a quango communication. It rather crawled under the wire. But governments and corporations are only just waking up to the benefits of humour. In business-to-business dealings it's still relatively untapped as a communications resource. People are still taking themselves far too seriously."

Bad design can
be upsetting
believes the new
Design Council


DESIGN COUNCIL MUG

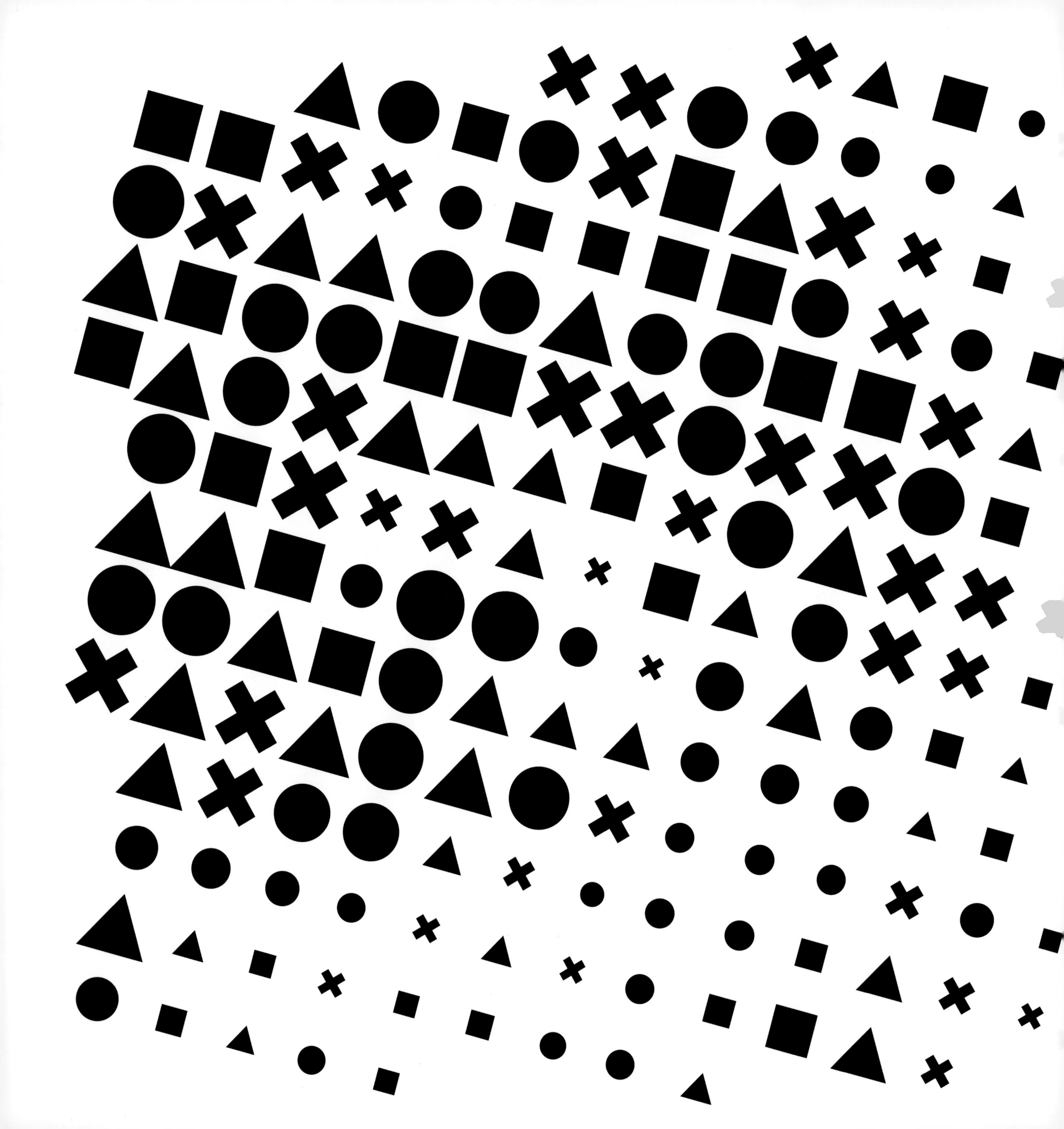

# PLAYSTATION DOT SCREEN CAMPAIGN

*The Sony PlayStation has inspired some highly creative work in many areas: advertising, point-of-sale, sponsorships and of course, the mind-bending games themselves. Simons Palmer were responsible for the original advertising, and when it merged with TBWA, Paul Belford and Nigel Roberts came up with this innovative dot screen design. To get the same effect as the poster on the side of the London terrace below, open the double-page spread on the previous pages, prop the book up, and walk as far away as you can. About 80 feet should do it...*

**Paul Belford:** "The PlayStation symbols – the cross, the triangle, the square and the circle – are well-known to all gamers. They mark the buttons on the handset that control a character's special moves. So, for example, on some games, if the manual instructions say: 'Press ▲▲■!', that means you press the buttons in that order and your character will kick the living shit out of his opponent in an explosive karate move that can only be countered by your enemy quickly pressing ✖● to avoid the onslaught... So they are really important to gamers.

"The symbols, of course, mean nothing to people who don't play video games, so they're a kind of secret. Every gamer will know that this is an ad for PlayStation.

"But what non-gamers will recognize is the power of the visual trick: the staring eyes. They look excited. Amazed. Terrified. Surprised. They look like the girl is living all the emotions that the games generate themselves. The message is very simple. PlayStation = Oh My God!

"This ad does what all good ads do: it distills information to its bare essentials and yet manages to communicate very powerfully to the target audience. It engages them, therefore it's memorable. It works so well it doesn't need to name the product – yet the target audience will know straight away what we're talking about. Gamers smile with a sense of secret recognition. It's an innovative use of a very established medium.

"The ad was inspired by a series we did a few years back for Waterstones booksellers, one of which featured an image of an eye which had been enlarged from a halftone black-and-white picture. The dots of ink from the printing process were clearly visible, so the image was made up of a series of black circles. This ad was pinned up on our office wall and when we began thinking about PlayStation, it was a small step to turn the circles into the PlayStation symbols.

"We then had to find a suitable image for the poster. Eyes worked best because they're such simple, recognizable, and yet highly emotive shapes.

"The client liked the idea, but we still had to fend off suggestions like 'can it be in colour?', 'can we show an image from a game?', 'can we have a packshot?' and 'can we have a logo?' All of which would have damaged the simplicity of the idea.

"The UK's always turned out good ads, and I think the ad work coming out now is looking more and more interesting. I don't think we're better at ideas than they were, say in the '60s, but technology has liberated us, and more advertising agencies are being more visually creative than before.

# SPIRITUALIZED CD PACKAGING

*When Spiritualized wanted to create innovative packaging for the Album* Ladies and Gentlemen We Are Floating in Space, *Jason Pierce turned to Farrow Design, well-known for their work with Kylie Minogue, Craig David, The Manic Street Preachers, Orbital, The Pet Shop Boys and William Ørbit. Farrow's work is famous for clean, clear communication and often employs a minimalist vocabulary. Jason wanted something that communicated a core philosophy of his: that music is medication for the soul. The good news was that the record company's marketing department saw the plus side of what was promising to be a very expensive idea. They reasoned the innovative cover would secure wide coverage in the style magazines and at the very least, reviewers would say: 'You gotta buy this for the sleeve if nothing else.' And people did.*

**Mark Farrow:**
"After talking to Jason, it entered my head that we could package it in the way that pills are packaged. Then I thought, let's take that idea to extremes.

"Well, in the climate record companies work in now, just being able to push something like that through is an achievement. It's increasingly difficult to do nice things. But in this case, the record company was up for it and very excited.

"Well, yes, I supposed it could be argued that there is an illicit drugs connotation, but really, we've done quite a lot to try to avoid that. From the outside it looks like a CD-sized pill packet for a prescription drug. I must confess that the idea of packaging prescription drugs really appeals to me. We've come up with a number of ideas that have that feel.

"You open the box and pull out a five-inch plastic blister pack covered in foil. You push the CD through it to get it out. We took all this to incredible lengths. We also made instructions that were printed by a pharmaceutical printer, because they're the only people who have machines to fold the paper as many times as you have to, to get it in the box.

"It listed the drug's side effects – i.e. what could happen when you listened to the CD, including: 'Delirium, a sense of intoxication, memory loss and temporary paralysis, etc.' And it said things like: 'What should I do if symptoms persist?' And went on to suggest listening to the other Spiritualized albums. We even had a prescription label giving the dosage...

"We then took it all a bit further, creating a foot-long box with two trays of six 'pills' which had individual tracks of the album on each. Only 1,000 of these were produced. They're now very hard to get hold of."

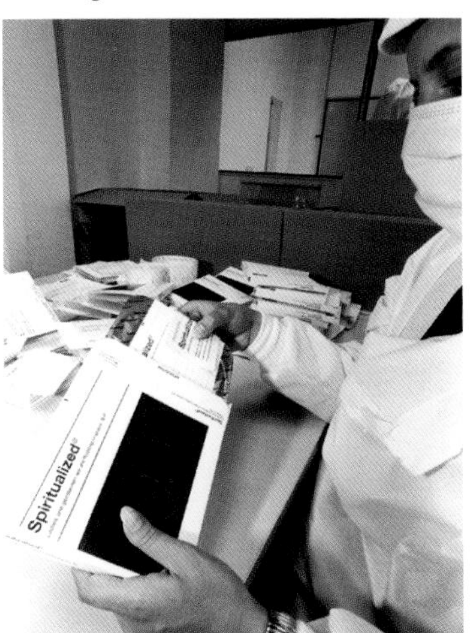

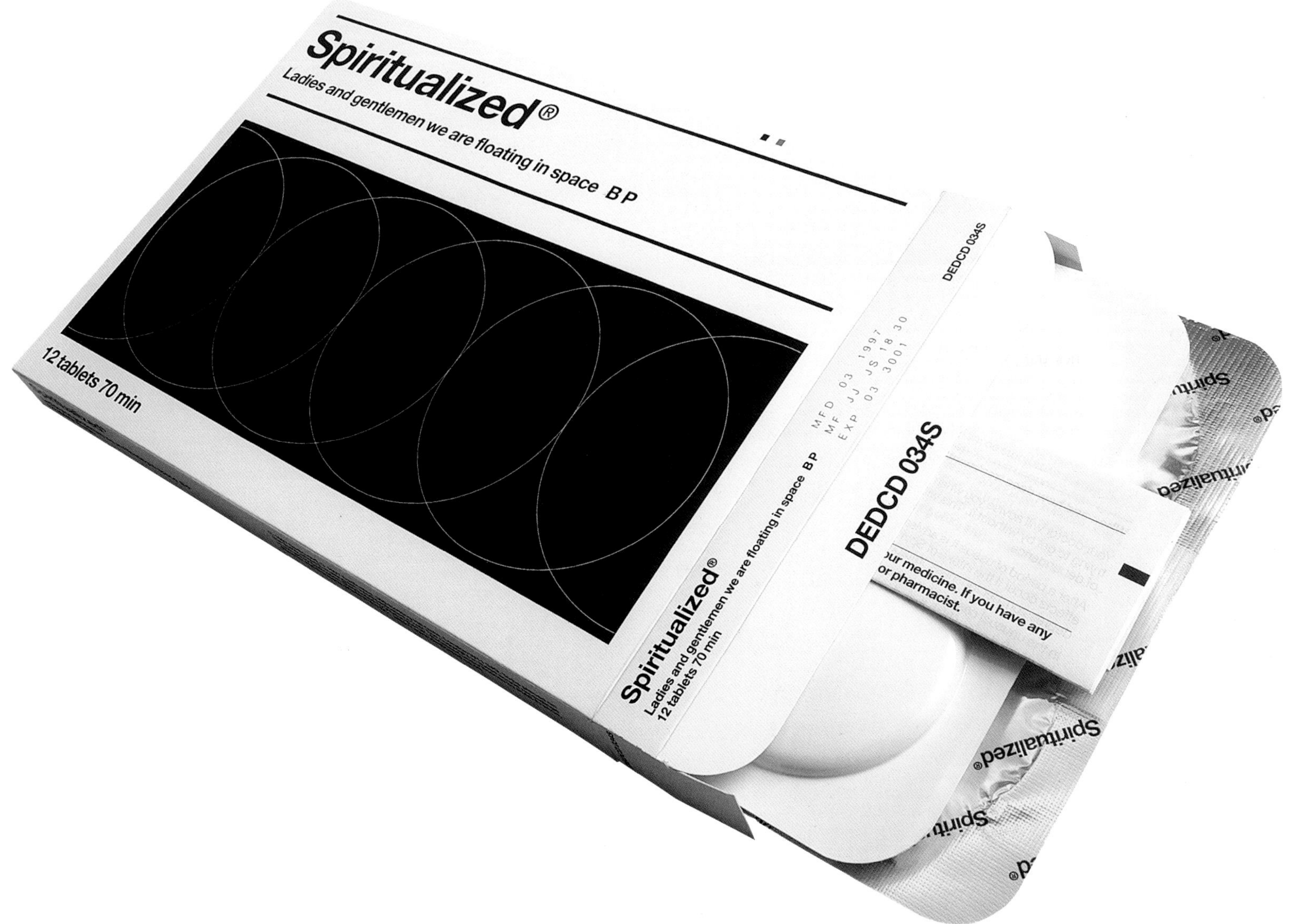

f c

uk®

# FCUK IDENTITY AND OXFORD STREET STORE

*Just a simple trick of the eye, two letters swapped about, and it has half a nation smiling – the other half staggering, wrong-footed. The FCUK campaign is a brilliant example of bold advertising carefully targeted at a young-at-heart audience. A campaign with a sexy edge. Sex sells – everyone knows it, but no-one better than Trevor Beattie at TBWA.*

*Din Associates has been working with French Connection more or less since it was founded in 1986. Other clients include Ralph Lauren, Selfridges, BAA and the V&A museum. The company's award-winning interior work on the FCUK Oxford Street store features a display system that is both highly flexible to work with and liberating to shop in.*

**Trevor Beattie:**
"If you go with a controversial campaign, you have to be brave enough to pick it up and run with it and then big enough to stick with it when the flak starts flying.

"I have a wonderful working relationship with Stephen Marks, and we have confidence in each other, so we were able to ride it.

"Stephen's brief made it a bit easier: 'Make me the most talked-about fashion store on the high street!' It's not every day you get a brief like that, so the response wasn't likely to be 'everyday' either.

"The idea was simple, really. It was staring me in the face. The company changed its name from French Connection to French Connection UK. I remember an internal fax from French Connection UK to French Connection Hong Kong. It came back FCHK TO FCUK.

"Having a good idea is like shining a torch. You throw light on something already there – that's how you discover it. It's like finding a £50 note on the pub floor. Someone is going to find it.

"Of course, we never thought it would take off in the way it did. In fact, for the first two months nothing happened at all.

"The first complaint wasn't about the transposed letters that implied a swear word, it was about the enormous amount of white space around the word on an underground billboard. Apparently it was dazzling the passengers on the platform.

"It was only in the second wave, some weeks later, when Linda Lee Potter picked it up in *The Daily Mail*, that it began to build. Rather marvellously, *The Guardian*, famous for its spelling errors, printed our headline as 'Fuck Fashion' – apparently because they had spell-checked it and the computer corrected FCUK to Fuck. A perfect 'Grauniad' moment."

**Rashied Din:**
"We've been working on all aspects of the FCUK brand. The brief has always been to put French Connection front-of-mind and position it as ahead of the game.

"It's very much a holistic approach: brand, packaging, identity work, new product development, store interiors, point of sale... we have input on all of this, and it's a team effort.

"FCUK is an in-your-face kind of brand, attitudinally. I think it's worked because of that.

"The shop itself was designed by Din Associates, headed by John Harvey, and Angela Drinkall. It's a hard, glass box with a highly flexible interior design.

"Everything is hung from the ceiling, so it feels light. You can see the floor right through from one side to the other. It creates a magical sense of floatation.

"The whole display system can be turned through 180 degrees. So one day you'll come in and see everything oriented towards the back of the store, and the next day it's all oriented widthways.

"It creates a great sense of freedom, and represents the youthful appeal of the brand, because young people are always looking for fresh experiences. It has a transient feeling about it.

"We've even suspended the cash desk from the ceiling, and the staircase is cantilevered, to make it feel like it's hovering in space.

"We really had to push the technological boundaries to get this to work. It's strong, hard, contemporary but very, very workable.

"And we've kept a graphical consistency on the posters and imagery that goes from the web page right through to the store. It's an instant hit for the punter coming through the door."

fcuk®
fcuk®
FRENCH CONNECTION
fcuk
allsummer
fcuk
fcuk
allsummer
fcuk

*Clothes made from paper? Are you mad? What happens when it rains? Don't be alarmed by the quirky work of Charlie Thomas. He's not expecting you to wander down the road in his paper anorak. And he's currently working on paper furniture...*

**Charlie Thomas:** "I have a mixture of interests and work. Most of it is generated by what a given client wants, but all the time I'm also working on my own self-initiated briefs. It's vital to have other interests, because they feed your paid work.

"It's also vital for me to work in collaboration – whether with a client, a retailer, a photographer or a stylist. Where you've got a number of people contributing, you've got an automatic generator of good ideas. You feed off each other. It's good to work with different people. You get this inside information of how things operate.

"The clothes are a comment on the process of creating fashion. It's like showing what's going on behind the scenes. They're like this: I draw a design, I make a pattern, I cut clothes out from the pattern, I run up a three-dimensional piece of clothing, I photograph it and so make it flat again. It gets reproduced in a magazine. The paper clothes are my take on the fashion process.

"Fashionable clothing has many lives, and sometimes the most important life isn't when you wear it, because you will probably never get to wear it. But perhaps you may look at in on a page. Clothes are not just to be worn; they become photographs, icons, a magazine shoot, a flashy advertising campaign. The paper clothes tell a story around these objects.

"I am preoccupied with longevity. I hate the disposable culture, the consumer culture that tries to make everything the same across the world. My paper suits are photographed and encased in Perspex. It's a comment on the disposable society.

"No, you can't wear them! They are just images. I used paper because, as a graphic designer, it was easy for me to use. It's accessible and cheap and I was skilled in manipulating it. It seemed very natural for me. The models wearing the suits had to be lifted into them. It was fun getting the models dressed – the models are as much apart of the process as the photographer. These clothes are about the journey – not the end product.

Design is changing since the digital revolution. Suddenly, overnight, everyone can be a graphic designer! Everyone had access to desktop publishing. It was a phenomenal thing to happen. It's a democratization of design. But there is a danger: I do believe in training people!

"In fashion there's such a turnover of images and trends. Things change and the forces that make those changes are outside of your control, unless you're lucky enough to be in a privileged position. External forces make fashion what it is – there's no real originality. But the stylists and photographers – to me they are the ones who have the control. They can make a design look good or not look good. That's the point I'm trying to make.

"Some fashion designers are moving away from the glamour of clothes and are moving into domestic furnishings. I find myself doing the same. I'm doing home products now. I'm continuing with paper, making small editions of paper furniture. I've also started to work with ceramics making decorative objects.

"There's a reaction setting in to minimalism. Decoration is coming back. It's like in the '70s we accumulated loads of junk and we needed to clear it way, and we used minimalism to do it. Now we're bored of empty walls and floors – somehow they've lost their edge – so decoration is coming back. But it's been informed by minimalism and it's more subtle. I think we are all more visually aware than ever before, partly because of the impact of the media."

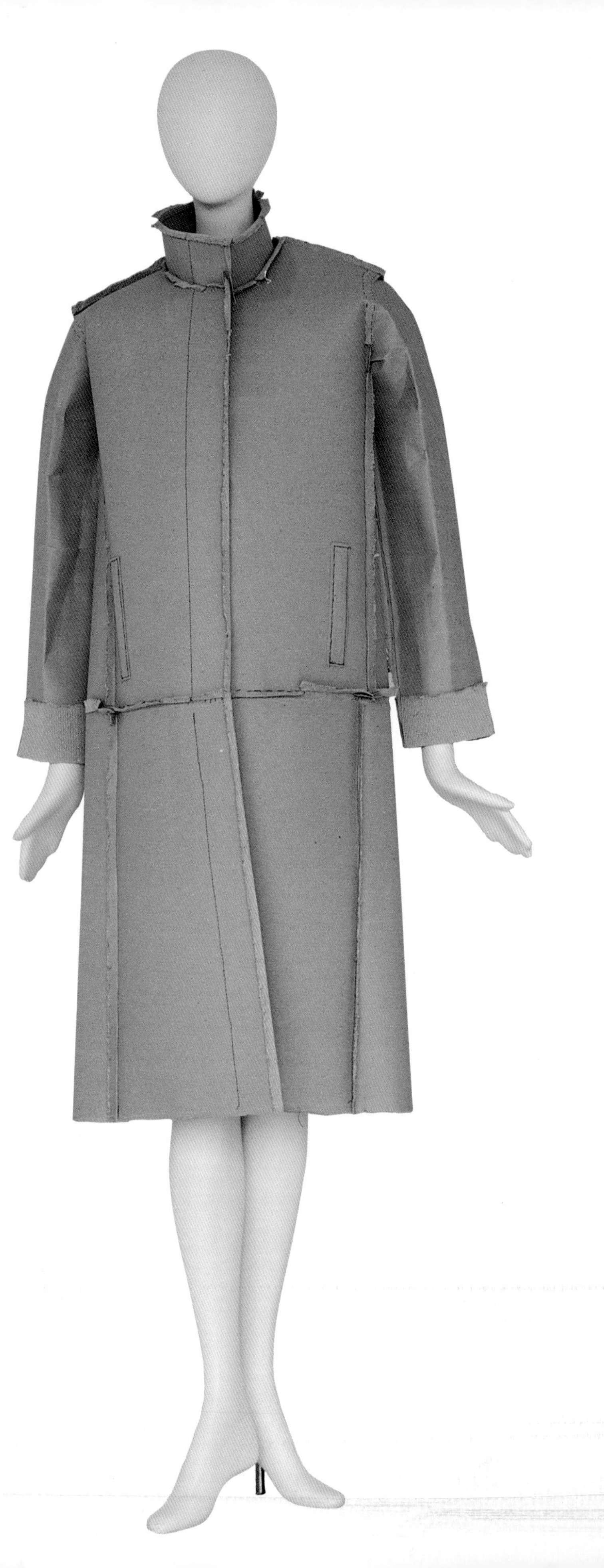

*Truth to tell, it's a PR nightmare trying to get publicity for a website. There was a time when new websites were sexy. Nowadays, big media take a lot of persuading to pay any attention to a new website, whatever the content. So when Britart.com arrived, offering art for sale on the web, journalists were not exactly champing at the bit. That was until Mother came on board. Their mission: under the direction of art director Kim Gehrig, was to make a noise. And they did.*

**Kim Gehrig:** "We had a pretty international bunch working on this. I'm Australian, Cecilia Dufils and Marcus Bjurman are Swedish, and writer Jo de Souza and Jamie Johnson were English.

"The aim of the campaign was to increase awareness of the Britart website – a place you can buy original art, from low prices to really rather high prices. We had hardly any money, so advertising was really out of the question. We needed to make a noise.

"We had quite a job to do. A lot of people don't much like art, and few buy original works – not because they can't afford it, because so much of it is cheaper than you think, but because they're frightened of it.

"So what we aimed to do was make people feel relaxed about art. We figured the best way to do that was to get them to laugh at it. But we didn't want to go over the top, or we'd alienate the artists! But we couldn't use arty language – it can so often be intimidating and condescending.

"Some time before this project, we made the 'Hooligan Kit'. This was an airfix-type model of a soccer hooly complete with beer can, two finger salute, etc. That secured a lot of press. It became our inspiration for this campaign.

"We came up with some simple gimmicks to send to journalists, to start getting awareness of Britart.com among the opinion-forming media. We sent them 'Preview Glasses', which were a pair of spectacles with a long hook sticking out of the front of them. The idea was you'd hang your artwork on the hook and move your head around. This way you could preview how your artwork would look in a given room. We did the same thing with VCRs – making a tape of artworks so you could see what they would look like with your colour scheme. It was all a bit of a laugh and got us some publicity in London's *Time Out*.

"Then we came up with 'Artalisers'. These were sheets of stickers that you could peel off and stick to your fridge, chair, door, wall, etc. The text declared the objects to be a work of art. It was poking fun at art, of course, but it was also increasing awareness of art and of Britart.com. It was helping people feel relaxed about it.

"We then did a sticker sheet in *Time Out*. It included Artaliser stickers for Badly Dressed Person, Boyfriend, Mobile Phone, Pint Glass, treating them sarcastically as works of art.

"We then thought: 'Let's take this idea outside.' So our writer, Joe de Souza, came up with this great, cynical, subversive, irreverent text which really did make people laugh and captured a lot of attention. We couldn't afford to do many – the plastic transfers were made by 3M and were very expensive. We concentrated on North London: Soho, Shoreditch and Notting Hill.

**Joe de Souza:** "I'd seen a TV programme about phobias. The psychiatrist had said one way to get over fear of spiders was to visualize the spider wearing a funny hat and spectacles. By doing that you turn the scary thing into something you can handle. With this we were doing something similar.

"This wasn't just 'Britart.com' stuck all over the place: this was engaging and smart. We got a lot of flak from the companies that own these bus shelters and poster sites – they felt we were undermining the established system of street advertising. I don't like being confronted by stupid things stuck on this that or the other – but we were doing something different. There was more of a reward. It had more substance. If people stopped and smiled and saw what we were trying to do, then I think it was worth it. We were saying: 'Look, modern art is not just a bunch of Hoxton trendies being pseudo-intellectual. Modern art can laugh at itself. Don't be scared of it. It's clever, and it's often fun.'

"It was about the democratization of art. Art is relevant, accessible and inspirational. We wanted to take it out of the gallery and put it into the high street where people could engage with it."

Railing 1971
metal rods, paint, hand prints.
300 x 100 x 5cm
Engaging three dimensional essay on containment.
art you can buy britart.com

Wall 1946
mixed media installation: bricks, tiling, wood, insulation, nails.
2256 x 425cm
Rebuilt 1956
art you can buy britart.com
Saturday
9th September
Darren Emerson
Giles Peterson
Tim Sheridan
(Dope Smugglaz)
Parks & Wilson
Andy Smith (Portishead)
Jason Bye
Stewart Rowell
David Phillips
Dave Beer
Huggy
Paul Arnold
DANNY TENAGLIA
DARREN EMERSON
Pavement 1962
concrete slabs, cement, shoe prints, dog excrement, chewing gum.
8000 x 15050 x 10cm
britart.com

# HUMANISM

# SNOWMAN SALT & PEPPER SHAKERS

*It's the little luxuries that count. Shin & Tomoko Azumi discovered a new principle in serving salt and pepper while developing a tableware series. The time-honoured tradition has always been to put the holes in the top of the shakers. But a search for a new approach led the designers to realize that, over the centuries, we'd been dispensing our spices in a rather cackhanded way....*

**Shin Azumi:** "We've been developing a tableware series for some time, and these pots are part of that evolution. The salt cellar before this one featured a hole, not on the top but slightly down from the top, on the side.

"This little detail was about changing people's behaviour. Because if you have holes in the top of the pot, you have to turn it upside down and shake it aggressively. But if we put the hole in the side, then you only have to shake it lightly. You can just tap it. It's a very minor detail but it made a big difference in terms of the interaction between the object and the human.

"For us, design is not just about material quality, shape or colour, but it is also about sensitive phenomena around the object and the way people react to it and behave with it. What we wanted to do was slightly change the manner of using the pot.

"In the new shaker, we found the holes on the side created a really strong impression. And we started to think about the boundary between the abstract shape of the shaker and the cartoony facial expression that was emerging. Without the holes, the shape was just abstract. Comfortable to hold, but not meaning much. With the holes – well, suddenly we could recognize it. And so the snowman salt and pepper shakers were born.

"Well, not *so* fast; it took about a year for them to emerge. But we find them comfortable, amusing, warm – even funny. We are still exploring this boundary between humanistic expression and abstract shape, but we think this series has reached its resolution."

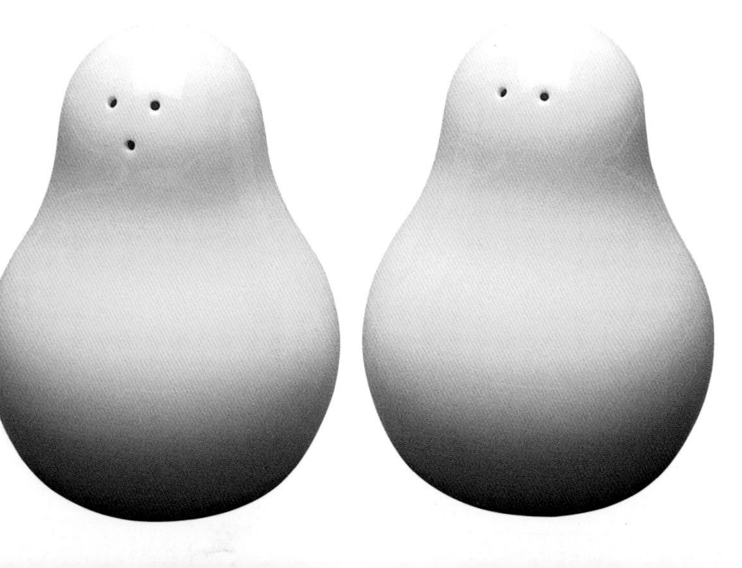

*Nick Park helped catapult Aardman into the big league with his immensely successful characters, Wallace and Gromit. His uncanny ability to put so much humanity into lumps of Plasticine continues to thrill and amaze. Who isn't looking forward to the new Wallace and Gromit film, due out in 2004?*

**Nick Park:** "It all started for me when I discovered that mum's home-movie camera took single frames. I'd always wanted to do cartoons.

"So I set the camera up in the attic and tried to copy Walt Disney. But that required so much tracing and painting and colouring-in that it began to put me off.

"And then I saw Morph – the *Vision On* TV character made of Plasticine and created, as it happened, by Peter Lord at Aardman. Morph wasn't the only active plasticine model.

"There were all sorts up to various tricks on the set, and they were so well done: wearing ties and collars – the sort of stuff no one bothered to do because it all gets smudged so easily. But it inspired me, and I began making my own Plasticine animations.

"I'd start with just a blob of plasticine. No script. The more I moved the blob around, the more ideas I got. Later, at the National Film School in London, these animations turned into Wallace and Gromit. I took them to Aardman, and got a job.

"When I started working on *A Grand Day Out* (Wallace and Gromit's trip to the moon), I had intended to make Gromit into an extrovert dog, jumping all over the place.

"But one of the first scenes I did involved Wallace using Gromit as a saw-bench as he cut up a door to make the rocket. Gromit couldn't very well leap about with that on top of him.

"The only thing he could really move were his eyes and eyebrows. I suddenly found I could do everything I needed just with those. All his character came through his eyes. I didn't even need to put a mouth on him.

"That was the breakthrough. The beauty of Plasticine is it can be made to do such beautiful and subtle things. It can appear so human.

"So much of the imagery, and indeed the script ideas, were based on books I'd read as a kid – Jules Verne and H.G. Wells. Victorian, Heath Robinson sci-fi. I have a passion for the detail of Victorian technology.

"There have been two pinnacles for me. The first came in *Creature Comforts*, a whole string of commercials for electricity. To this day people think they were for gas – I've got no idea why.

"They were based on recorded interviews I'd done with students. The first was Frank (the tortoise) who I interviewed about electricity. I took my inspiration from the soundtrack – that dictated the visuals.

"When he tapped his fingers, I'd reproduce that in the Plasticine tortoise. When he sounded glum, I'd make the tortoise look like it was miserable. When he swallowed, I had the tortoise's Adam's apple gliding down his throat. These simple things are a joy to watch in animation.

"The best of *Creature Comforts*, I felt, was the Brazilian jaguar in the pavilion. I had interviewed a Brazilian student about British food, weather and accommodation, and his voice sounded so depressed and fed up. I really just followed the soundtrack.

"Comic timing is the key. As Chuck Jones once said, 'the difference between a joke working and not working is one frame.' And unlike computer animation or cartoons, you really do only have one shot at it. Two or three is the max. You can't keep improving it, unless you have unlimited time and money.

"For me, the best of the Wallace and Gromit films was *The Wrong Trousers*. We were a small group who made that film. We did something special there.

"And the penguin! Somehow we managed to achieve a real sense of evil with him. The secret lay in the fact that he had no facial expression. There was something cold and disconnected about him. Sometimes less is more.

"*Chicken Run* was very ambitious and I'm glad we did it, but it was very much a learning process. I found it hard to let go and direct this incredibly skilful group of people. There was a lot of dialogue to handle. I found it hard to communicate with the team. Though I think the film worked in many ways, it was certainly a steep learning curve.

"Now I'm working on a new Wallace and Gromit film, *The Great Vegetable Plot*, and that feels much better. It's like being back on home turf."

HOVERWELLIES
PROTOTYPE

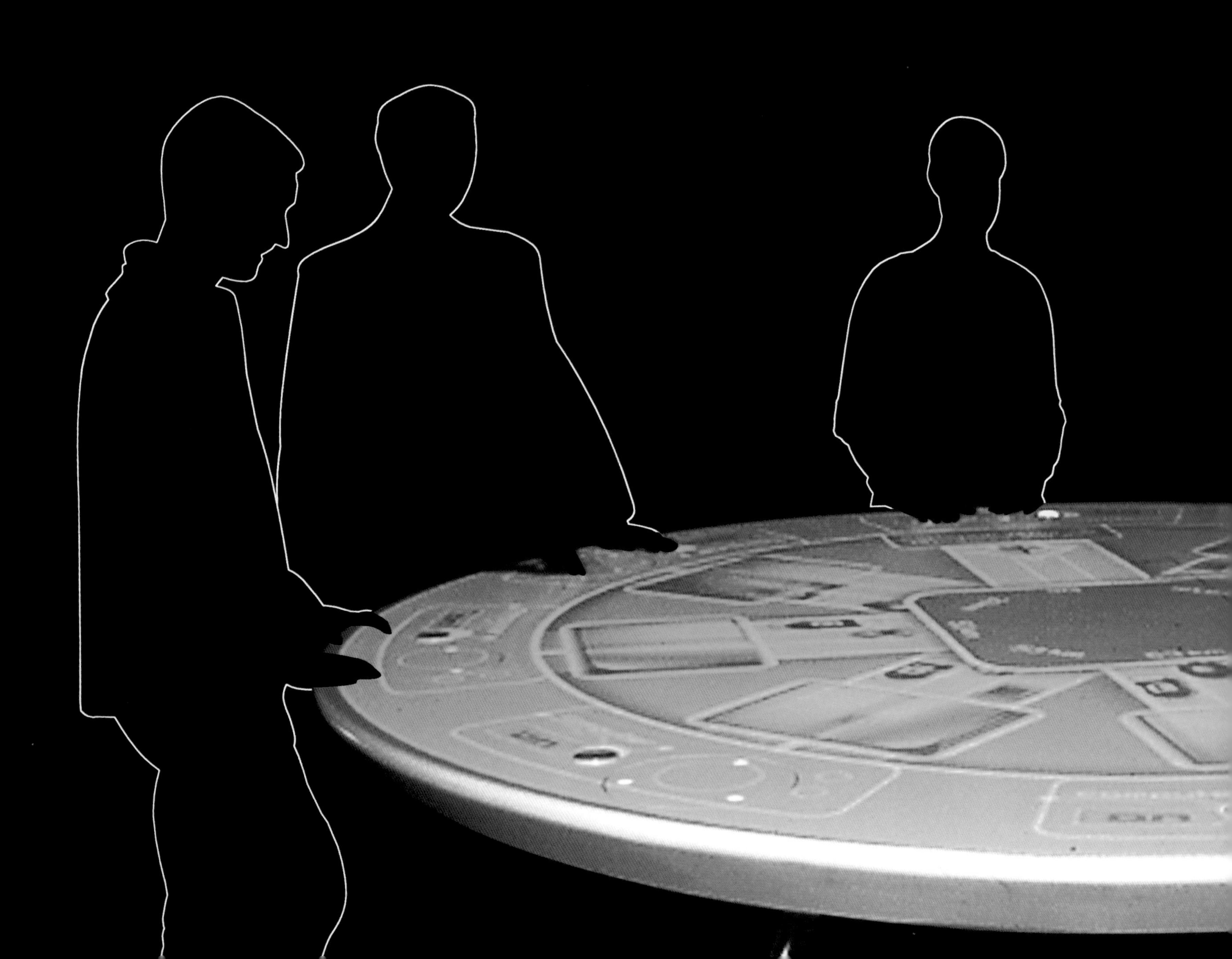

*The Science Museum has recently opened the Welcome Wing, dedicated in the main to modern science, where most of the rest of the museum is historically focussed. It is famous for its beautiful machinery, so Casson Mann felt bound to create something of a similar quality to house its displays. The company created Digitopolis, about the digital world, and used the concept of the binary code and the silicon chip to create a gallery that is like a giant motherboard. It also created Bloids, organic-shaped interactive display units to evoke interior parts of the human body. And on the third floor, there's the games room.*

**Roger Mann:**
"It's a kind of gaming space. There are three tables. On those tables are projected interactive multi-user games. Only one game can be played at a time at any given table.

"Each game deals with a potential future scenario. It might be about future life, and how you can choose the sex of your baby by taking a pill to select or deselect male and female sperm. It's a future issue, but it's virtually upon us.

"Then there are games set in 2020 AD talking about foreseeable stuff. Automatic cars, tagging your children with satellite bugs so you can keep track of them, men having babies – all contentious, thought-provoking stuff, raising social issues about the impact of science.

"The technology and the games lure young people to them. People can vote on the issues – is it a good idea that men have babies? The cumulative totals are displayed.

"The concept for the gallery came from us, and then we started working with the software developer's Itch, which is a specialist in intriguing game structures.

"The table has a white surface with buttons and wheels in it. The whole table can become anything that's projected onto it. Full-colour graphics and video animations move in front of you to create a new world. Then you interact with it.

"The dwell times in these galleries were record-breaking – far more than any other gallery at the museum. Which is great, because so often people just spend a few minutes in any gallery."

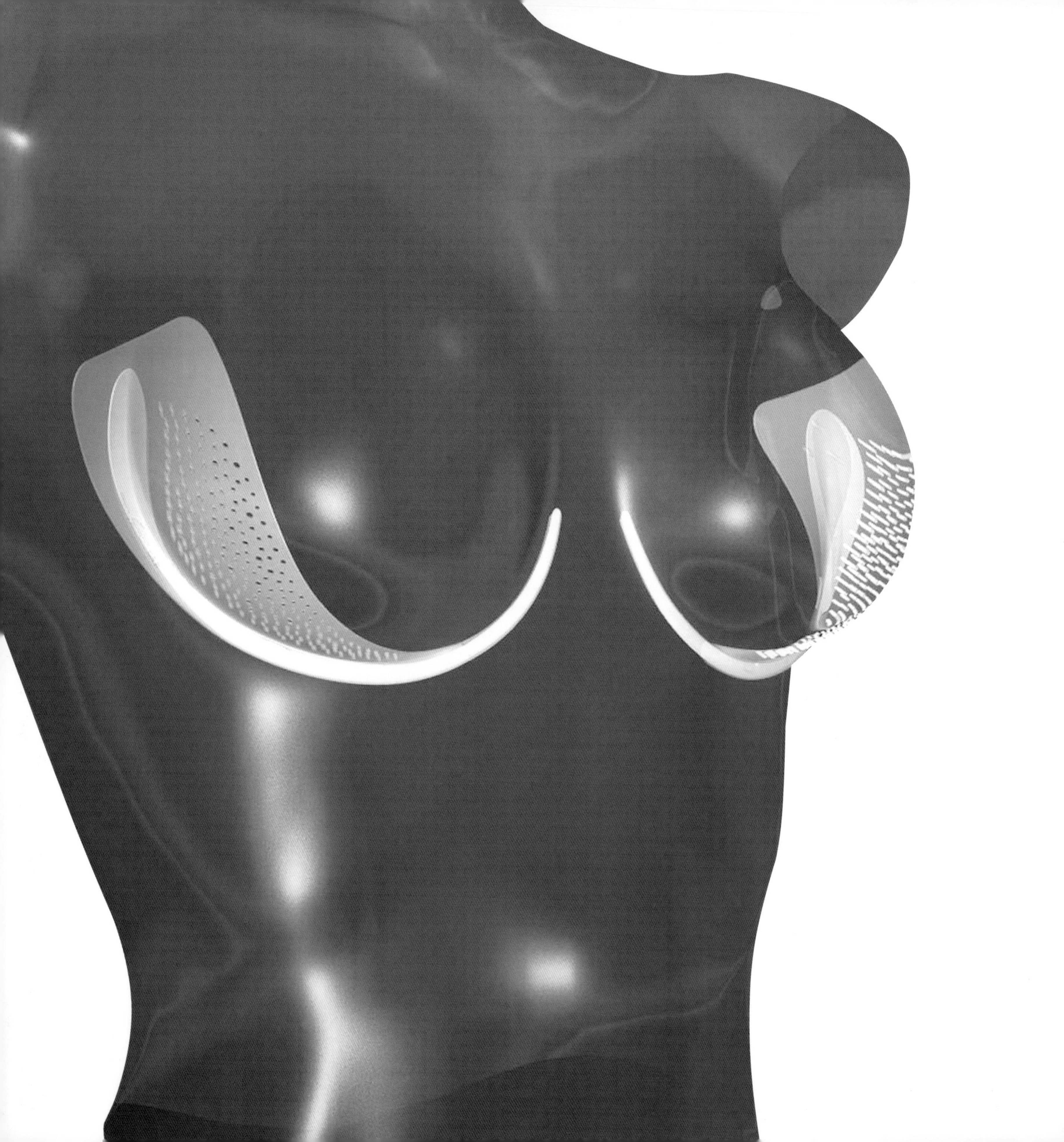

*A wonderful example of design cross-fertilization comes from Seymour Powell and its Bioform Bra, created on air for a Channel 4 series on design. The company's two designers were asked to look at a series of household items and improve them using design thinking. They demonstrated how creative techniques taken from one design arena can generate undreamed of solutions in another.*

**Richard Seymour:** "We began looking at sports footwear and, by a sort of contrast, bras. The difference isn't only anatomical, it's technological. Adidas and Nike have gone through the roof technologically. But bra manufacturers – frankly they're antediluvian.

"The bra sits uneasily between fashion and mechanical necessity – it rocks in both directions, rather like the stiletto heel. From a bio-mechanical point of view, it's quite nasty, but women put up with it because it achieves the effect they want.

"We did some research, and found that around 75 percent of women were wearing the wrong-sized bra. And it gets worse the bigger your breasts are. I can tell you it's quite a tricky thing to bring large breasts under starter's orders.

"So we came up with the Bioform – basically, a pair of supporting inserts. It's like having a pair of hands coming around the sides of the breasts, lifting from beneath, and providing the lateral support larger breasts need to avoid that underarm migration – that east-west sag.

"We knew nothing about bras before we started this. But to be able to stand outside the problem and not be hidebound by existing knowledge is a major advantage. The technology transfer alone was revolutionary in underwear. Injection-moulding is pretty banal in other areas, but in lingerie – wow! It's not easy to do this sort of thing from within the industry. Your starting point often militates against it. It's unlikely injection moulding solutions will occur to you when your factory is heavily equipped with sewing machines.

"So designers need to have a powerful ability to persuade. 75 percent of any project is preparing the client for the shift he/she is going to have to take."

**Dick Powell:** "We quickly focussed on the underwire as the villain of the piece. It's a nasty bit of kit. It's sharp, for a start, and can be very uncomfortable. So we moved to marry the sort of mould blending technology that you see in scuba flippers, and even a frizbee-style flying ring to create a supportive keel.

"We did experience a huge fear of failure. I mean, we were flying in the face of experts who knew it all. But one thing that puzzled us was the cup-sizing system. It seemed a bit dodgy to us. The moulds look nothing like a human breast. No one seemed to know its origins. We were thinking – hang on a minute, how have we got to this point? So we began to think the fact we don't know anything isn't much of a hindrance! If we need specialist knowledge about bras, well, these people know what we need to know. The question is, what can we bring to it which *they* don't know?

"We have a process called the 'Creative Workshop' or the 'Creative Event', in which we generate ideas. And the secret is to generate, and not to question. Evaluate later.

"Interesting ideas, when you start to measure them against a matrix of requirements, seem happy to tumble into place, and side issues to your central problem somehow get solved, too.

"We've been working so long together we've developed an instinct for them. When they come by, we go: 'Yes!' A hallmark of a good idea is that even though it may be built on one issue, it tends to solve more than one.

"We use the shorthand of drawing. We can both draw, and with drawing you can visualize something very quickly. And we ask: 'What if we did this?' And then we might draw something demonstrably stupid.

"You might say something like: 'Wouldn't it be nice if we could support the bust with – a skyhook!' And we explore that. 'What else could do the job of a skyhook?' They're classic Creative Event phrases. 'Wouldn't it be nice if...?' Or 'What if we could...'

"There are three fundamental steps to design: idea, belief (proving it to the client) and embodiment. It's the old Taoist theory. It works for us."

*Innovative products require innovative packaging. Lewis Moberly, the award-wining London based design firm, applied similar clear and creative thinking to come up with a completely new approach to presenting a bra at point-of-sale.*

**Mary Lewis:** "This is radically different. If you went into a department store and looked at the bra category, you'd see wall-to-wall ladies wearing their bras – a very predictable set of imagery. This bra is revolutionary. Therefore the branding has to be equally revolutionary to match the stance of the product. So rather than mimicking what others have done in this area, this packaging celebrates the components.

"The idea is simply to show what the product does and to capture the technical distinction behind it.

"It's like putting the inside workings of the bra on the outside. The Pompidou approach. We've taken the component and photographed it as a still-life. It's beautifully lit and intriguing.

"The pack is transparent and easy to open, and that solves a major problem connected to bra packaging. Women do tend to pull bras out of their packages and have a good look at them. They want to feel them, to get a full sense of them. So shops often end up with a lot of tatty boxes with bras stuffed back into them.

"So we placed the opening on the side of the box, so it's much easier to get the product in and out, because you're pulling from a deeper part of the box. This way the coding doesn't get disturbed or torn.

"Also, because it's open, people can see the colour. Therefore there's no need to code the product. And there's no confusion that results from the photograph showing a black bra but the product being pink!"

*Quentin Blake, the Children's Laureate is perhaps most famous for his illustrations of books by children's writer Roald Dahl. But he also illustrated* 'Learning Journey', *a series of guides to the National Curriculum, conceived with the aim of demystifying the National Curriculum for parents. They have been produced by the Department for Education and Skills who offer them free to parents.*

**Quentin Blake:** "The Ministry were very pleased. They said: 'It's great the way you solved this difficult communication problem.' But I didn't know it was a difficult problem. It all seemed perfectly natural to me.

"I approached the job more like an illustrator than a cartoonist, guided by the content. I was also prepared by two circumstances. The first was that I trained as an English teacher, so the school context was familiar to me, and the second was that I had done so many books for children. Those books often involve relationships between parents and children. And often the parents read the books to the children. So I'm pretty familiar with working the triangle of book, child and parent.

"The trick to making cartoons is empathy. They work best if the cartoonist can put himself into the situation and so encourage the audience to do the same. The message of '*Learning Journey*' was along similar lines: 'Be empathic. Be interested in your kids' experiences of school. Take time out to get into their world'.

"The idea is to get across enthusiasm and passion and fun. The message is: 'Look: it's not laborious to do these things. You can enjoy doing them!' So I take a phrase out of the book, and then get into the situation and exaggerate it.

"Let's say I see a bit of dry text that says: 'See how long a plant can stay alive without water.' The text then runs through the experiment describing one plant being watered and the other not. So I draw a girl looking glumly at her plant, which is nothing more than a sad, withered little twig, and a boy looking up over his watering can at this beanstalk of a plant that nearly reaches the top of the page. Far bigger than it would be in real life.

"The trick is activity and expansion. Putting action into the scenario and knowing how much to expand it, though there must be some connection to reality. It's a creative process, I guess. It doesn't really happen to me unless I am drawing. I don't wander round the streets laughing at situations and exaggerating them in my head. But it's a different story when I've got a pencil in my hand.

"But above all, the whole project was about accessibility. I did something similar at the National Gallery when I was Children's Laureate. I made a series of pictures that was all about getting young people to look at art without worrying about feeling whether they should be there or not.

"My drawings acted as an intermediary, saying: 'Come and look. You don't have to take art too seriously.' It worked like a charm, and the Gallery got twice the number of visitors it expected. Cartoons can act as a good intermediary, and can open up texts, making them more accessible.

"We're quite good at this in the UK. I think it's something to do with our lousy weather. In France and Italy, everything is crystal clear in the wonderful Mediterranean light. But we've got a lot of fog and mist and rain. There's lots of ambiguity here – nothing is clear-cut. Just because it's summer doesn't mean it's sunny every day. It'll rain for sure as soon as you get the barbecue out. Well, you've got to laugh! I think that contributes to our seeing the funny side."

# PECKHAM LIBRARY

*The original brief for Peckham library required "a building of architectural merit that will bring prestige to the borough and a welcome psychological boost to the areas. It should be a throroughly modern building that is ahead of its time but also one that does not alienate people by giving an appearance of elitism, strangeness or exclusivity. Local people must be able to relate to the architecture and design as well as the services provided and they should feel pride in, affection for and ownership of the building." Not easy. Will Alsop won the 2000 Stirling Prize with his brilliant answer.*

**Will Alsop:** "It was a competition between us and about five other architectural firms. We won. I don't know why, but we did. But I'm very thankful. It gave us the opportunity to redefine and explore what a new civic library might be.

"The site we were given was between Peckham Hill Street and a canal. It was on a route between the nearby Health Centre and the shops. We didn't want to create a big block you had to walk round; that might work to disenfranchise the shops. So we made it possible to effectively walk through it, by creating this big square with a large portico. It seems to have worked. The shops are being refurbished, and they seem to be getting a new lease of life.

"A sense of location is so important. The library's actually quite high up, so we wanted to make as much use of glass as possible to give the people of Peckham views into London from inside, to help them visualize the fact that they really are part of Central London, not just holed up in some anonymous suburb. This is all revealed as you ride the lift into the upper library. You can watch the London skyline come into view. So the act of rising through the library is an important part of the experience.

"This was put together very much with a gut feeling that grew out of a lot of work with local people. The ground floor is a one-stop shop. There you can go, talk to people about your problems and pay local taxes. Admittedly, paying taxes is not a popular thing to do – but people seem to prefer doing this sort of stuff here than in the more imposing environment of the Town Hall.

"Externally, the implied space of the portico works well. The two-metre high stainless-steel letters make it pretty clear what the building is about, and we've created an orange sunshield which some people have compared to a beret. Two internal pods burst through the roof and that creates more internal space and more external drama. The blue light at night is particularly effective, shining up against the stainless-steel mesh. It looks like nothing else I've ever seen.

"There's a generous sense of space. There are meeting spaces sufficient for small performances. There's a library dedicated to their wonderful collection of Afro-Caribbean music and that's connected to the children's library, a great place for curling up and sucking your thumb while books are read to you. They have breast-feeding classes in there.

"The building as a whole has acted as a catalyst for more investment into that area. They're now going to build a community hall and flats next door. The library has registered 3,000 new readers since it opened. That's got to be good!"

WHITTEN

WWW.MOUNTSTMARYS.ORG

*As part of the Joinedupdesignforschools pilot project that demonstrated the effect of bringing professional design into school environments, Elmwood designed a website for their local school, Mount St Mary's in Leeds. Elmwood's chief executive, Jonathan Sands and his team worked with their client pupils to improve Mount St Mary's communications, pointing the way towards a future where professionals and pupils could work together to mutual benefit.*

**Jonathan Sands:** "The first problem was that the school had never commissioned a design consultancy before, and clearly they were shocked at how much information we needed.

"For the Joinedupdesignforschools pilot to work it was stressed that we should treat the children as we would any other client. It was a vital part of the process. We always feed and water our clients, so whenever the student client team came to our offices, we'd lay on biscuits and chocolates and fancy goodies. Well, the kids looked like they'd died and gone to heaven. You could just see the Christmas glee on their faces. It was most amusing.

"The best thing about the whole project was watching the children grow as it went on. During their first visit here they didn't say a single word. We asked them questions about their school, and what they wanted on the website, and they just stared back like rabbits in headlights.

"We quickly learnt that kids find big meetings intimidating, so we changed our tactics and slowly their confidence and self-belief grew and grew. Soon they recognized that we were nothing but big kids, really, and began to take ownership of the project. We established a rapport and understanding and they really blossomed and came out of themselves. This was a major benefit of the whole programme – perhaps the most important element.

"The aim of the exercise was to help communicate Mount St Mary's to the local community, so we wanted to make the website as fun and lively as possible. It was designed to engage the kids, but more than that, to be truly *owned* by the kids. So we animated the children, and, using their voices and their faces, made them the website figures who guided you round the school.

"This project generated pride. The school is proud of the site, and the children are proud of their school for having such a cool website, and having had such an important role in its production. And we're proud to have been involved. Watching the smiles on their faces as we presented their ideas back to them in a form they hadn't quite envisaged – it was very rewarding.

"The design industry is all grown up now. We can weather downturns better than ever before. And big corporates are buying up the small independents. There is danger here and opportunity. Designer entrepreneurs work best when running their own business. There's a risk that British design could become bland and homogenous now that the designers are in big corporations. But there is the possibility that the same designers will have a powerful impact on big corporations and, using their massive resources, designers could move design to a new level."

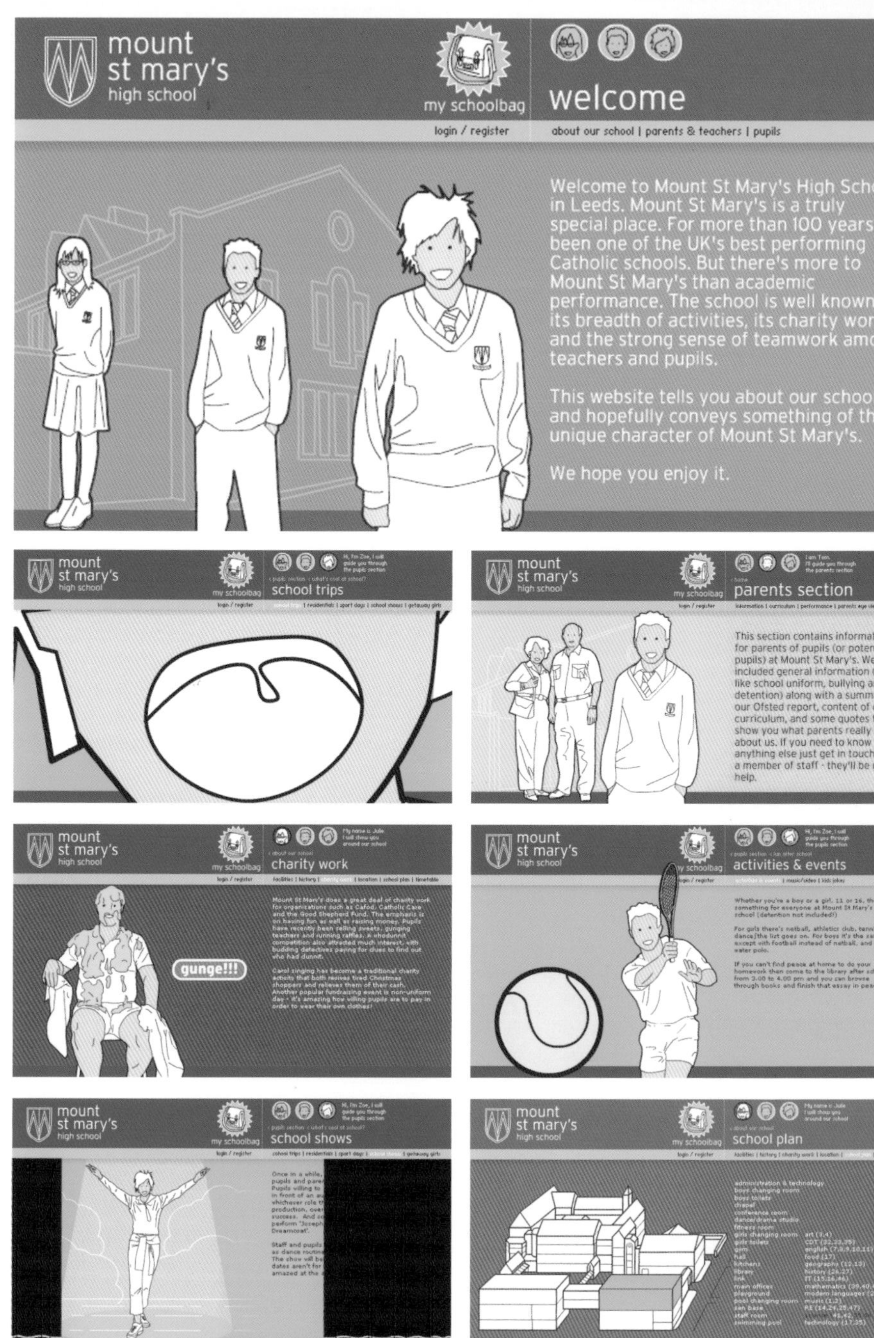

# ANYWAY UP CUP

*Mother Mandy Haberman invented this cup when she became frustrated with the way her toddler's drinks leaked in her handbag. She managed to get the attention of a major supermarket when she sent it full of Ribena and upside down to one of their top buyers in a box. She said: "If this hasn't leaked by the time you get it, call me." But the product hit the big time when she turned to Sebastian Conran for a redesign.*

**Sebastian Conran:** "I was flipping through the *FT* when I spotted an article about this woman who had designed a leakproof baby cup.

"So I thought – well, great idea – except that it looks like any other baby cup.

"So for the first time in my life I called someone up and told them 'I can design this better for you.'

"Why make this another piece of baby product? Why not make it look like something you might serve your guests with?

"Well, the received wisdom then was that babies wanted silly faces. But as a parent I don't always want to have my house littered with cartoon-adorned baby plastic. It's bad enough with all the toys!

"Why should kid's stuff all look toy-like? I really wasn't convinced.

"I knew the babycare and the domestic houseware market really well. So we came at it from that point of view, going for classic forms.

"They're the sort of shapes one takes for granted now in this business, but at the time. When we came out with it, Mandy's partner said: 'I'm not sure about that; that's a bit different isn't it?'

"We took the cup and gave it a contemporary design. We made it cheaper to manufacture and we made it into something that, to my mind at least, visually looked the part.

"Translucent colours seem so obvious now. But then people said: 'Ewww! It will make the orange juice look green!' They really couldn't cope with it.

"But I couldn't handle the primary colours people were advocating. You put primary colours together and you get Toys 'R' Us!

"It worked. Sales went from 250,000 a year to four million a year!"

# LANDSCAPED GLASSWARE

*The downside to increased longevity is that the simple things in life become harder to do. Lisa-Dionne Morris has found a way of making life easier for the victims of arthritis, rheumatism, strokes and other disabilities.*

**Lisa Dionne Morris:** "When I design, I design for people, with people in mind. I do not design in isolation. This glassware was developed for people who have severe forms of impairment brought on by strokes, and for people suffering from arthritis. It's all about helping them move out of physical disability, to feel they can be independent and use everyday equipment.

"So much equipment for the disabled is uninspiring. Some users even feel it can be insulting. It pays no heed to the psychological effects of being unable to do things you once took for granted. And people with disabilities want pretty things as much as the able-bodied.

"I developed it using a lot of trial and error. Every time I came up with a design, I gave it to the trial group and got their feedback on how it could be improved. The trial groups were made up of people with various disabilities. I learnt a lot from their comments on handling and weight. For example, they have a lip which helps people carry them one-handed. They are designed to be held in a variety of ways – so whatever your disability you will find a way to hold it.

"I've also tinted the glass, because if your vision is impaired, the edge of clear glass is difficult to see. It also looks good."

"People found suddenly they could hold glasses they couldn't hold before. It was if their dexterity had suddenly increased. The glasses feel secure in your hand. That's good for disabled people and also for children."

*We live in the global village, but it is a congregation riven with prejudice, hate and misunderstanding.* Colors *magazine is a fascinating medium dedicated to showing how people live together. It examines communities across the world and tells their stories in pictures and words. The editor, Fernando Gutiérrez, believes clear communication is the best way to achieve the understanding and compassion the human race so desperately needs.*

**Fernando Gutiérrez:** "Above all, *Colors* magazine is about human community. It's not about famous people and it's not about the latest gadgets. I prefer to work with young photographers and journalists. We brief them and off they go to do their thing. It's very visually led, but it is not a big design statement.

"I wanted to draw in people from different cultures. It's a very human take on the things going on around us. Through reading this magazine you can see clearly people's experience related to their community, and the world community.

"It's a unique opportunity to do a magazine that reaches people and talks about people in a different context. It's financed by Benetton research, but we have complete independence. There's no censorship and no imposition. I carry advertising from other brands. I strongly believe the magazine must stand on its own two feet. It must have a sense of reality. It must be self-sufficient. It feels better that way. Then it can really exploit its independence.

"I started off as creative director. I had first worked on it six years ago with the founding editor, Tibor Kalman. There was a moment in between when his successor took a more sensationalist approach. I felt the credibility suffered.

"*Colors* started off addressing AIDS, religion, race, poverty, living on the street. Those themes were very strong in the 1990s and of course are still important today. But it was tired. It needed a new way of communicating important things.

"So I focus on how people live, the experiences they have. Those other themes weave naturally in and out of the stories as they occur in reality.

"Community is important. Society is currently very geared towards individuals. We have this celebrity culture pumped at us: 'He's great, and she looks fab, and aren't I cool?' But celebrity and wealth are not important in the real experience of life. Sharing is. It's pleasurable and full of reward. I try not to get political. I want communities to speak for themselves.

"Globalization is double-edged. Perhaps it's good we are closer together, that we understand each other better. It's what this magazine is about. But global greed, obviously, is not so good.

"I try to avoid letting ego into the magazine, and I think it's important to underplay the design aspect of it. I work visually and also work with words. I want to put something across in a commercial context.

"Photography is a beautiful medium. TV and video rush by the eye, but pictures stand still. You can study them and look into them. I am a great believer in photography and the words that go alongside pictures.

"The magazine is always tailor-made. We use no stock; it's all commissioned. The editions come out once every two months, and they're distributed in nine languages.

"To do something that's very human and that's not about ego. That, to me, is a great privilege."

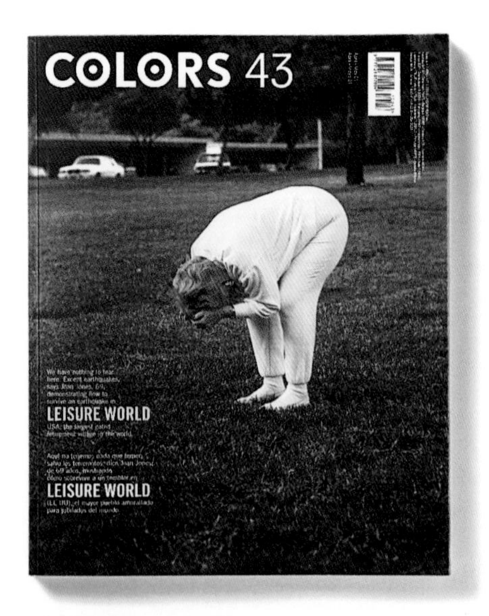

Doesn't it bother you, riding your bicycle over graves?
No, they are dead. Nothing bothers them anymore.

Ça ne te dérange pas, de rouler sur les tombes avec ton vélo ?
Non. Ils sont morts. Il n'y a plus rien qui les dérange.

Sur sa bicyclette en bois [illegible] traverse le cimetière de [illegible]

*Combien t'a coûté ce vélo ?*
*Cinquante shillings [illegible]. Mais ce qui m'embête, ce n'est pas le prix, c'est le garde forestier. S'il me voit avec cette bicyclette, il va la casser en deux et me la confisquer.*
*Pourquoi ?*
*Parce que, pour faire ce vélo, on a coupé un arbre sans sa permission.*

Tout le monde dans le camp joue au chat et à la souris avec le garde forestier. [illegible] pour la cuisine, des médicaments pour les guérisseurs traditionnels, des matières pour toutes les constructions. L'infrastructure du quotidien repose sur des [illegible], qui s'épuisent à vitesse grand V.

*Qu'est-ce que tu imagines quand tu es sur ce vélo ?*
*Vous me demandez si je fais semblant que ce soit un vrai vélo. La réponse, c'est non.*
*Pourquoi ?*
*Avec un vrai vélo, je n'aurais pas besoin qu'on me pousse. On ne peut pas faire comme si [illegible] n'a pas de puissance.*
*Si tu retournes chez toi, au Burundi, tu emmèneras cette bicyclette ?*
*Non. Il y a beaucoup d'arbres au Burundi. Je pourrais faire tous les vélos que je veux.*

**IDRIS BERAS**

MONTENEGRO

*Privat*

CROWDALL STREET, LONDON N1

PURCELL STREET, LONDON N1

HOXTON STREET, LONDON N1

PURCELL STREET, LONDON N1

## THE MOST DIFFICULT THING IN THE LAST 100 YEARS WAS GIVING UP MY CAR KEYS

## LO MÁS DIFÍCIL EN ESTOS 100 AÑOS FUE ENTREGAR LAS LLAVES DEL COCHE

"I did it on August 20," Jim Purcell continues, "on my 100th birthday. I ask myself how can anyone reach 100. I don't feel any different inside, I don't know how I should act—I've never been 100 before." [illegible] that age brings the wisdom to cope with the problems it creates. "I only did it because the license had expired. I wouldn't have done it by choice."

"Giving up a driver's license has far bigger consequences than it might seem," says 84-year-old Brenda Ross, mayor of Laguna Woods. [illegible] Loneliness and depression quickly follow.

"Loss is a big underlying issue as we age," Leisure World's resident social worker, Mary Colclough, explains. [illegible]

Aging amplifies the fact that loss is inevitable, and irreversible. Rosanne (Cody) Mehrer, 50, knows this. [illegible]

"The worst thing about aging is the series of losses you experience. [illegible]" [illegible] "She had these big old tears running down her little face."

«Lo hice el 20 de agosto», prosigue Jim Purcell, «el día en que cumplí 100 años. [illegible]»

«Entregar el carné de conducir tiene consecuencias mucho más graves de lo que podría parecer», dice Brenda Ross, alcaldesa de Laguna Woods, de 84 años. [illegible]

«Las pérdidas son un problema fundamental de la vejez», explica Mary Colclough, una asistente social residente de Leisure World. [illegible]

[illegible] «La pasaban unas lágrimas enormes carita abajo».

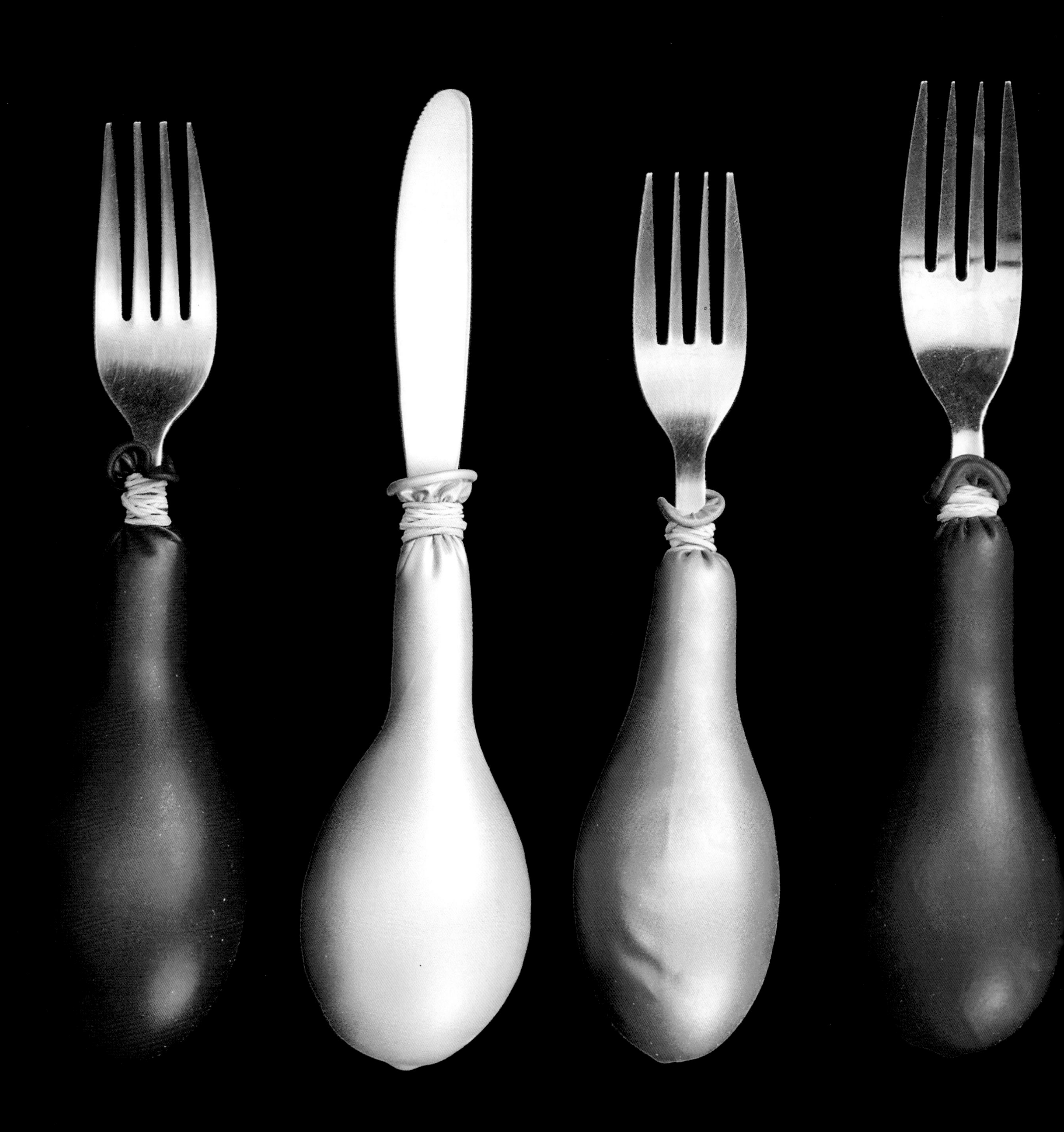

# ADAPTABLE & DIY CUTLERY

*Have you ever broken your wrist and then tried to eat a meal? It's not funny. It's even less amusing if the disability is long-lasting or even permanent. William Welch has designed a brilliant set of cutlery that makes it possible for physically disabled people to feed themselves. And then he created a Do-It-Yourself set that you can make for the cost of a balloon, some flour, and a rubber band.*

**William Welch:** "I felt there was so little cutlery available for disabled users. And what there was had plenty of function but no aesthetic. I did a long research project, looking at how people were using cutlery and what they thought of existing cutlery and the general opinion was there was some stuff out there but it was clumsy. They looked more like garden tools than tableware.

"I wanted to improve the functionality and make them more appropriate for a dining environment. Anyone could be disabled, either permanently from birth, or temporarily as a result of an accident. It doesn't mean they have to be condemned to using ugly cutlery!

"It became clear that people with disabled hands needed something that could adapt to their shape of their hand. So I developed large, soft handles. I even added wrist straps to aid people with weaker grips. The straps gave people - say, stroke victims - the ability to use cutlery again. Being fed by someone else is often felt to be a great indignity.

"My design philosophy revolves around integration, functionality and desirability. These pieces are meant to look fun but elegant. People might actually enjoy laying a table with it.

"And then I came up with the DIY make-it-at-home range. This is for people with temporary disabilities – say if you've broken your wrist or something. All you do is take a balloon, fill it with flour, put your spoon, fork or knife in it, and tie it up with a rubber band. The flour–filled balloon gives you the grip. You can even use it for a toothbrush or a paintbrush. It'll cost you less than £1 for all the pieces. The full instructions for making your own temporary cutlery are on my website and you can download them for free." (www.wwelchdesign.com).

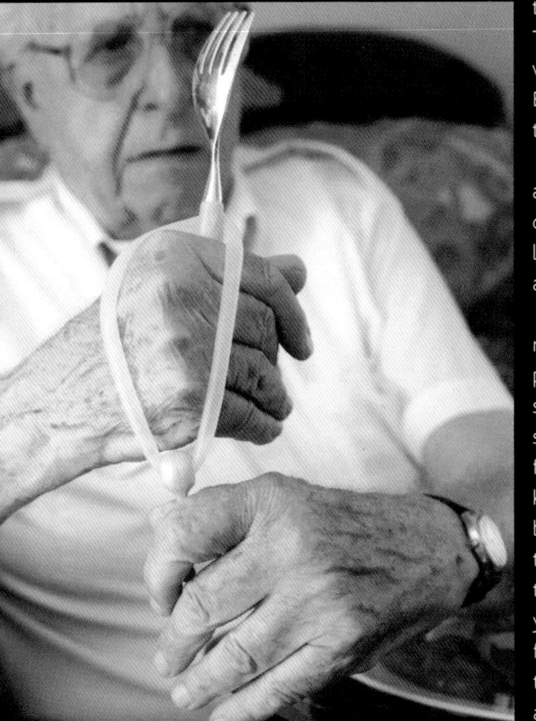

# 'CD ROM' PRINTED LEATHER BOOTS

*These fun, witty boots, designed by Helen David are guaranteed to bring a smile to your face. Helen was born in Brighton and started the English Eccentrics fashion label four years after leaving Central St. Martin's School of Art. She has designed costumes for the Ballet Rambert and won the British Fashion Award for Glamour in 2002.*

**Helen David:**
"These boots came out of a print design for a scarf and shirt range we called 'CD Rom'. Then I began thinking about putting the design onto a circular leather handbag and then onto boots. This is very difficult technically and we had a lot of trouble making sure the leather was primed properly. Eventually we got it to work on soft leather.

"My work is about applying patterns to various parts of clothing on the body. I thought boots would be a fantastic way of wearing patterns. It's quite the opposite of the way a scarf works, where the pattern happens at the neck. Here the pattern is happening around the feet, which is both exciting and unusual.

"The wonderful thing about the boots for me is the way the design curves around the ankle and the heel, echoing the curved lines intrinsic to the design. Quite a fun idea!

"The colours came from my seasonal palette for that summer. These are, I must admit, fair-weather summer boots. Footwear used to be more decorated than it is now, but it wasn't very functional. But the press got very excited about these boots, as they did about the circular bag. They saw them as witty and fun. I certainly had fun creating them.

"I don't think we're really at a high point in design. I think we're being innovative, but all in the same way. The prevailing style of London fashion at the moment is a little bit like everyone's doing the same look. It's a hybrid look – part of it is to do with looking back to Edwardian Victorian era – and another part is an '80s revival."

# TRANSFORMATION

# GATESHEAD MILLENNIUM BRIDGE

*Newcastle boasts one of the most spectacular river views in the world, not so much because the Tyne is so impressive, but because the series of bridges are breathtaking. Now this remarkable view has been further enhanced by one of the most innovative footbridges in the world, created by Wilkinson Eyre architects.*

**Chris Wilkinson:** "The inspiration for the bridge came from my partner, Jim Eyre. We were in a competition to win the commission for this foot and bicycle bridge. We knew we had to come up with something very strong and dynamic to win. This was going to be adjacent to the other two important Tyneside bridges and they are known the world over. So the context was very powerful.

"What also made it interesting for us was the contrast between the two banks of the Tyne. Newcastle Quayside is a thriving place, but the Gateshead side is comparatively quiet. Gateshead Council was especially keen to promote their side of the river. They wanted the bridge to be iconic, and to help them attract attention and investment. Their desire was a major spur for us.

"We felt that the most likely way of creating something iconic was going to be through the opening mechanism which allowed shipping to pass through. There were several other constraints in the brief. It was going to be very difficult to take support from the bank – especially on Newcastle Quayside. And it looked like we were going to have to build a fairly severe ramp to provide sufficient clearance over the river for smaller vessels when the bridge was being used by pedestrians and cyclists.

"Also, we'd been inspired by some earlier work of ours. When we were building the Hulme Arch Manchester Gateway, we were originally going for a circle segment as the shape. Then we thought a parabolic curve would look more attractive, and the engineers came back telling us that such a design would be more efficient. The shape changes in size and shape across the length of the arch to deal with load paths.

"All these factors led us to thinking about generating something really new and innovative. Jim came up with the bright idea of an arc in plan and section. A horizontal pivot mechanism would open the bridge like an eyelid, or like a motorcycle visor sliding over the top of its helmet. The way it works is the pavement and walkway rise up so that the visor shape of the structure lifts high up over the river. We think this is a world first – to our knowledge it's never been done this way before. The method helped solve a whole range of problems. And it's energy efficient and cheap to operate – costing less than £4 for each opening.

"The whole bridge is one great moving part, rather than just a section of it. We've put the pedestrians on the inner walkway, and cyclists use the outer. The pedestrians are separated from the cyclists by a stainless-steel fence which acts as a windbreak from cold winds. The bridge can even clean its own litter. As it lifts, it all rolls into special traps.

"It really is a wonderful addition to the existing bridges, giving Tyneside a multiple bridge vista that is, perhaps, unrivalled in the world."

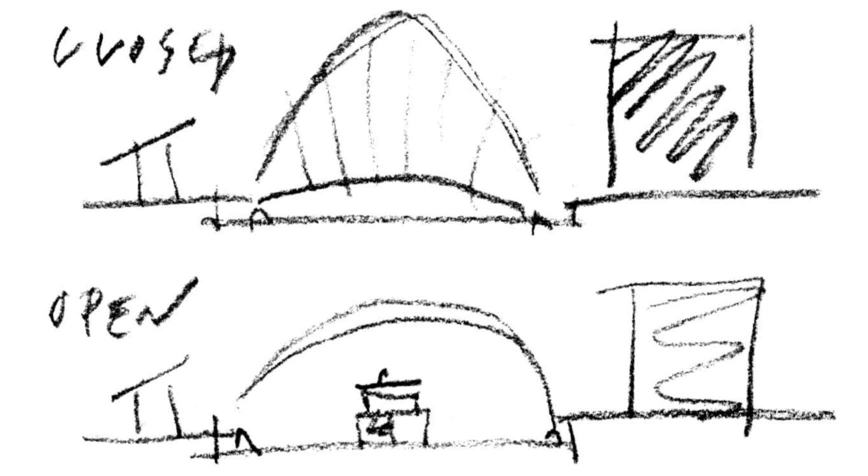

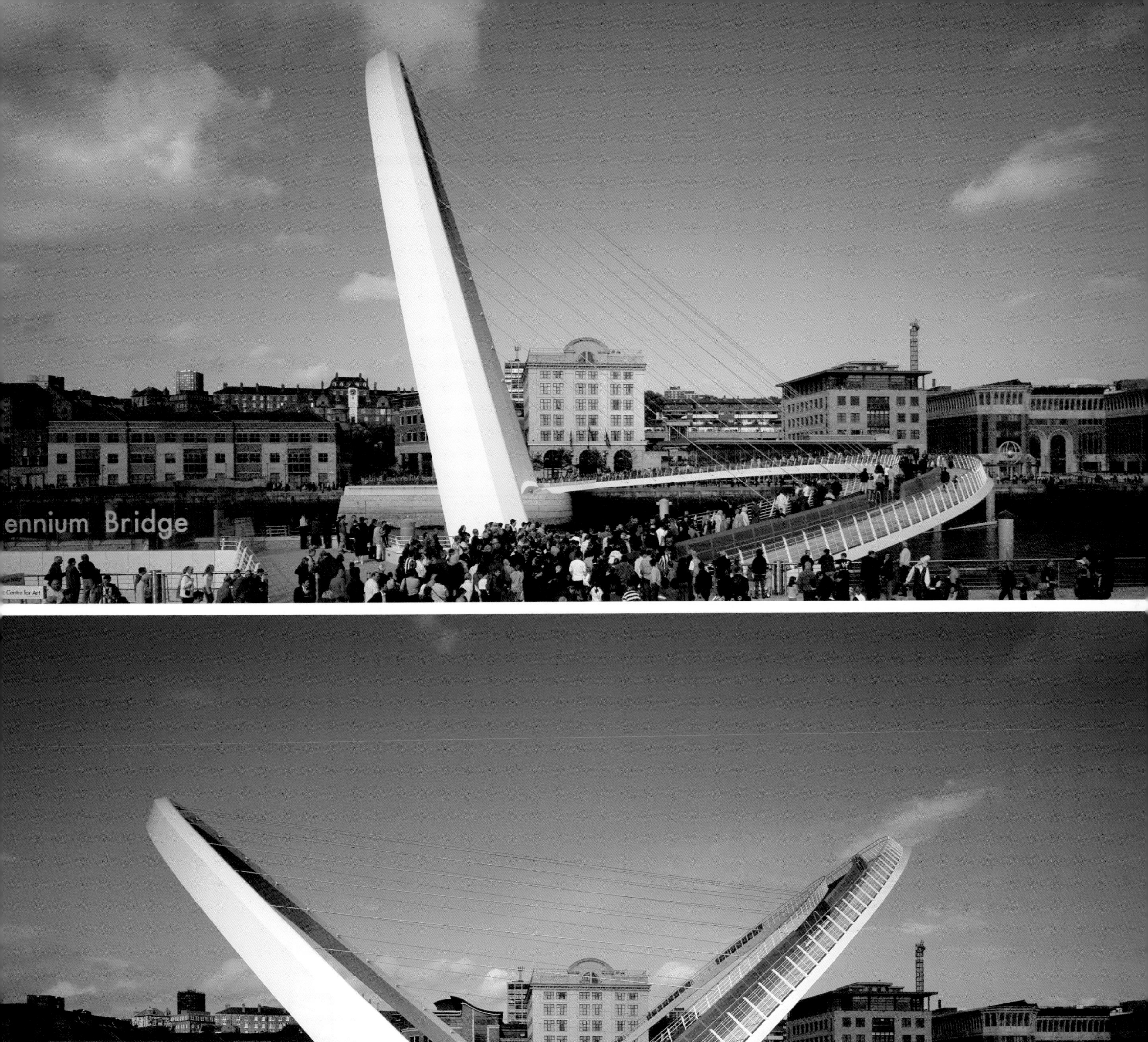
ennium Bridge

EE IT
BE IT

# PLANK STOOL

*Furniture design. Haven't we seen it all? Well, Thomas Heatherwick proves we haven't with this clever and precision-worked sculpture that functions as a table, a seat or a plinth. Thomas is nothing if not versatile, creating the world's first bridge made entirely from glass, and designing aesthetically pleasing mobile-phone masts. To make the Plank Stool, Thomas had to use a wide range of skills: design, carpentry, cabinet-making and precision engineering. It is a wonderful example of minimalist furniture that can change its form – a transformation that delights the mind. It is sculptural in its appeal, but unlike most sculpture, it has a clear function. And, most beautifully, it is clearly what its name suggests: a stool made from a six-foot plank.*

**Thomas Heatherwick:** "Perhaps I played too much with Rubic Snakes as a child! But the idea really came from my being somewhat disengaged from the world of furniture design. There's so much of it! I almost didn't care what stylistic decisions were being made. Cute little coffee tables! I don't even drink coffee.

"I started off down a different path. I thought: 'What would be the simplest form? How can I get away from thinking about whether the table should be red, or blue, or curvy or curly? Wouldn't it be fantastic if one could make a single piece of timber become the entire piece of furniture?' I wanted an idea that would force all the ideas through one logic.

"I was experimenting with paper at that time. I was taking a strip and folding it at right-angles to the direction. Then I saw with slighter angles how a spiral could begin to form. I began to see that on a straight plank of wood I could create a twist that would spiral round and form something larger. Then I moved to cutting up a plank of ash, and putting rotating joints into it.

"The most deceptive facet of the piece is its accuracy. The tolerances are very, very high. This is more engineering than cabinet making. For if you get the tolerances wrong, it's very easy to land up with five floppy bits of wood. There needs to be exactly the right amount of friction to make it strong and to stop it from flopping.

"I love the maths on projects like this. I love plodding through and calculating how to make the mathematical side work out. And I really do enjoy working in microns rather than millimetres of tolerance. This is unusual in furniture.

"We made 15 prototypes. I made the first two myself. After that we started looking for someone else to do it. But I couldn't find anyone who could. It was really frustrating! The first prototype took me six weeks and we knew it had to be made quicker than that! Eventually we found a company that could make it to the tolerances I wanted. And now they make it better than I was able to.

"You can set it in various positions, and use it as a table or a seat. To be frank, I'm not too bothered about how it's used. Just having it around as an interesting object is fine by me."

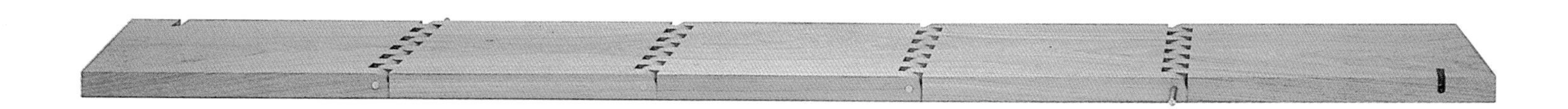

*Space planning company ETC wanted to communicate that it could make office space work better, that it could create environments that encouraged group working, that stimulated efficiency, and that could be quickly changed or adapted. It turned to Tonic, for a website design that would communicate all this. A tall order as Tonic's design director, Simon Heys explains...*

**Simon Heys:** "This was all new to us. ETC showed us the research documents, explained the theories behind how people use space and how they move around an office. They explained it was actually important where the photocopier goes, where the printers are. They showed us people walking between the furniture and how spaces should be planned around the people's needs.

"Well, this promised to be quite difficult to explain on a website. Then we hit on the solution. We needed to have people moving around a virtual office. Well, we tried it but we didn't like the way they turned out – it felt angular and cold and mathematical. We needed to create something more alive.

"We brainstormed it, and during that process, concluded that in real life, people are driven by prioritizing their desires. For example, in your world, let's say you want to stay up late and watch a film on TV, but you happen to be totally knackered. The desire to sleep wins out – you've prioritized your desire, forfeiting one pleasure for another. This was something we could simulate mathematically.

"So we reproduced this on the website. There are 14 different characters and they all have different desires and actions. So, for the receptionist, his or her main desire might be to sit at the desk and work. The phone rings – triggering her desire to answer the phone, and she picks it up. And the call might generate a desire to make some photocopies, so off she goes to the photocopier. By the end of the day she's fed up and wants to go home. So she reacts to her desire to walk out of the office. So it goes for all the characters.

"It was incredibly exciting when we first saw them working. It was like we'd created these people and set them free! All the maths and logic and the coldness of computer websites became invisible."

WWW.ETC-UK.COM

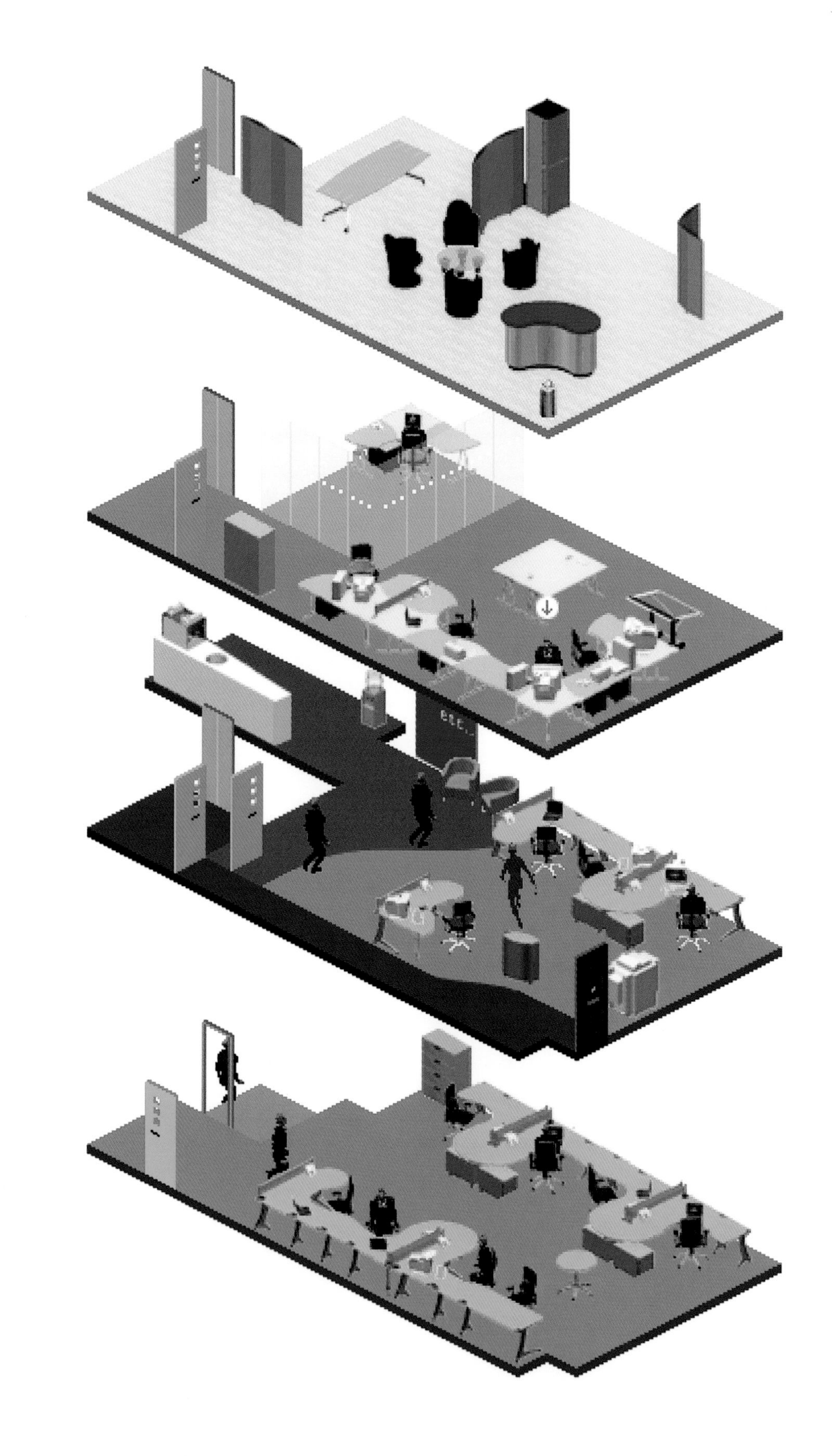

*One definition of transformation could be to take something that has one function, and give it the ability to turn into something with an entirely different function. This is exactly what happens with Nina Tolstrop's Post Present – a present that not only arrives in the mail, but IS the mail itself.*

**Nina Tolstrop:** "It's a present in a postcard. It comes in a plastic envelope. You post it to your friend, and then they take it apart and make it into a T-light holder.

"I always try to have a surprise, an innovative twist in my work. I like my work to make people smile, and I nearly always give it dual purpose, a double meaning. I recently made a dressing mirror that turns round and becomes an ironing board. That makes people laugh, but it works. It's a great way of saving space!

"It all springs from the moment I sit down with scissors, card and glue. I play with it, and then the shapes start coming out. I have no clear concept in my mind when I play. In this case I was playing with the idea of postcards, and what can be done with them to make them more fun.

"I guess no one would expect a T-light holder to be made out of cardboard, or for that matter, to come out of a postcard. For a start, it all seems too flammable. It doesn't burn, of course. We tested it. It takes the heat from the bottom of a tealight without any problems.

"It's a comment on the flat-pack world we live in. I thought: 'Let's use the packaging as the product.' I hate waste, and I love recycling. Design trends worry me a little at the moment. It seems all so wrapped up in globalization. I think there are too many products around. That's why here at Studiomama we are so keen on products having more than one use."

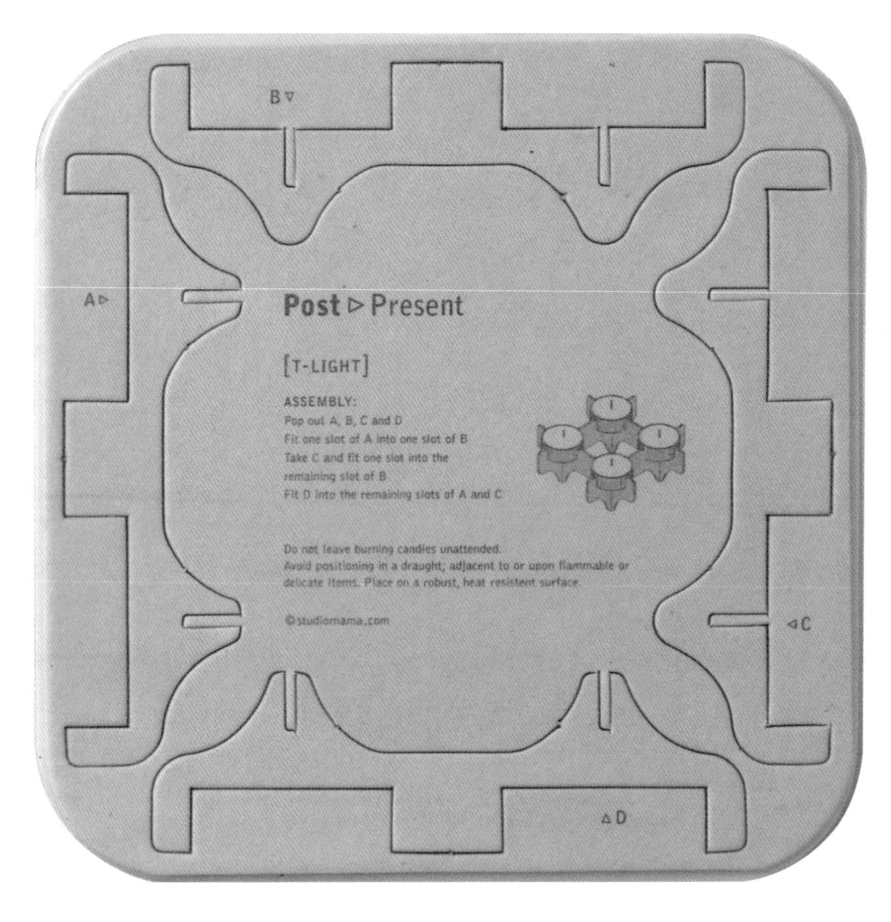

B▽
A▷
Post ▷ Present
[T-LIGHT]
ASSEMBLY:
Pop out A, B, C and D
Fit one slot of A into one slot of B
Take C and fit one slot into the
remaining slot of B
Fit D into the remaining slots of A and C
Do not leave burning candles unattended.
Avoid positioning in a draught; adjacent to or upon flammable or
delicate items. Place on a robust, heat resistent surface
©studiomama.com
◁C
△D

# LLOYD'S REGISTER BUILDING

*Lloyd's Register for Shipping is a large building on an historically sensitive site in the City of London. With considerable skill and care, Richard Rogers Partnership has created a building that pays due deference to the existing architecture while managing to be a modern, energy-efficient, custom-made office block. Its form has arisen directly from the vision of Richard Rogers himself and the skill of architect Graham Stirk.*

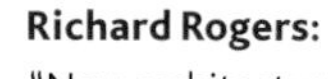

**Richard Rogers:** "New architecture is vital for society's well-being. I was born in Florence and came to England in 1939. I've lived in a world surrounded by modern art and architecture. And I've never had a problem with the shock of the new. I saw that architecture could be artistic and could reflect and change the way we live. That has always driven me. And I have always been fascinated by cities – why we leave them, why we return to them – the relationship between citizens and the people who leave cities.

"We're entering a new era. There is this immense drive towards a sustainable environment, and there is a movement to encourage people to move back into cities after a tremendous battle with the car and also with an industrial environment (which has been more about brawn than brain). Changes have to be made and are being made to improve the quality of life.

"As an architect, one develops one's own language, for good or for bad. When we did our first house we probably had a couple of hundred variations. Nowadays we know much more about the dead ends. The danger, of course, is that in the confidence of one's knowledge and experience one can overlook the things one should be looking at. But architecture is very much about understanding constraints and turning those constraints into positive action.

"So the shorthand has changed. It's emerged from the relationship between flexibility, growth and change – the idea that nothing is constant. This has pushed us towards technological expression, which today has become as much ecological as technological.

"At the same time we're in a far more fluid situation, where a church can be a nightclub and a nightclub can be a church. There is no longer that clarity of image. But there are other things you can hang on to – geometry, rhythm and environmental relationships, structure – and they have always driven me.

"I tend to be an optimist. There are tremendous battles to be won. But it is increasingly being recognized that design goes hand-in-hand with social problems. The physical goes with social.

"Britain and Europe are in a good position - probably better than the States. In the '60s you went to America for new ideas. But now industry there has such a hard hold on what they think design is about that there's little room for architecture and urban design."

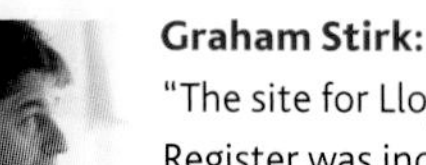

**Graham Stirk:** "The site for Lloyd's Register was incredibly complex. It was surrounded by listed buildings and façades, some of which had to be retained. We had to demolish buildings at the core and then rebuild the back of some of the surrounding buildings. We had to develop a system of building to fit the space, a system that would allow us to step away from the historically sensitive areas.

"It was a challenge to create harmony between a modern vocabulary suitable for an energy-efficient building and the Edwardian Baroque and the architecture of a nearby 18th-century pub!

"We resolved it in part through what we called the 'Alice Through the Looking Glass experience'. Although you can see the building from the less historically sensitive aspect, it is invisible from the more sensitive views. You access it through an alleyway. And it's a surprise. It suddenly appears and you are in a new, exotic world.

"It was hard to build. The building was largely prefabricated and all the component parts were passed through two temporary openings. It was a bit like those old *It's a Knockout* competitions when pianos where demolished and posted through a letter box.

"Looking at it now there are a number of things I love. I love the clarity we achieved in such a complex situation. It's an easy building to understand. I like the open atria, the indents rising to the sky. I like the colouration. I love the energy technology – the automated louvred façade that shades the building from the sun, allowing us to develop a system with lower energy requirements."

*We're pretty lucky in the UK. Because we live on a militarily powerful island we have never really had to face the plight of being refugees. But in Cyprus they know all about being refugees. Hussein Chalayan's family had to flee their home. His family's plight, and the recent ethnic cleansing in Kosovo, inspired the table skirt.*

**Hussein Chalayan:** "Having to leave your home at gunpoint is an horrific idea. And some of the horror comes from the things we are forced to leave behind. I was fascinated by what people protect and how they preserve them in times of such crisis.

"A lot of our work is based on movement and changing environments. This developed from that theme. The whole performance was based on having to leave your home in a time of war. What possessions would you try to hide if your home got raided? The performers camouflaged their favourite clothes as chair covers. Then they put the clothes on, and the chairs themselves turned into suitcases. The table turned into a skirt, made up of circular mahogany-veneered pieces opening up like a picnic cup.

"We had Bulgarian singers performing ancient prayers using throat song. Some of the performance was watched through a screen, which I think worked to convey the surreal feel of television reporting, with its editing and censorship.

"I think it's a bit far-fetched to call myself an artist, but I'm not sure I'm a designer as such, either. I direct ideas. We create things people can use. They're not necessarily practical. They don't always have a long life, but they serve a purpose. I think when you are creating things that can be produced industrially, then you are a designer.

"My ideas come from experience and life observations. Sometimes I am a detached observer, and I like to dissect prejudices. But something has to move me emotionally before I can get to the design stage.

"People have now realized you can turn creativity into business. I think that has its plusses and its dangers. The danger is that once things become too formulaic, they begin to lose their spirit. They are exciting at first, but after a while they become so much marketing."

# TABLE SKIRT

# IL RITORNO D'ULISSE IN PATRIA STAGE SET

*Ian MacNeil is one of the world's leading theatre designers, and his work has appeared from Munich to Broadway. He has also collaborated with The Pet Shop Boys on the design work and videos for a recent album. In* Il Ritorno d'Ulisse in Patria *(Ulysses' Homecoming, for the Bavarian State Opera) he has transformed the various sets into powerful expressions of the psychological subtext. The effect is visually and emotionally dramatic.*

**Ian MacNeil:** "Monteverdi is claimed to have invented opera, but what is great about this is how he managed to avoid the opera clichés. The emotions he communicates are not stylized – they are extraordinarily recognizable. He managed to take the sublime and the base of human experience and put it all into one piece – a wonderful expression of human duality.

"It was inspirational for me. I was looking for a way to express the sublime, the epic and the intimately human. I was also inspired by the space – the auditorium at the Bavarian State Opera is beautiful without being lush. A southern, almost Italian version of Bayreuth.

"My job is to give the director the space to play with, to provide an environment in which emotions can be expressed. The director's job is to relate the figures to that space. We intended to have nothing in it at all, really, we were just aiming to play off the huge parquet floor. But one by one we brought in a series of iconic objects. Because so much of the piece involves just two people singing, it was possible to create a dynamic that was at once epic and intimate. The singers could move down from the back stage towards the audience over a distance of 100 metres. You could hear the voices transform as they came towards you. It was wonderfully engaging.

"We managed to be both simple and iconic, creating a series of distilled images. The sets had a dream-like quality.

"In one scene, the parquet floor is erupted and curved towards us like a giant wave. This is for the scene when Penelope finally relents and admits that she recognizes Ulysses, after going through three hours of dismissal, anger and denial.

"I'm pretty good at male shapes. So here, for once, is a female shape. It's a beautiful, threatening curve. It's about a woman's power to forgive and to yield. A wave like that can excite you and can kill you. It's a huge, yielding female. It's a bloody dangerous shape!

"The ineluctable wave - it's frozen but poised to crash. On an emotional, intuitive level, it's sexual, the rising of a wave of passion from the depths. It is subconscious knowledge and desire bursting up. A wave is an embodiment of power reaching its climax and falling away.

"But that's to intellectualize it. Certainly, when you are conceiving such a work it is wise not to over-articulate it. I can be over-intellectual and find I have to suspend that tendency in order to do my better work and create an event that is essentially dreamlike. When it's good, music theatre is a pretty direct conduit to the emotions and our irrational selves. It doesn't work if you over-rationalize it on your way to releasing it. You have to operate on instinct.

"In this context, Penelope finally acknowledges Ulysses and he is at rest. She sits down and puts his head in her lap. It really is intensely moving. Not grandiose but very connecting.

"I see the Trojan war as a vast male menopause, where a load of middle-aged men just need one more adventure, and they're engaged by the myth of a woman who's worth fighting a war for! So they leave their real lives behind. Some don't return.

"Ulysses is symbolic because he lives half his life away from family and wife and then finally returns. It's a great myth.

"Design is about making life better - that's what it's for. So the fact people understand design more now is, generally, a fine thing. With this in mind I went along to the radical fashion exhibit at the V&A with great anticipation. But I saw the stuff as wilfully weird and even cruel, like it was made purely for the sake of reaction. It was beautiful, but in a decadent, cruel way. I find it disturbing. I don't know what it's for. Broken glass against a female skin. It seems we have to be shocked. I reacted to it, of course. But I find myself asking: 'Why?' It's certainly not about making life better".

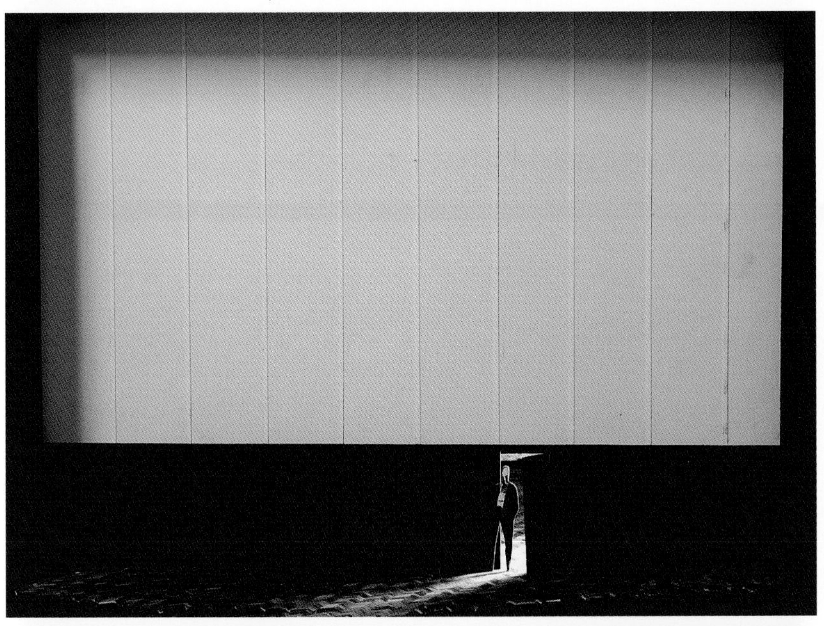

# MODULAR KIT SHOES

*What's more important to you? The shoes you wear or the sofa you sit on? Should the person fit the car or the car fit the person? Rosemary Wallin thinks we've got our priorities all the wrong way round. She's using her lateral approach to draw on design thinking from a range of disciplines to generate a new approach to footwear.*

**Rosemary Wallin:** "Comfortable footwear is every bit as essential as a comfortable sofa or a comfortable room. If you have uncomfortable shoes on, it doesn't matter how nice your sofa is or how beautiful your building. The only thing you can think about is that your feet hurt.

"Shoes are complex – trainers have up to 150 parts. Women's shoes are especially problematic. If they are high heels, they need a shank, a sprung-steel under-arch to act like a backbone. This is not usually connected to the heel, so if the shoes are subjected to strenuous use, there's a high risk the heel will come away.

"I began to think of equivalent structures and came up with Tupperware. The lids are flexible, the body rigid. I was away! I came up with a flexible stretch upper that was very comfortable. It moved like a pair of tights. Then I thought, if you make the heel and shank removable from the upper, you could put the upper in the washing machine! In short, my focus changed from the design of a good shoe to the design of a shoe that fit a person's life.

"So I set to work using Alias, a CAD programme used for developing cars. And I thought of the shoe as a structural problem, like a bridge. Except this was a bridge bearing massive, perpendicular, continually shifting weight.

"The result? I came up with the modular Kit shoe. The shoe is, as the name suggests, made up of different parts. You can take it apart and put it back together as you want.

"In this shoe, you pull the heel back and it slides out with the shank: and hey, presto you have a pair of slippers. The soles are made of polyurethane and the uppers from one piece of stretchy material. So simple.

"It's so versatile. A woman could buy this shoe and then select a different heel height, or even a range of heel heights. The future lies in mass-customization. That's where technology is taking us."

*The Falkirk Wheel rotating boat-lift is not only a first: it's beautiful, it's functional and it's in central Scotland. There is such harmony in the shapes, such grace and economy in the movement, that it looks more like a sculpture than an operating boat-lift. For that, believe it or not, is what it is: an ingenious means of moving boats from one canal to another. It is a wonderful thing that such artistry can be put into something so functional. Tony Kettle of Robert Matthew, Johnson-Marshall and Partners was the man who designed it – and he used Lego to help him do it.*

**Tony Kettle:** "This is the first rotating boat-lift ever built, and the first boat-lift to be built in Britain since the Anderson Boat Lift in 1895. It reconnects East and West Scotland, Glasgow and Edinburgh, the Forth & Clyde Canal with the Union Canal.

"The level difference between the two canals is some 300 feet. All sorts of options had been considered, from a stairway of locks that would take at least one day to complete, to a proposal like ours, which included a rotating lift.

"The idea simply is to pluck the boats from one canal and lift them up to the other one, and vice versa.

"Our concept was this linear route or spine that connects the two sides of Scotland.

"The existing aqueduct is very thin and elegant, and we wanted the one that fed the lift to be equally elegant, in a modern idiom. A beautiful, flowing thing, like the spine of a fish.

"We thought that at the point where it breaks and makes the connection between the two canals, it should be something of a celebration.

"So we were driven both from an aesthetic point of view and from the requirements of the mechanical engineering.

"We wanted something sculptural, something that gives a sense of movement and rotation, and this is the function of the hooked leading edges.

"People have commented that these forms resemble Celtic symbols. Well, I think it's interesting that they look not dissimilar to such forms, but really, that is coincidental.

"Originally we were considering that these hooked edges could also act as counterbalances – they were to be water tanks.

"But the team came up with an hydraulic driving mechanism which only requires the power of two electric kettles to turn it. So we didn't require a more complicated drive system.

"We also developed a simple mechanism for maintaining the horizontality of the caissons – the containers holding the boats. I had a solution in my mind, but couldn't communicate it to the engineers.

"So I went home and sat down with my six-year-old daughter, and together, we built the idea in Lego. The solution is a five-cog system which allows the caissons to rotate in the cradles, but not to swing back and forth. It didn't rely on gravity.

"Sometimes the best concepts are the simplest. When I had first tried to explain it, I hadn't been able to get it across. When I showed them the Lego model they looked at it in surprise and said: 'Well, yes. Of course! We understand that!'

"The work has some of the qualities of a timepiece. I see it as both a work of art and a piece of structural engineering. A lovely collage of curves and movement in one composition.

"And there's another dimension. We have all been very used to looking at still images of this mechanical device.

"But when it moves, something special happens. All the reflections change as the curves hit the water.

"How can I describe its effect? The closest thing I can think of is a kaleidoscope. It's mesmerizing.

"I also love the way the aqueduct appears to shoot through the hoops with no apparent support. I think the hooks add an aesthetic drama.

"I remember as a schoolboy working up the ladder locks on the Grand Canal. It took all day. This happens in 15 magical minutes.

"I think design is in recovery after the terrible fallout of the '60s, with the rise and fall of the tower blocks.

"Now there's a new confidence, and it doesn't have the arrogance of the '60s, in which people and their lives were so ignored. I think the revolution is just beginning."

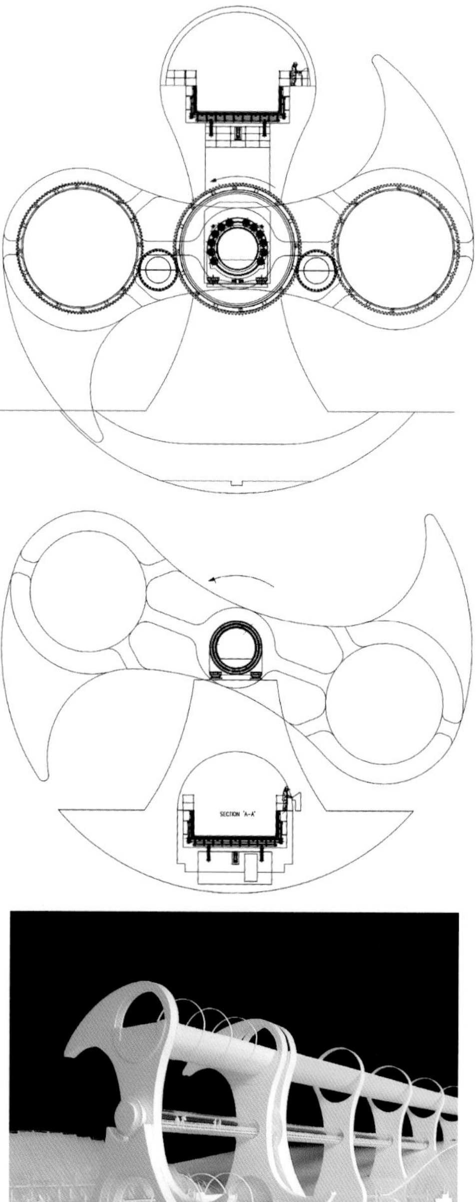

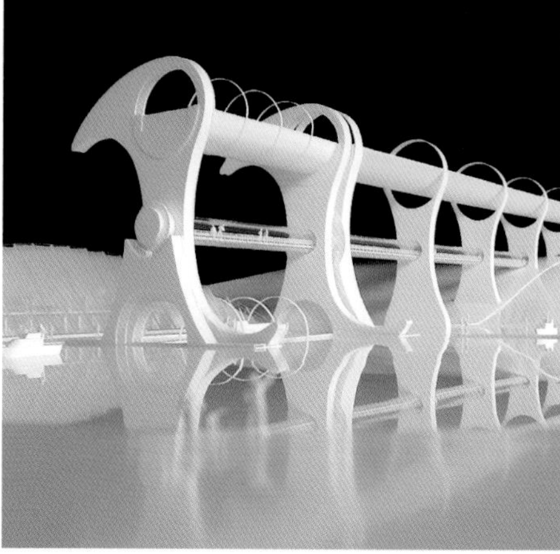

# FLUIDITY

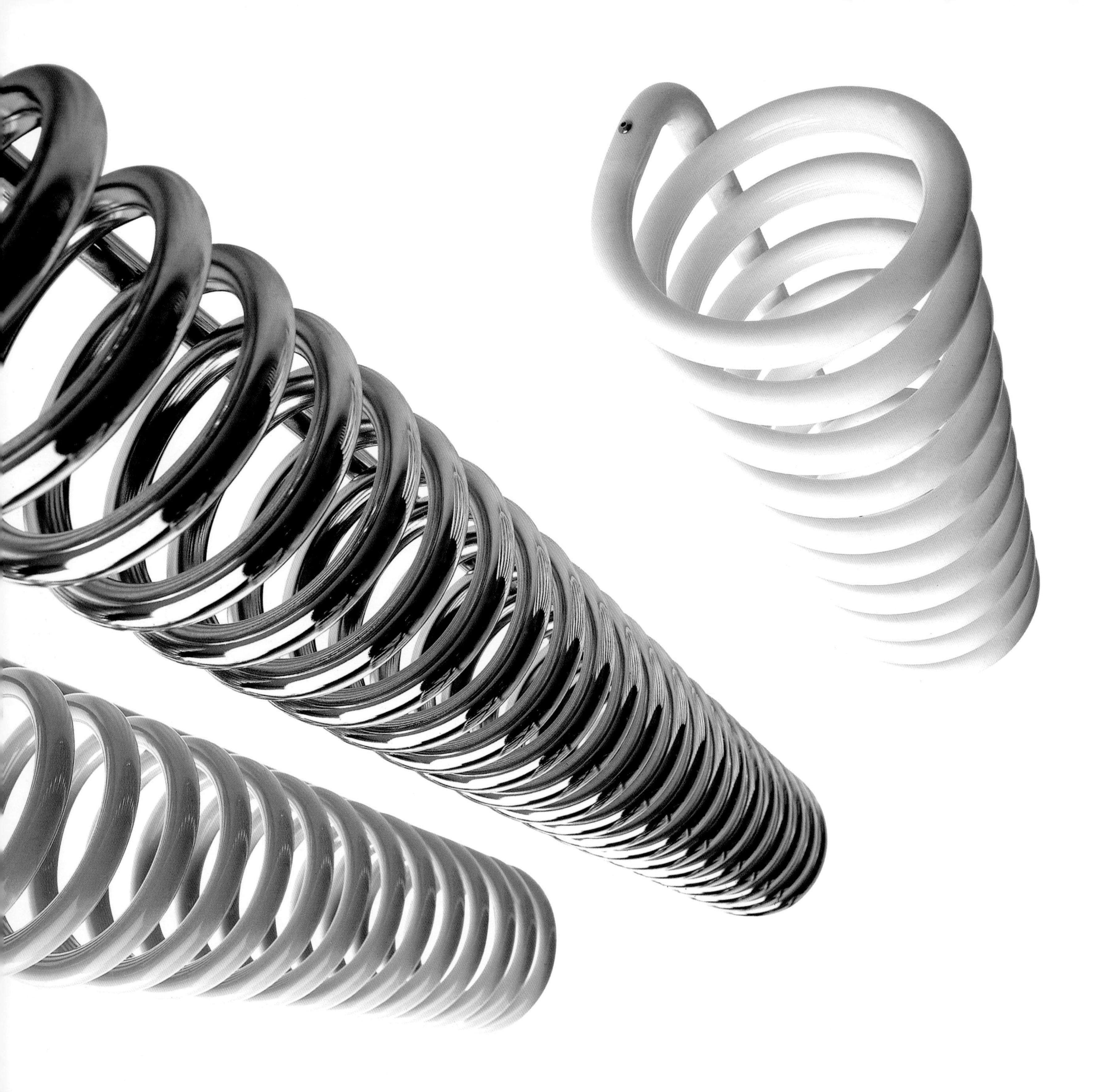

# HOT SPRING RADIATOR FOR BISQUE

*What could be more fluid than a spiral containing liquid? Fluidity suggests change and dynamism, and these domestic radiators are exactly that. As you move past them, the reflections shift, and they almost appear as if they are turning. This novel approach to radiator design is the brainchild of award-winning designer Paul Priestman, perhaps best known for his design of the Virgin trains.*

**Paul Priestman:** "The idea originally came from looking at existing towel radiators made from cut-and-welded straight tubing. These are expensive and complicated to make. We thought: 'How about making the tube into a coil? Then there wouldn't have to be any cuts or welds.'

"Also, lurking in the back of my mind was the fact that I had always been amazed by people spending lots of money on light fittings and other decorations, and yet always seeming happy to put up with the bog-standard, boring panel radiator. Things are changing, of course, because people are considering interior design in more detail.

"The shape is absolutely functional. They are used upright – they won't work on their sides – and they create a chimney effect, drawing up cool air from the floor and warming it.

"But the spring shape is alluring, and springs are such fascinating objects. If you walk past them or round them they actually change – the highlights change. The curves seem to twist and move. I've seen people at exhibitions walk past the Hot Spring and just automatically reach out and touch it. Of course, springs suggest power – the coiled spring – and ultimately heat is a form of power. And somehow the shape is friendly. People see it and smile. It's a radiator you could hug!

"One of the things I find satisfying about the design is the fact that people look at it and say that it doesn't look designed – it looks like it just happened. That's when design is at its most successful: when it's not superfluous, when it's not just decorative. The shape is totally interlinked to the manufacturing process – you can't take any part of it away. It's unembellished and yet it looks good. And it's been enormously successful."

FORCE 10 FABRIC

*The rolling contours of a weather map: we're all intimately familiar with them, though we might not know exactly what they mean. But we are all aware they suggest incredible power – the closer the contours, the stronger the wind. And when Paul Simmons of Timorous Beasties made them into wall fabrics and curtains, it generated a storm-force energy.*

**Paul Simmons:** "For a while, we had been working on traditional fabric designs with a slight twists. We'd been taking traditional repeats but blowing them out of proportion. The flowers would be pretty but suddenly would become not so pretty. They'd become triffid-like.

"Force 10 was a change for us. It was designed originally as curtain material. Well, there's a natural link between curtains and weather patterns outside the window...

"The weather map is a modern icon. We watch them all the time on TV. Concentric circles, contour lines... We thought it would be a simple design, but it ended up quite complicated and every bit as much work. But it was a good challenge to make something so complex that could work, say, as wallpaper. TV weather patterns just move across your screen. They don't have to line up with other weather patterns!

"It took a lot of trial and error to get it right. We designed them by sticking thin black tape onto paper. We found it easier to do it by hand. We ended up designing quite a few patterns.

"Somewhere along the line the designs hit a nerve, and felt right. The Force 10 graphic seems to have a lot of appeal. Of course, the weather is important to the Brits. It's especially important to the Scots! Some fear the design can be a bit overwhelming, but if you do just one wall in this material it has a dramatic impact. It counters the square geometry of the average room, changing the room's whole feel. The curves have a smoothness that people love.

"Most people like maps. I've always been inspired by them. My uncle used to have huge OS maps on the wall of his bedroom. I used to sneak up and look at them often.

"Is the UK a good place for creativity? Well, I wouldn't want to be anywhere else."

*Look over the page. The wonderful image from the Guinness ad that begins with the spellbinding line 'Tick follows tock'. As Walter Campbell, formerly of Abbott Mead Vickers, explains, this ad works because of its mythical richness.*

**Walter Campbell:** "One thing that creates the ambience of Guinness is the time it takes to pour. So we started playing with the idea of waiting, and out of that came the idea of 'good things come to those who wait.'

"We did a press ad about a guy hunkered down, looking out to sea, with a surfboard on his lap. He was waiting for the seventh wave, a magical wave. The client said: 'I like that image. Can we do that on TV?'

"In the meantime we were working on 'SwimBlack', the ad which features the old boy who dives in when the pint starts being poured and races to his brother's bar before the last drop falls in. We were building the bar, and discussing pictures to put on the walls. We came across the painting of Neptune's horses, riding the waves. We thought: 'Yes! Let's bring that to life.'

"We wanted to layer the film and make it rich, give it depth and resonance. We were thinking of *Moby Dick*, the obsession of it, and the danger of it. At one stage we thought of having a whale make the wave.

"It was superbly directed by Jonathan Glazer. The music was by Peter Rayburn. We had listened to around 2,000 tracks, trying to find the right music, and we were considering Led Zeppelin. But Peter knew Leftfield and proposed the-as-yet unreleased number, 'Phat Planet' - 'Phat' being a Jazz term for rich, hitting the groove.

"And the words: 'tick follows tock follows tick follows tock' carried the sensation of waiting, of time passing slowly, almost suspended, in slow motion. It had suggestions of Joyce from *Portrait of an Artist as a Young Man* and the novel's terrible sense of eternity, of something threatening that may take forever to come.

"'And the phat drummer hits the beat with all his heart....' We were looking for the sound inside the surfer's head when he's on the wave. Like a super-pulse going through his head and ears. It's a very emotional pulse: dynamic, unstoppable, reaching an epiphany, a glory.

"You've got to push constantly. You've got to keep looking for the missing ingredient – you have to sense when it isn't quite there. Finding the right thing, like that music, often opens up new doors, new perspectives.

"We'd hit a rich vein. 'The Dream Club' film carried the same sense of generosity and community as 'SwimBlack'. And so did 'SnailRace'. The preposterous idea that people were waiting for the snails to race. It's a fairy tale, but one that came true! Our first film took Guinness's market share from 4% to 5.5%."

"People feel a sense of generosity and affinity when watching these ads. Some ads talk down to you, but these are inclusive. Somehow they feel warm. And people respond with an internal nod: 'Yeah, I want to be a part of that.'

"I think these ads could only work for this beer. They're very subtle and they're very powerful. And Guinness has a tradition of dense, clever, emotional ads. So here's to your dreams..."

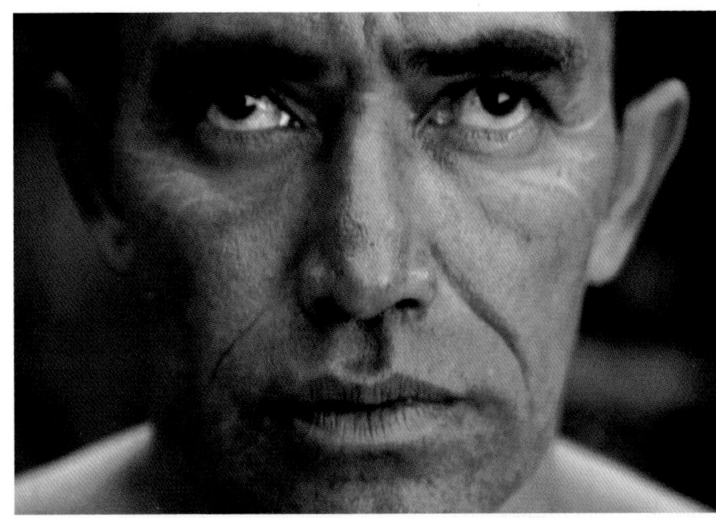

# NICHOLAS ARROYAVE-PORTELA VASE

*Fluidity is at the heart of Nicholas Arroyave-Portela's thinking. The changing contours in the natural world fill him with a sense of beauty. For him, fluidity is all about life, death and the movement between those two states. The shape of the vase pictured is influenced by the shape of the water it contains. His ideas have their root in the philosophy of the Far East.*

**Nicholas Arroyave-Portela:** "Fluidity is at the centre of much of my work. I had a philosopher friend at college who used to come back and talk about metaphors and how ceramics might be metaphorical. She would quote Lao Tzu: 'The water that flows into an earthenware vessel takes on its form.' It's a beautiful idea.

"But I wanted to subvert it, to see not how a vessel's shape influences the form of water, but how water can influence a vessel's shape. I did experiments with plastic bags – seeing how the water would distort it, what effect its weight had on the bag. Those textures led me on to dehydrated fruits – where the water has been sucked out by heat. Like dried figs and prunes, all wrinkled.... And apples slowly drying in the sun, gradually developing lines and wrinkles.

"And there were literary influences. Philip Larkin's 'Skin' – how, as we get older, we 'must learn our lines' – the lines on our skin brought by anger, amusement and sleep.

"Lines. Lines made by water. Look at the snaky ripples on a beach – how the water has affected the sand or the mud. They're like contour lines. Landscapes fashioned by water, curved and liquid. Some people say my work reminds them of the opening sequence of *The English Patient*: when the plane flies over the sand dunes.

"For me, fluidity is contemplative. It's about change and translation. It's why I like water: it can be tranquil or violent. It's very much a state of mind – a bit like an abstract painting. It could be so many things, you'll never tire of looking at it. That's what I'm aiming to create: objects you never tire of contemplating.

"I had a fairly standard background. I came out of college with a ceramics degree. The show I did for my degree had all the germs of what I'm doing now. Then, I was more into large-scale pieces, which required me to throw them, coil them again, and throw them again in order to achieve the skin. I developed my technique and throwing skills so I could throw larger pieces in one go.

"I gradually got orders from big firms for my smaller pieces. Then I realized that I was going to end up as a one-man band for manufacturing, effectively working for about £1 an hour. I didn't fancy that!

"Well, if you look past the hype you have to conclude that, yes, there is a creative revolution. I went to college during the rise of Brit art. But what is sad is that it's not taken advantage of. There's some fantastic creativity coming out of colleges, but the big companies are not snapping it up; they're letting it die. So many of my friends have had their worked ripped off, plagiarized. There's no redress and it's very frustrating.

"The education system is throttling creativity. When I went to college, there were grants. Now people come out saddled with enormous debts. They can't afford to take up work in the vocational industries, like ceramics.

"The only option I saw for someone like myself was in making one-off pieces. Well, that was an unreal thing to expect. Happily, it worked out. It hasn't for so many others."

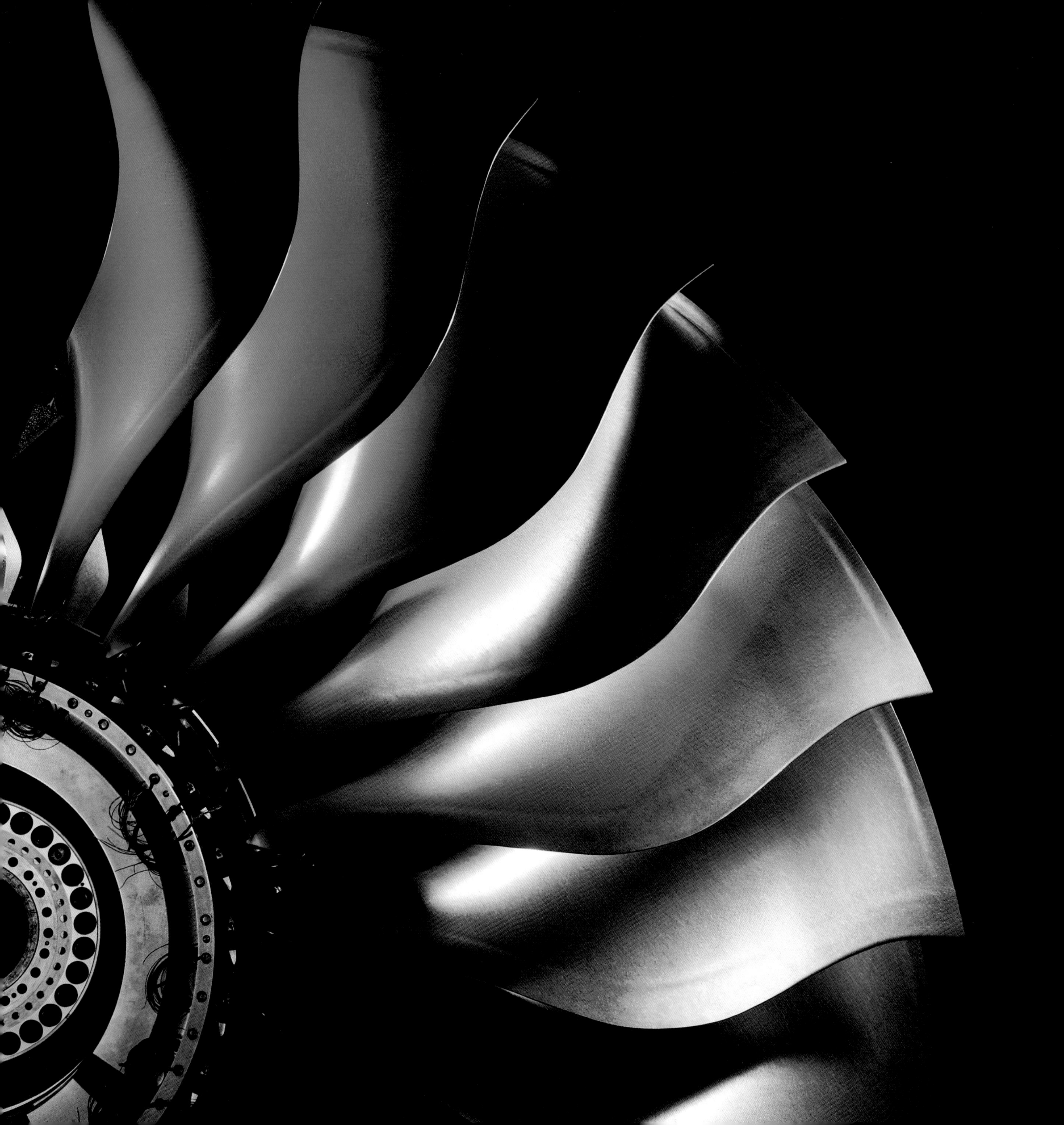

# ROLLS ROYCE 'SWEPT' FAN BLADES

*The Rolls Royce Trent engine is probably the best commercial aircraft engine in the world. Light, quiet and super fuel-efficient, each version of the engine contains literally hundreds of pathfinding innovations. One of the most difficult problems was the creation of the large fan blades that suck the air into the combustion chamber. In order to meet Rolls Royce's efficiency targets, Chief of Fan Engineering Integration Tony Lloyd coordinated a team that worked on both the design of the blade and its safe and secure integration into the rest of the aircraft. And the result was not only enormously successful, but also stunningly beautiful. The perfect design?*

**Tony Lloyd:** "This was all about getting the curves right. If you get the blades' contours wrong, you'll get dramatic losses in efficiency. Conversely, if you get them right, efficiency gains become equally dramatic. The fan blades' function is to suck air in and compress it, so providing thrust for the engine. The struggle is to climb up the efficiency curve.

"More efficiency means lower fuel bills, less pollution and higher profits. It's as simple as that. How did we do it? Put as simply as possible, the curves were achieved by the use of computational fluid dynamic software – in short, a computer programme that optimizes the fan blade shapes in order to minimize losses. The result was the dramatic twist in the blade, the profile that sweeps in a slender curve both backwards and forwards.

"Getting the blade tip right is critical. When the aircraft is cruising, these tips are slicing through the air at over 1,000 miles an hour. And that means they generate sonic booms, powerful shock waves over the top half of the blade. Control of that shock wave is the primary means of controlling efficiency losses, because the turbulence caused by the shock wave causes more friction, more drag. This beautiful blade is nothing more than a compromise – an effort to achieve minimum efficiency loss over a range of extreme conditions along the length of each blade.

"The complex shape has been made possible by another Rolls Royce innovation, for the blade is effectively hollow. As you go up in engine size, you cannot sustain solid metal blades. So we have developed hollow fan technology.

"The blade is made of two panels joined together by solid state diffusion bonding – another Rolls Royce innovation. The 'glue' is made of titanium and 'dries' into a honeycomb which acts as a 'web' – like a system of girders. We then 'inflate' the blade, pumping in inert gas under extreme pressure, blowing the panels outwards until they touch the conforming die. This produces the wonderful profile, the beautiful curves. And it creates a blade of incredible strength.

"But then it has to be strong. The force acting on the tips is so enormous, it's equivalent to hanging 10 London buses off the end of each one. The energy produced by the blades is enough to power 3,000 family cars. The four Trent engines on an average Jumbo generate sufficient energy to power the city of Derby. When the blades are up to speed, they suck 70 tons of air through the engine every minute - 70 TONS of air.

"The blades are made this way, and this strong, partly to combat 'soft body ingestion': if a bird hits one of these fan blades, it has a local impact load of some 20 tons. Hard to believe? Well, the blades are doing 1,000 miles an hour, the plane, say, 500, and the bird, say 30 – so that's a combined impact speed of over 1,500 mph. The bird is therefore acting like a high-velocity dum-dum bullet, made up of flesh, bones and water. There have been cases in other aircraft where a bird has broken the fanblade and destroyed the engine. But these blades are so shaped as to deflect the bird rather than breaking on impact. The shape is subtly designed so that the distribution of thickness in the metal within the blade allows a controlled deformation and the blade rides the blow.

"Of course, it is possible to be hit by something harder than a bird. Fan blades can be broken, despite their strength. Should that happen, the broken blade parts are aerodynamically designed to take a particular exit track, and so are safely contained within the engine carcass, allowing the engine to be shut down safely.

"The Swept fan blade was built for the 8104 Trent engine and will now go on the Trent 900, set to power the new generation of airbuses and jumbo jets."

*Image-makers Warren du Preez and Nick Thornton-Jones are two of Britain's leading creatives, producing extraordinary work that flows from a fascinating philosophy. The quality of their work is dictated by their concept of 'hypervisuality'. These are images that do far more than merely represent objects. They speak with a deeper resonance, aiming to communicate at a subconscious level.*

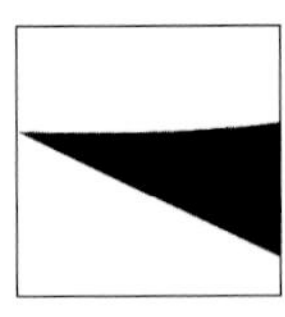

**Warren du Preez & Nick Thornton-Jones:** "I think we are right in the thick of a creative renaissance fuelled in part by a technological revolution. I believe we're entering a transcendental era where communication will work at subconscious levels and work so much better for it.

"But still, there's a lot of shit around. Ads so often just insult the intelligence of the audience. So much is stale, and so much else is just smoke and mirrors, cheap visual tricks.

"But audiences are highly sophisticated; they have massive visual vocabularies now. And through that vocabulary, through that increasingly hypervisual awareness, you can really communicate with incredible power.

"Our creativity comes from our will to explore our creativity. And from hard work - we are very disciplined and work very long hours.

"We have a sense of community here, of mutual support, and we've maintained this cottage-style mentality. We believe in keeping things small and in-house.

"We love to work with clients who have something to say beyond their ego - people like Björk who are so visually aware. People who understand human kindness and common respect.

"And we like to take our time. We like to push the wrong buttons, but for the right reasons. It's how our creativity works.

"We might take an image and turn it upside down and look at it inverted a million times just to understand why we're doing it.

"Sometimes we'll hit the answers straight off. Sometimes we'll be investigating it for a week, looking for that hypervisual resonance. But I have to be careful about intellectualization. It can fuck things up and create havoc in my head.

"We're talking about a revolution. The old school buggers can't jump into the digital domain. They're trying, but they don't really understand what they're doing. Sex is the only vehicle many of them understand how to use.

"And there are a lot of new, talented graphic artists hammering at the doors. Soon the gates are gonna give and a flood of new talent will burst through, chomping at the bit. Like a river, it will wipe all these old-school egos out the way – a new wave of hypervisual creativity.

"We work by holding each other up, supporting each other, rationalizing with each other. We both have good eyes and are very visually aware.

"We fight for the time to digest and discover a job. Time is so valuable to us.

"And we don't call them jobs, we call them collaborations. We work *with* our clients – the creative handshake. It's worth taking time to get to know the client, because if you can understand the person, then you are going to be able to tap into his/her subconscious and communicate far better.

"We are very fucking lucky – we are beyond lucky. We work with trusting, loving people. Fear cripples you. But we are able to keep our confidence up because of who we work with."

# SONY ENTERTAINMENT HEADQUARTERS

*The Sony PlayStation has had an incredible impact on the marketplace, and that market's only just beginning. As the PlayStation2 spawned the next stage in the on-line digital generation, Sony Computer Entertainment decided they needed a European HQ in London that did justice to the product and its vision. They called on Fletcher Priest Architects to accomplish the mission.*

**Keith Priest:** "The job to create an appropriate base for PlayStation was run by Antonia Infanger and Ruth Lonsdale. What we tried to do was on the one hand provide the normal working requirements of an incredibly busy office, and on the other to inject into the workspace the subversion inherent in the brand.

"So there's an element of playing with the audience, joining them in a few in-jokes. PlayStation aficionados see things that corporate visitors don't even notice. The advertising plays up to that and so did we.

"So if you go into the toilets you might notice that there are two basins. And on the basins are four taps. But as you go to the taps you may notice the handles are shaped like a square, a triangle, a cross and a circle - the four PlayStation symbols.

"As you walk by, there's no great big Sony Europe HQ sign. But you might just spot the manhole cover. It has ■▲✖● in raised letters on it where 'Westminster' or 'Scunthorpe' might have been embossed. We know someone did spot it because the first one was pinched not long after we put it there.

"The foyer features this wonderful curved screen. But it's actually see-through – your PlayStation contact can watch you arrive from Golden Square. It actually conceals a rather ugly bronze and marble screen. PlayStation rents the building, so ripping that out wasn't an option.

"This introductory arena leads onto the core of the building: the central column of stairs, lifts and toilets. The toilets have another interesting feature: there are three doors - one for males, another for females, and the third? Perhaps it leads to the third place.

"The boardroom is suspended in space two storeys up in a timber hull. It looks out over a lightwell above the internal garden with its PlayStation blue benches and lozenge-like tables that glow mysteriously at night.

"The presentation suite is painted in lenticular reflective paint, so any wall can become a screen. The room can be changed from a meeting for 30 to a meeting for 300 just by moving a few screens. It's great watching people do it. They just take it for granted.

"It's a bit like good health. They're not aware of it. They'd only be aware if it didn't work. They use it naturally, and that's how it should be.

"Is there a design revolution? There's always a design revolution. It was always true and it always will be true.

"Certainly the digital revolution has made a difference. And I imagine there was a minor spurt when Letraset came in.

"Certainly it's easier now for more people to work on one piece of work. But it also means it's easier to produce a lot of bad stuff very quickly.

"Good stuff is as hard to produce as it's ever been, and good stuff depends on creativity and serendipity and the glorious collision of it all."

*Harvey Nichols has a reputation for good windows, and Thomas Heatherwick was delighted to secure the commission to celebrate the 1997 London Fashion Week with this dramatic display. Thomas was so fascinated by public reaction to his display, that he would get on buses that ran past the store just to hear what people were saying. Some said it was a series of animated bones. Others said flames. Or legs. Or even Twiglets...*

**Thomas Heatherwick:** "I worked with structural engineer Ron Packman. The road is like a wind tunnel and there was serious risk of it all just blowing away. We had to develop an approach that would make the stuff appear like it was going through the plate glass. In the end we went for Aeroply, a timber which is only 0.8mm thick, and a core of expanded polystyrene in the middle. But we couldn't find a manufacturer to meet our requirements, so we had to make it ourselves.

"I spent a lot of time carving the forms. I wanted to create a wave effect, but then I thought: 'Well, that will be boring!' We needed something that had vigour and life – that looked animated.

"So I created something in a continuous strip, with these legs stepping through the glass. It had great dynamism. It's not about anything more than that, really.

"I'm currently designing a Buddhist temple in Japan, which will store the remains of 2,500 people. It's amazing that a Japanese religious organization should come to a British designer to create something that will be there for the next 500 years."

NICHO

NICHOLS

# CITY CUTLERY

*"A fork, a knife and a spoon. Well, what's so great about that? We use them every day." That, of course, is the whole point. Because if all everyday objects were designed as beautifully as this cutlery, life would be a much more pleasant experience. David Mellor's cutlery is so perfectly balanced it's a delight to hold. It is a triumph of form and function.*

**David Mellor:** "We started off with the city cutlery. We wanted to create a shape that felt good to handle. Most cutlery is made out of flat material, but we wanted something more comfortable.

"Cheap cutlery is not easy to work with. And if you thicken the pieces up and make them solid, well they're more comfortable to grip, but they're too heavy.

"When you look at the knives, it all looks like one piece, but in fact they are made up of three parts. There's the hollow handle, the blade and stock, and there is a weight inside the handle that gives the knife its perfect balance.

"It's taken a lot of care to get the balance right.

"These are difficult to make and there is a tremendous amount of minute processes involved.

"The handle is made from two half-shells welded together round the stock.

"We've developed a special machine to make it all appear seamlessly curved, like it's fashioned from something entirely solid.

"I sometimes wonder whether the cutlery is a proposition at all. But everyone wants to carry on with it.

"After the city cutlery we moved on to the kitchen knife, which effectively is the same thing but on a much bigger scale.

"Now this is much more of a commercial proposition!

"Is there a design revolution? Not in cutlery. The opposite. We're now the only firm in Sheffield making modern cutlery.

"We're working on a new design now, which is completely different. We call it the 'Flat Four', and it's all made in flat sections, giving the cutlery the opposite look to the city range.

"It's kind of from the sublime to the ridiculous!"

*Few designers are as versatile as Ron Arad who can turn his hand from designing products to buildings. So it's no surprise he has begun to forge an entirely new direction in furniture. He has created a fantastic series of sculptural pieces using vacuum-formed aluminium, represented here by the B.o.o.p table. The process makes it possible to create a delightful sense of fluidity.*

**Ron Arad:** "B.o.o.p – it stands for 'Blown Out Of Proportion', and that describes the process by which I've made these pieces. I developed it after I came across vacuum-formed aluminium, used for the aerospace industry and the wings of a Morgan car. It's not normally used for furniture.

"I noticed that when they formed it, they 'inflated' the aluminium to iron out wrinkles. I was fascinated by that process of blowing aluminium. I started thinking: 'What if I could blow this aluminium through shaped holes, rather than rectangular frames? You might connect them, and get a landscape. An organic, curvilinear landscape.' The word 'organic' is much abused. There's a lot of 'vomit' stuff that calls itself organic. But it applies here.

"It was interesting to do things you can't do with techniques like press forming. To press metal, you normally need a male and a female part – one receiving and one pushing. You don't need this if you are blowing it. So, blown aluminium has a mystery about it. People look at the large pieces I produce and are baffled by them, because they know that no one in their right mind would make such a big press tool.

"We made an aluminium blowing tool to make large objects. You can reverse the tool, which means you can make shapes back-to-back, with cavities in them. And because the 'superform' aluminium is rich in magnesium and doesn't tarnish, it means you can polish it and make it look like stainless steel.

"I take the blown pieces and cut and weld them, making bowls, tables. It's just a question of cutting and reorganizing.

"The curves are derived from the process. The table has areas for beer glasses, and depressions for fruit and peanuts. It's not a piece that pretends to be the most practical of tables, but it's not the most impractical, either. You might have a problem playing ping-pong on it, but then you can't have goldfish swimming in a ping-pong table.

"I think the process is interesting, and it gives rise to its beauty, its reflectiveness, its curvaceousness, its seamless transition between the flat and the indented. People from my profession had no idea how it was made. There's a magic in it."

# PRECISION

# BUDDY ANIMATRONICS

*When Jim Henson's Creature Shop was asked to create a gorilla for the title role in the film* Buddy, *it was the obvious choice. The Creature Shop is a leader in the world in animatronics – the electronic animation of puppets. The new creations bear little resemblance to the wire-guided frogs and pigs that founder Jim Henson created decades before. Now the realism is breathtaking. John Stephenson, executive vice president, Jim Henson's Creature Shop Worldwide, explains how it's done.*

**John Stephenson:** "It's incredibly strenuous what that man has to do inside that costume. But when the cinema audience watches, they must only see total reality. The difference between the way an ape moves and a human being moves is enormous. Every single bit of musculature in the body is considered – and considered in conjunction with how the human inside is going to be moving.

"Buddy's head, is the zenith of 15 years' design work. It's extremely well thought out, like a Porsche or a VW. Year after year those cars are improved, and so it is with our animatronics. In the days of *The Dark Crystal* we did it all with string and bits of aluminium.

"We can now do incredibly impressive close-ups with animatronic heads. And a lot of it is down to the Henson performance-control system, which operates all the facial movements.

"The man inside is talking all the time to the outside operators. So we spend a lot of time rehearsing. Vocals have to be added in post-production. Breathing is strenuous in there. Frankly, the job of being inside is pretty horrific: really you can't see very much and it's incredibly hot and claustrophobic. And we shot this in the heat of Los Angeles. The actor, Peter Elliott, overheated quite a lot. We had oxygen on hand should he need it.

"Digital technology isn't really a threat – we now do as many digital effects as we do physical. We're not wedded to physical technology; in fact, the best results are often achieved by mixing the two. Our aim is to produce a great image on screen. We don't really care how.

"We are always trying to get on-screen perfection. I think if we ever did get it, we'd probably all die."

*Alexander McQueen, the wild child of world fashion,* l'enfant terrible. *But behind that rather superficial image is an incredible creative mind. He is undoubtedly one of the greatest talents in fashion ever to emerge from these shores.*

**Alexander McQueen:** "This whole show was inspired by military themes. This coat, made of leather cut into strips, has the feel of armour. It's very strong, very structured. It was inspired by the great coats of the First World War. It was the silhouette that interested me.

"I believe in empowering women with my clothes. I believe in giving them strength. But I also love the softness of femininity. This show was about both: the hardness of the military male side balanced against beauty and elegance. I also used soft wools and Edwardian lace in the show.

"I find I take my inspiration from so many places. It could be the way a woman walks in the street. It could be a bizarre book from a bookstall in Rye, strange images from a Parisian flea market. I don't like modern magazines – I rarely read them.

"The American artist and war photographer Joel Peter-Witkins has been a powerful influence on me. His imagery is so layered, so deep. And it is very dark. I remember from the 'Mirror Box' show last year using an image of his. This was when the glitterati of the fashion world arrived at the show and watched themselves in a massive mirror for 45 minutes before anything happened. I guess I was forcing them to look at themselves.

"And then the mirror lit up from within and you could see the models inside this pristine, clean room. Then it was the models' turn to look at themselves, because the audience disappeared behind a mirror reflection.

"At the end a rusty old box falls apart and a voluptuous model emerges, covered in moths. A heart-beat rhythm pounds out. The lights go out and the audience sees itself in the mirror, then the lights flash on and the moths lift off. The lights go off again, the audience sees itself again, the lights come on again, they see the girl and the moths. It was almost subliminal in its impact. The final shot is of 40 models pressed up against the glass box, looking at the audience.

"I can't start work on a show until I have a clear vision in my head. I visualize the show and the presentation. Then it's 'OK, this is it!' and off we go. I know I ask the impossible. 'A ring of fire, please!' 'A 60-foot mirror box!' But I know that when people are challenged and want to rise to that challenge, they will do what the show needs. Anything can be done if you really want to do it. I don't believe in compromise.

"The business is growing massively. We're in partnership with Gucci now and they've injected a lot of money. We have a new store in Japan. Another in New York. Now our show is part of Paris Fashion Week. The fashion scene is strong in London but the Paris fashion profile is still much higher.

"Other fashion designers? I have tremendous respect for Rei Kawakubo. She's been in this industry for 20 years, and she constantly pushes the boundaries and turns things on their heads. I don't see the point in a fashion show that is only different from last year's show because the hems are one inch further down the leg.

"Some people think I'm all about shocking people. But it's not about that. It's about getting people to think, to question, and to ask where beauty really lies.

"Sometimes my best work goes unrecognized. Well, that doesn't matter. It takes people time to take it on board. But ultimately, my shows are about the clothes. I understand how to cut a suit or fashion a dress. It's my craft. I love it."

LEATHER COAT

# WHEN OBJECTS WORK

*When Objects Work – WOW. That simple word trick sums up the power of John Pawson's work. Famous as an architect, whose modern, pure and austere style always amazes, he turns his hand occasionally to designing the finer detail. It's important to him, he says, to get everything to balance, to feel right.*

**John Pawson:** "I like generous proportion. Everything is slightly longer, slightly deeper, slightly heavier than you might expect.

"A Belgian company asked me to design the sort of tableware things that don't need to be put away – that can be left on tables or sideboards. I did five objects, objects that worked. They were all containers, and they all had a duality about them.

"The bowl has a sculptural quality about it – not something I had necessarily intended. I like the way it can be positioned. It can be set horizontally or at a sharp angle. It's made up of a bronze sandwich with sand inside to give it weight. There is something sensual about it. Sensuality puts people in a good mood.

"The UK has always enjoyed a huge wealth of talent. Perhaps it's the atmosphere. Perhaps it's the gene pool. Recently people have begun to specialize a lot, but I like to keep my design skills as broad as possible. I like to design every bit of a project, because another designer might, with a small detail, upset the balance.

"What drives me? Creating things I'd like for myself."

*David Adjaye was recently described as architecture's rising star of the avante-garde. His work is known for its precise, modern style. Here he talks about a bathroom he's created as part of his conversion of houses in Kensington Palace Gardens, in the heart of fashionable London.*

**David Adjaye:** "In this bathroom I guess I'm investigating the idea of luxury - how to make a new kind of luxury. A bathroom is, for me, a very interesting place. I wanted to make one that was more about a room and not just about splash-down and splash-up.

"I didn't want it to be just about bodily functions.

"I wanted it to have pieces of furniture in a space that was very specifically curated.

"The client allowed me to redesign all the sanitaryware, and add some sensuality to the functionally. The loos, the shower chamber – everything has been remodelled.

"I used dark timber, which gives it a 'room' feeling, a rustic quality, which balances well against the white, pristine objects.

"It dissolves two ideas together and that to me is really important. You can walk around and not feel like you are in a bathroom – but in a 'room' in which there are bathroom fittings. It's difficult to define.

"To me, ideas must be precise. I am concerned to make things well, and accurately, and to a high standard. I was very rigorous about delivering the central conceptual idea.

"For me, the central conceptual idea here was the way the plan form of the room is replicated in the skylight.

"The skylight organizes the space above just as the bath organizes the space below. This works to give a specificity to the room. Such conceptual precision leads to pleasant surprises.

"I once did a different project for an artist where we designed the bathroom with an opening ceiling – you could shower in the rain or the snow. I like the idea that the functional becomes something sensuous.

"I like the idea that a home isn't: 'Oh, here's the functional bit, and here's the nice bit.' I want home spaces to be a sequence of pleasurable experiences."

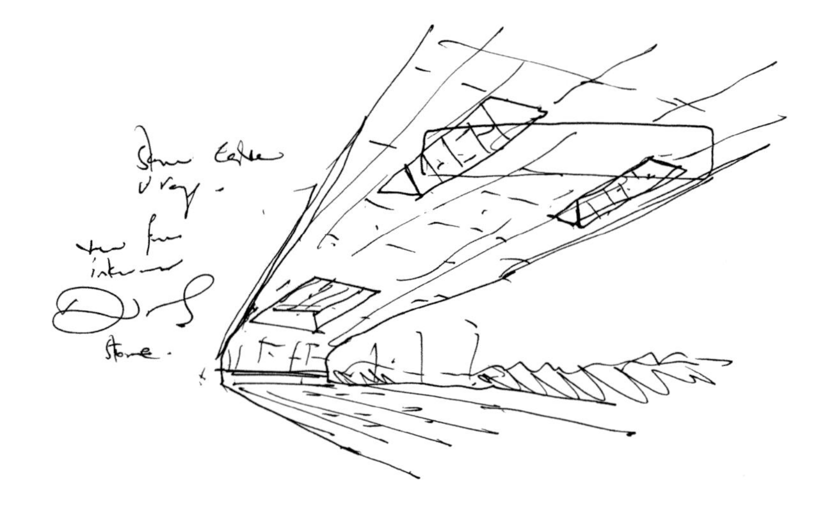

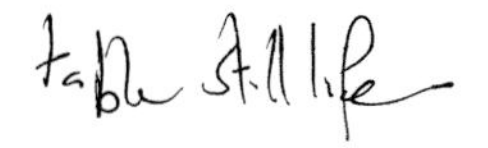


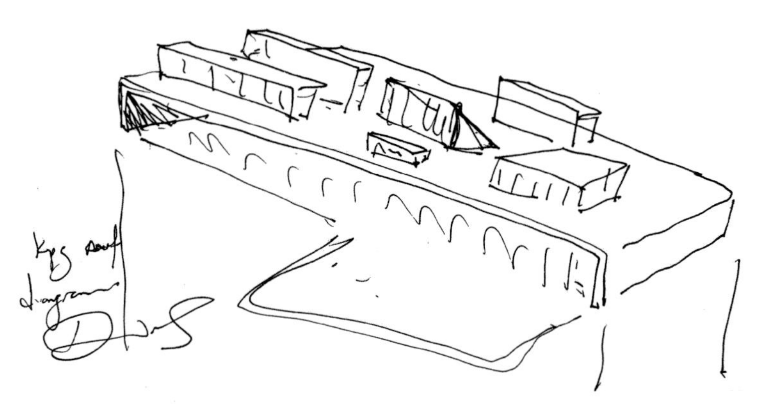

# SIM STACKING CHAIR FOR VITRA

*Jasper Morrison's classic designs have made him a legend in the industry. Recently he's designed the new Hannover tram, the 'air chair' (a low-cost, one-piece, injection-moulded chair using a new gas-injection plastic technology) furniture at the Tate Modern and a recent solo exhibition for Flos at Yamagiwa Centre in Tokyo. His hallmarks are precision and proportion, and these chairs are set to become classics in themselves.*

**Jasper Morrison:** "This project for a stacking, linking chair, took a very long time. It's hard to say why, except that some projects go very smoothly and others need time to come right.

"Vitra had asked for the chair to fulfil stacking and linking functions and after thinking it over I realized I wanted it to be a descendant of the GR40, probably the best stacking linking chair in existence, but with an outdated ergonomy and too much weight.

"Sometimes it seems more valuable to try and evolve things rather than try and create something from zero. Sometimes, as well, chairs breed other chairs and typologies become established.

"I like the way objects seem to have relations and ancestors, and if a development of an old model is done with good intentions and achieves something more than the original, I think it is justified."

# X-ACT GLASSES

*Wine glasses do have style, but the truth is they are a pain. They rarely survive a fall, even on a tabletop, and how many times has a glass broken in your hands as you washed it up? Julian Brown has come up with a new approach: a glass that has all the style of a wine glass, but all the practicality of a tumbler.*

**Julian Brown:** "This came out of a commission from the German company FX Nachtmann and its glassware brand, Marc Aurel. They wanted short-stemmed drinking glasses. I saw an opportunity for a pathfinding fusion between the traditional stemmed goblet and the modern tumbler.

"Working between the two cultures, I was looking to generate something easy to use, casually beautiful and less pretentious than the wine glass.

"In essence, I've simply fused the two. The trick lay in playing with the proportions. The new glass has a completely new feel. It's solid, machine-produced lead crystal with a short, modestly substantial stem, which is a really nice place for your fingers to play, and a reassuring shape and feel to the conical vessel.

" And the glass has a surprising tactility. It's quite heavy – the foot especially. It is, I am told, the world's first stacking wine glass. Of course, some other wine glasses stack, but kind of in the way cars stack: not very well. This is very definitely a wine glass but equally good with water and juice. We think it's created new territory between two polar cultures.

"It's what you might call a democratic wine glass. We wanted to call it 'Volksglass', but the German company had some problems with that. In the end we agreed on X-act, which reflects the clear and precise geometry necessary for its stackability.

"Is Britain in a design revolution? Well, frankly I think we're just catching up. And because we've arrived with lots of great ideas, it looks like a new wave. But really, the Italians were where we are now 10 years ago. Creative pragmatism - that's what the Brits are good at: down-to-earth creativity. But we have no monopoly on fantasy and creativity. Perhaps we've just started speaking an international language of design."

# CREASED TOTEMS ROMAN BLIND

*Karina Thomas and June Swindell of Salt take great pleasure from 3D - so much so that they have created a set of Roman blinds that fold up and down in a startlingly three-dimensional fashion. Some say there's something reptilian about the way they move, like scales linking together.*

**Karina Thomas:** "This is a 3D working Roman blind. It started off as a flat Roman blind, a knitted 100% cotton fabric with integral aluminium rods. But my passion is for 3D, and I soon found myself converting the piece into a sculptural landscape of hills, sea and sand, with all the multiple units interacting. It works as well!

"Most of our work at Salt has this ability to move in space. June Swindell and I love this sort of animation. When you pull the blind up, the curve of the aluminium forms a bull's horn. It tips downwards towards you, and when you've got all these multiple shapes choreographed the same way all tipping towards you and receding, it appears so complex, and appears so precise and scientific, though it is actually quite simple. A lot of our products have a kind of dance, but you have to use them to really understand this.

"When you open it, when you start to pull it up, because it looks so three-dimensional you think you are really going to have to strain. But in fact it's easy, and anyway, you are distracted from any effort by the incredible performance that is taking place as you haul. Let it down and immediately it reforms into the landscape effect. It really is a new experience each time you do it."

*It's amazing the impact architecture can have on a community. When work on the Canada Water Bus station began, the locals said they didn't want it. Now that it's finished and its beautiful structure stretches out like a seagull's wings, local people say they like it. They say that it looks like somebody cares about them. For that, they have to thank Eva Jiricna.*

**Eva Jiricna:** "To be absolutely honest, I can't say I had a special vision. I'm not the sort of person who wakes up in the morning with a revelation: 'Yes! This is how the bus station is going to be!'

"I have to put on the table the brief, limitations, the possible interpretations, and out of those I slowly and logically work towards the final image.

"And the image that evolved was that of a bird. And the body of the bird supports its wings. It was logical. We could only support the roof from a series of columns in the centre. The wings (the roof) would have to spread out over a large, unsupported, distance, and kind of flop in the air until we could stabilize them. So the central pillars had to act as a sort of spine.

"Then we worked through the process of making the space underneath the roof. We now needed to make this heavy object at least semi-transparent, because we wanted to bring light through it down to the station.

"Well, they need daylight. People don't feel so aggressive in daylight. And people abuse places they don't like.

"The two key problems were transparency and support. We had substantial loading problems. Uplift from the wind, snow on the roof. It required precision engineering to get it right. We made the pillars in the shape of elongated crystals, which rise up between the glass wings. Some say it's working to an aesthetic. To me, that is so, but it's more about solving problems of light and loading.

"I had no reason to hide the structure. If people want to look at it, they can. It helped the elegance of the total project somehow that the structure was visible through the skin.

"The structure is based on the principle of how we are all constructed. We're just following natural principles. Everything in nature is controlled by simple structures. People like to see structure looking right – if it looks wrong, then people instinctively feel uncomfortable. They don't necessarily know why. But they know when something looks right. And something that looks right is often beautiful. It's rare that something is beautiful and yet looks wrong.

"Architecture is the marriage of professionalism and talent. It is very different to art, which has no rules and no limits. It doesn't always require precision. I don't consider myself courageous enough to abandon precision. It is my guide - precision, and perfection of details. I suffer if I don't achieve it!"

*David Watkins and Wendy Ramshaw worked together on the paper jewellery project. It is, says David, a celebration of the ephemeral beauty of paper as well as a fun form of body decoration.*

**David Watkins:** "When we first designed paper jewellery back in the '60s, we were motivated by our desire to use processes outside the mainstream of jewellery production. The idea of printing jewellery really appealed to us. We wanted to create things that were fast and simple and fun and inexpensive. And throwaway – the throwaway concept was intriguing at the time

"These ideas were developed and brought up-to-date for the recent Thames & Hudson book. I say book, but really it was more of a package, since you were meant to take the book apart to make the jewellery.

"I think I might have been inspired by a party trick. I now remember that my grandfather used to bet us a penny that he could pass his whole body through a playing card. Easy money, we thought. But then he'd pull out the scissors and snip and slit away until he managed to create a huge portal big enough for him to step through.

"The trick with paper jewellery is to play to the beauty of the paper itself. You must celebrate its thinness, its flexibility, its printability and its lightness. Spirals work well because they grip the arm and are flexible enough to take account of different sizes. Some pieces include concentric cuts permitting a piece to be passed over your head.

"Perhaps it won't last very long, but while it lasts it will be beautiful."

*They look like a row of fantastical musical instruments, but they are not. They are finger rings living what Wendy Ramshaw calls their 'off' life. They are mounted on specially tailored stands that create sculpture on the dressing table.*

**Wendy Ramshaw:** "What you see here are finger rings on their stands. You unscrew the top to slip them off. The stands are important. They are part of the piece when the rings aren't being worn.

"Jewellery has two lives: one when it's on you, and the other as an object. It has an animated life and a still life. An on-and-off life.

"You need to take care wearing these rings. They are large and delicate. These particular pieces come from a series of drawings done for a Japanese client who gave me a commission in 1993 to create a small collection for him to celebrate the end of the century. I didn't make them – I did something else for him. But in 1999 I pulled the drawings out and got to work.

"I guess they are somewhat anthropomorphic. They are somewhere between plant or living form and robotic or bionic form. A hint of plant and a hint of human. And a sense of growth and movement.

"*Curl and pod*. Well, clearly it's halfway between machine and plant. It has a softness but it is also very hard. It's made in white gold. (The stands are nickel alloy.)

"It has four rings in it. You can take it apart and put it back together differently. My work has a lot of cones and arrows in it. They communicate dynamism and direction.

"*Ladder and wheel*. This is three rings. The wheel is navigational - it looks like it might be spinning. Yet the ladder makes it a very stationary piece, though there is a lovely sweep and curve

"*Plant*. This is the simplest of all. It's somewhere between machine and organic growth, so when you put it on, your finger it works as a link between man, metal and nature.

"I think these are hopeful. They aim to make you smile - a sort of English sense of the whimsical. But they oscillate, I think, between threatening and entertaining, hard and soft."

*It's the car to die for. Some have described it as simply the best sports car in the world. Certainly it is one of the most beautiful. The McLaren F1 has set many a young man's heart racing. But that's hardly surprising – it was born in the copybook of a young man's dreams. That man was designer, Gordon Murray.*

**Gordon Murray:** "I started off in arts. I'm firmly of the opinion the thing has to look good, and that good looks should be integrated into the engineering design. The F1 came out of a sketch I did at college. My old college books were full of sketches, but this one stuck in my mind as a good idea. I was fascinated by packaging – the balance between maximum accommodation and minimum space. So I put the driver in a central position, flanked to the rear by two passenger seats in an arrow formation.

"Being in the middle gives the driver a sense of absolute control, a true racing feel. It's especially good for driving around the UK's windy roads where good visibility down both sides is really useful. And it's much easier to drive accurately in relation to the road edge. And, of course, it offers big production advantages. They range from the fact you don't need a left-hand-drive version to the fact there is no pedal offset to cope with wheel bulge. And you don't need to put a speaker balance button on the stereo! We made a point of leaving that off...

"Packaging dictates it all. The mid-rear engine location, the low scuttle [dashboard height], the distinctive roof-sited air-intake which feeds directly down to the engine... The doors are dihedrally hinged, and when they open, swinging outwards and upwards, they lift out part of the roof and the door to make it easier to get in. All very different thinking.

"We wanted to give the car a sense of animal power, like a leaping big cat: powerful in the haunches. And I was adamant about giving the car shoulders, a tumblehome. Most supercars run the sides straight into the windows, but I wanted a pronounced tumblehome to set it apart from saloon cars.

"We wanted the car to echo an F1, with the front quite round and sleek but becoming more mechanical back towards the powerhouse. What we desperately sought to avoid was the generic boy-racer with wings and spoilers. It had to be a smooth classic along 1960s line. If you can use the fluid, classic curves without being overtly retro you'll have a design that won't date. Look at the knife-edge designs, say, of the Lamborghini Countach: wonderful, wonderful car, but it does look a bit dated now. This car was simply about 'no compromise'. Everything about it is the best you can get.

"Do I have one? Er, no... but I have access to one. It's no longer in production. When it was, it would have set you back £640,000. Now it's up for sale for around £1.1 million."

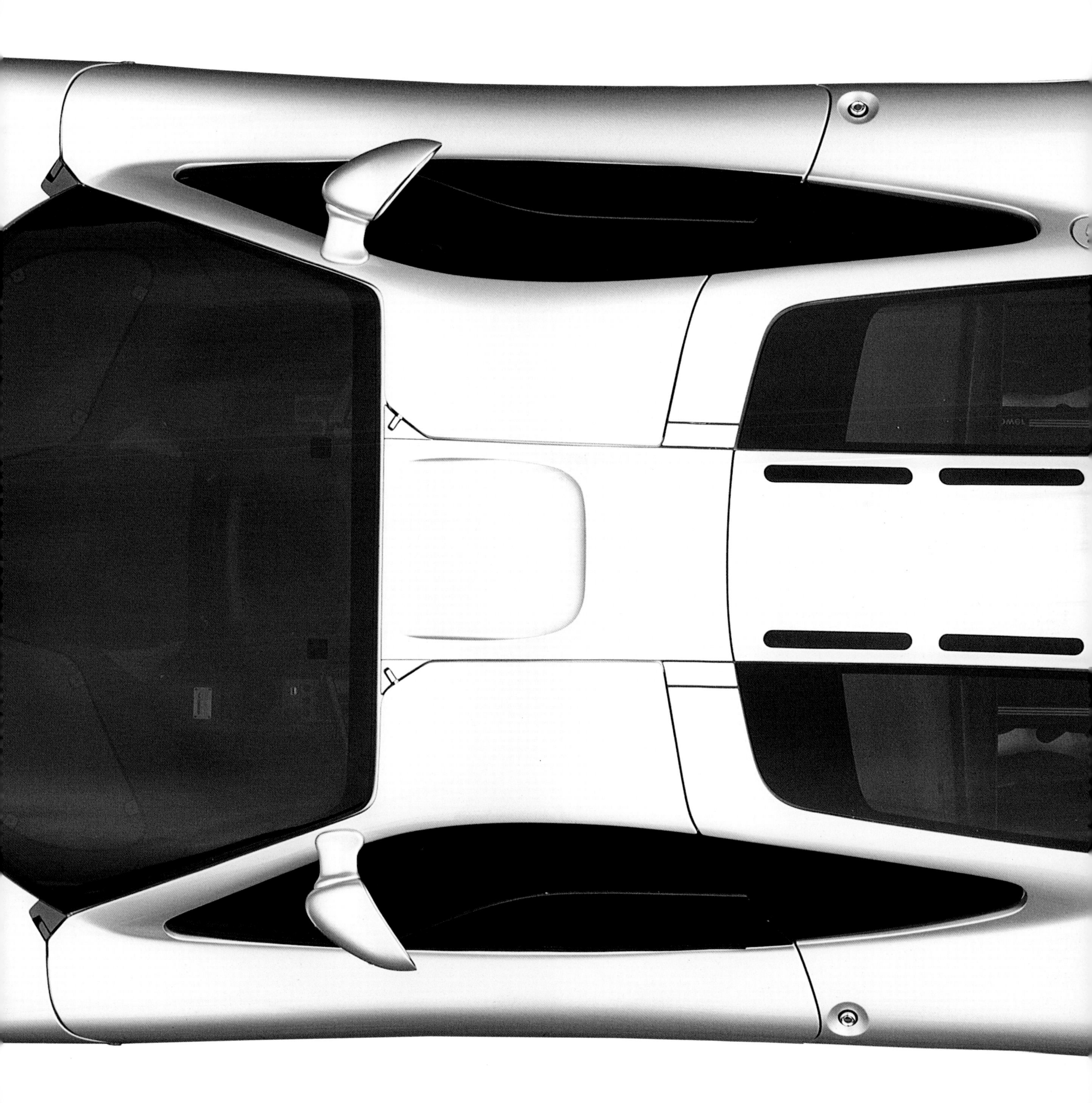

# TRANSPARENCY

# FIGARO STAGE SET

*The use of transparent screens in this performance of* Figaro *at Glyndebourne had a powerful impact on the action on stage, and created new dramatic tension. Richard Hudson explains why he chose this approach, and why, if he did* Figaro *again, he'd take a different tack.*

**Richard Hudson:** "This is the second time I've designed *Figaro*. Then we did it in very bold, bright colours. It was a completely abstract set, and was effectively colour-coded.

"This time I took a completely different approach. We started off with a big, empty, cream room with windows, and large gauze screens. The screen delineated the human dimensions of the room, creating a domestic feel.

"Transparency is at the heart of the idea. The opera is all about people coming, going, hiding, jumping out of windows, about things going on in rooms that other players aren't aware of, but that the audience is. Like in Act Two when the countess and Susanna are in the bedroom. We can see the count arriving before the she enters the room. It builds tension where perhaps before it might have been invisible. And we can see the hiding places, like when Susanna locks herself the closet.

"And when the count gets angry with the countess and bundles her out of the door - we can still see her there, singing through the gauze.

"One's primary concern is to help the director tell the story clearly, so I don't like to put unnecessary things on stage. I'd rather pare it down and keep it simple, so it can be told in an uncluttered way. Let the art breathe.

"The lighting designer was absolutely brilliant. She's an American, Jennifer Tipton. She has a wonderful ability to light a set in such a way that you are unaware where the light is coming from. She imbues the set with a magical quality. There's something about the nature of her light. The costumes are often white, and it's hard lighting white costumes on a white set; you tend to lose the details. But she manages to sculpt with light and give it a three-dimensional quality.

"You can approach *Figaro* in so many different ways. If I was asked to do it next year, yes, I wouldn't hesitate to try something new."

*Danny Lane is perhaps the most impressive exponent of glass sculpture in the world. Born in the USA, Danny has worked in the UK for over 20 years. His work appears in museums all across the globe, but among the most impressive is the balustrade on the stairs leading to the mezzanine floor at the Victoria and Albert Museum's Glass Gallery.*

**Danny Lane:** "The alternative title to this is: 'Look, ma, no handrail.' The lack of a banister adds a sense of danger created by the fact that the balustrade is glass. Each pillar is capped with an oversized dome nut, a tactile knob-like ending to each column.

"I never sat down and thought about the transparency of this, but I do love using glass. It's a material that modifies light. It can even transmit it, and it creates colour shadows. I love it!

"The pillars are built like a series of stacked CDs, partly because to cast such a column in solid glass would require about five times the budget. And there'd be that nauseating anxiety that resides in perfect glass, the: 'Oh, my God, I've chipped it. It's ruined!' reaction. With this construction, if you chip it you can unlock the pillar and replace the piece.

"I'm interested in what glass means to us psychologically. Materials generate different responses. Rusted steel, spotless stainless, textured glass – they all create different reactions. Glass occurs in nature, created by volcanoes. The Egyptians were using it 5,000 years ago. It has a special meaning.

"The techniques for cutting and forming glass haven't changed in a hundred years. You still scratch it with a harder material, create a flaw, and abuse it from the other side with a hammer. I've been a slave to this technique.

"But you can't get it done by ordinary glass factories anymore. It's better to train people to do it.

"The engineer, Harry Roberts, gave the balustrade the final test. He looked at it and gave it a serious boot. It wobbled, but wasn't damaged. It's the interesting thing about glass. The normal reaction is: 'Be careful! Don't touch it!' It's seen as precious and fragile. It is, of course, neither. Thick glass is very strong."

*The British Airways London Eye provides views right across Europe's largest city and has become such a much-loved landmark that it is hard to imagine a London without it. Everyone who's 'booked a flight' testifies to the wonderful experience it offers: the slow, stately revelation of London as the transparent capsules rise inexorably and gracefully up to the zenith. It was created by Marks Barfield Architects.*

**David Marks:** "It all began with a competition to commemorate the millennium. The Architecture Foundation and *The Sunday Times* were looking for designs for a landmark, and Julia Barfield and I read it, and were excited by it. We had the time to enter it. We thought it would be a good idea to give London a vantage point. Most cities have a good viewing platform, but London lacked one.

"Once we'd thought of that, it was a quick progression to the idea of a giant observation wheel. It seemed to be the most efficient way of getting large numbers of people up high, especially if you made it continuously moving. And a wheel is such a powerful millennial symbol. It suggests the Wheel of Life, with people rising up and coming down through time. It's a symbol of regeneration and renewal in many cultures.

"The other plus, of course, is that a giant wheel makes a perfect counterpiece to the vertical and rectilinear idiom of a cityscape.

"We started discussing where. Julia said there could only be one place: the South Bank. It hadn't occurred to me, but once she said it, it was obvious.

"We formed the Millennium Wheel Company and started looking for contractors and operators. And, as we progressed, *The Evening Standard* backed our idea, and then Bob Ayling and British Airways.

"The wheel has some interesting French connections. The first was the fact that we had a competitor in Paris. M. Campion declared his wheel in Paris would be one metre larger than ours, and the 'War of the Wheels' began. The Mayor of Paris had to step in to calm down M. Campion's ambitions and they settled for a wheel half the size.

"But the real contribution came from Poma, a French cable-car company, which had the skills, technology and safety record to build our capsules. They were innovative and they wanted to do it.

"What we were planning had never been done before. We didn't want the capsules to swing about like gondolas on a ferris wheel, suspended on gimbals and moving under gravity; we needed them to move mechanically. This would allow universal access. They would be perfectly level and stable.

And we wanted them mounted on the outside of the wheel's rim, so that when each capsule reached the top there would be no structure above or around you, just an uninterrupted 360° view of the cityscape (*see overleaf*). This called for some clever engineering.

"Julia's idea of a riverside site also meant we could bring the components in by river. It sounded wonderful, and in practice, after some teething problems, it worked.

"But it was, as ever, not as simple as it looked. I remember one meeting in which I was presenting to the Port of London Authority our plans to put the wheel up. I was using a scale model.

"Well, the harbour-master listened patiently, got up and said: 'Here, let me show you a model of my own.' And he showed me a cut-out model of Southwark Bridge and how our floating crane was going to have a maximum of one foot clearance under the centre arch and the river bed - providing we got the tides right and the wave height was low. But he didn't stop us; he just laughed and said: 'You're going to have to be incredibly lucky to get away with it.'

"Well, as fate would have it, we were, and we did."

The Science Museum is grateful to the following organisations for their support and expertise without which the Digitopolis exhibition would not have been possible.
How does digital technology affect you?
intel
Principal Sponsor
AGFA Agfa
Major Sponsor
Discover what makes digital technology so useful. Explore its power and look into the digital future.
Chris Baber
Birmingham University Industrial Ergonomics Group
Andy Bower
Robert Buckley
Chris Burgoyne
Cambridge University Centre for Mathematics and Theoretical Physics
Canadian High Commission
Gillian Crampton-Smith
Royal College of Art Computer Related Design Dept
Rae Earnshaw
Bradford University Electronic Imaging and Media Communication Dept
Don Foresta
Jodelle French
Goethe-Institut
Keith Ingrams
Cranfield University Radiography Dept
Abe Mamdani
Imperial College Electrical and Electronic Engineering Dept
Thankyou
Doug Masterton
Leeds Council Education Dept
Philip Miller
John Naughton
Cambridge University Wolfson College
John O'Reilly
University College London Electronic and Electrical Engineering Dept
Donald Peach
Cranfield University Radiography Dept
Paddy Redding
Ministry of Defence
Peggie Rimmer
CERN
Thad Starner
Georgia Institute of Technology
St Joseph's School
Chelsea
Andy Tait
Kevin Warwick
Reading University Cybernetics Dept
Thankyou

*When Casson Mann wanted to solve the problem of creating vivid signage at the Digitopolis Gallery in the new Welcome Wing of the Science Museum, it turned to Graphic Thought Facility and Andy Stevens. They came up with electronic signage that had never before been used in exhibition spaces.*

**Andy Stevens:**
"The problem with Digitopolis is that most of the exhibits are light-emitting. Casson Mann didn't want any extra light – the sort of light you need to read signs – because that would diminish the impact of the displays.

"So what we needed to come up with was graphics that emitted their own light.

"The good news was that we were involved early. On some projects you get asked to tack the graphics on at the end of the project, but in this one it was possible to make them integral.

"Hugh Morgan came across this material called EL – electro-luminescent. Basically it's a thin substrate which can take phosphorescent inks that will glow when an electric charge is passed through them.

"It's the same sort of technology that you might have in your digital watch.

"The EL rep came round and showed us how it worked on a transparent car dashboard.

"You could see through the oil gauge and speedo to the glowing colours that illuminated the instruments and then to the circuit board-style connections. It looked amazing.

"So we thought: 'We can use this as a graphic tool.' In fact, EL has been used on a museum as a backlighting, but never as the actual lettering.

"We silk-screened the letters onto the signs using the EL ink, wired them up and watched them glow inside their glass cabinets.

"It was very efficient. We didn't need to bring new wiring to the Digitopolis displays, because they were already powered up doing their own thing.

"And it looked good to expose the workings of the technology.

"Hugh got very involved in the intricacies. As an agency we're becoming experts in a variety of weird sciences. It's great to have an opportunity to play with stuff like this."

# PAULINA WEDDING DRESS

*Why is this woman wearing a straw bale round her legs? Your first reaction, and it's perfectly valid, might well be that this is a perfect example of fashion gone completely mad. Welcome to the world of Arkadius, a fashion designer fast emerging as the most promising talent in the London scene. So why is a straw bale and a see-through wedding dress NOT a really silly idea?*

**Arkadius:** "The collection this dress comes from was inspired by the Polish countryside, where I spent time with my grandma as a child. There I lived among straw and hay and the ritual of gathering. The wedding dress is the final piece in the collection.

"For me, the dress is about innocence and restraint. I think restraint is part of the central meaning of marriage. So the bride's arms are constrained, and the straw bale restricts her feet. The straw signifies the beauty of nature cut down, reaped, and bound up. Some people feel the straw suggests fertility and sexuality – a roll in the hay. That's not what I intended, but people make their own interpretations.

"To me, the transparency is also about the purity and unadorned lightness of the bride. It signifies virginal innocence and a sexuality in a light, open, innocent way. The head-dress is like a bird's nest. Again, it's innocence, like virgins feeding birds in the countryside.

"Could someone wear it to a wedding? Well, they could try! But really, such pieces are not about that. 70 percent of the collection is highly wearable, and 30 percent is about testing the boundaries, about inspiring creativity. Sometimes fashion designers get heavy criticism for their more outrageous designs. But these pieces aren't really meant to be worn; they are meant to inspire new ideas and new directions, to give rise to a creative chain reaction.

"I like the unexpectedness of this dress. No one thought of putting straw in a dress like this before! And its impact has been equally surprising. It secured more coverage than a famous diamond dress that was rumoured to have cost £1 million. But this only cost five pounds to make!

"London is the only place in the world for fashion now. In Milan they would ignore me."

*Caroline Dent has created a wonderful fabric out of what most designers would think is a dreadful material, a fabric the warp of which slips and slides. The effect however is beautiful, and Drift and Wave sums up the elemental look to the material. Dent it seems, is making her mark...*

**Caroline Dent:** "It's very sheer. It's made from a polyester monofilament yarn in the warp – like a fishing yarn. It's transparent and slippery, and designed to create tight and loose areas of weaving across the cloth. The weft is cotton. As the fabric moves round the rollers, loose areas move and shift. The tight areas stay in place and you get this controlled distortion.

"I love perversity. I have taken something that would normally be looked on as fault – thread slippage – and turned it into a design tool.

"I see fabric as an engineering material really – I liked building dens as a child! Some textile designers are very colour-motivated, but I like the mathematical side of things. How you can use yarns that shrink and slip by given percentages to make something interesting happen. My aim would be to create fabric that intrigues, so people will have to come and look closely, so they will want to feel it and to see why.

"UK is going certainly through a design renaissance. I left college 20 years ago and the opportunities for designer makers were few. Things have changed dramatically."

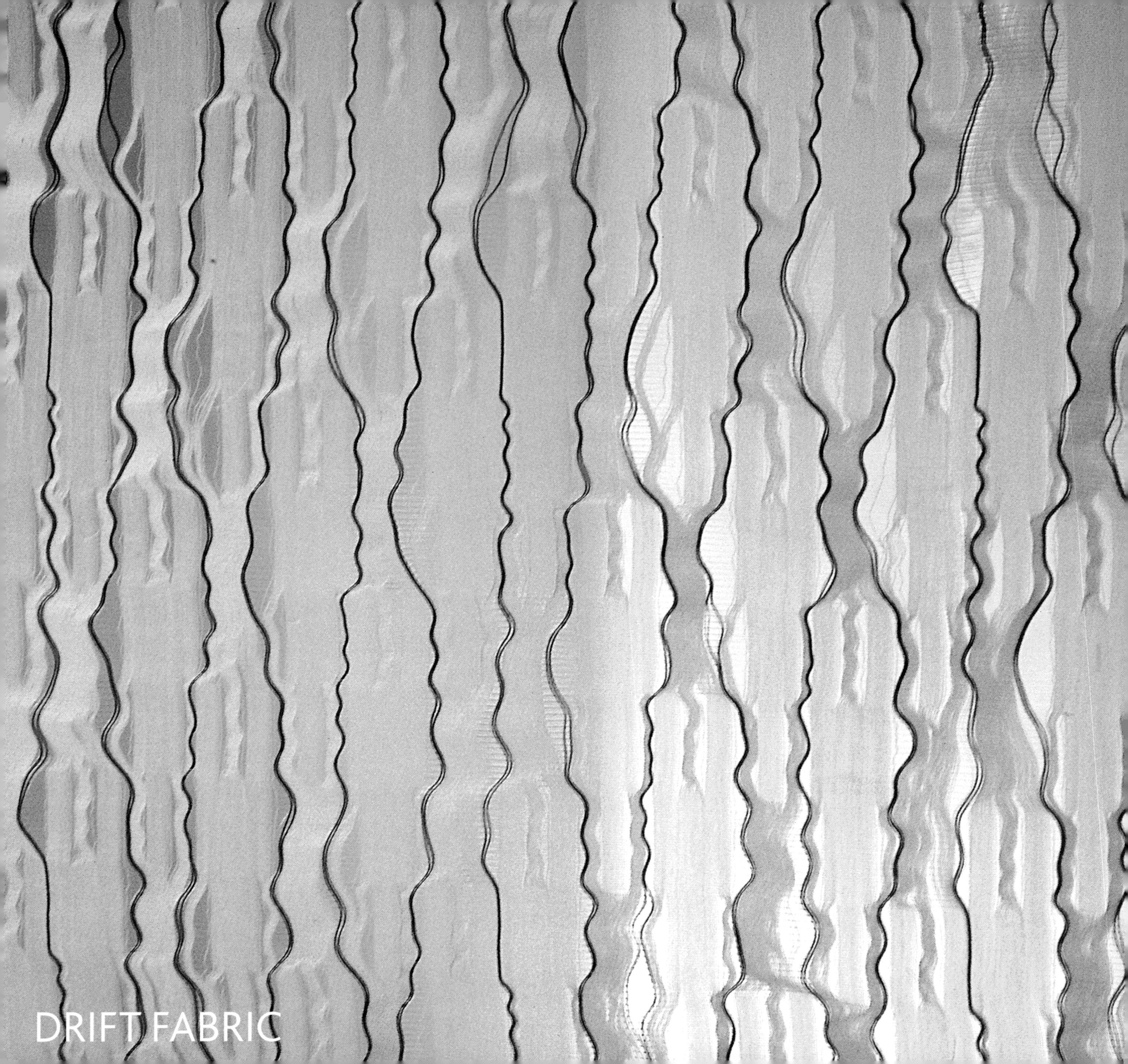
DRIFT FABRIC

# PERSPEX CHRISTMAS CARD

*What did you get for Christmas? I got a stamp. It wasn't even on an envelope. I'm not complaining. It was probably the most original Christmas card I've ever received.*

**Thomas Heatherwick:** "Well, of course, we do Christmas cards every year. For 2001 we thought: 'Let's do it different.' And we talked about what a Christmas card was: a picture, some words and a stamp. So we got to thinking about how we might boil the Christmas card down to those bare essentials. We thought, 'All you really need is the stamp itself. It's already got a Christmas picture on it. All you need to do is write the address and greeting on the back.'

"But we realized it would get lost in the franking machines and probably never get through. So we went to our local post office, the Mount Pleasant sorting office in central London, and were invited in to the philately department. They were incredibly enthusiastic.

"Between us we came up with a way of suspending the stamp, and the frank, in an icy, transparent resin. It had to be the right amount of resin because the whole thing couldn't weigh more than the stamp would pay for.

"We cast them in individual moulds so each would be a little different. The Post Office were amazingly proud of them. They were even a bit too loving, bubble-wrapping them and trying to ensure they didn't get scratched. Our idea had been just to produce them and chuck them in the post."

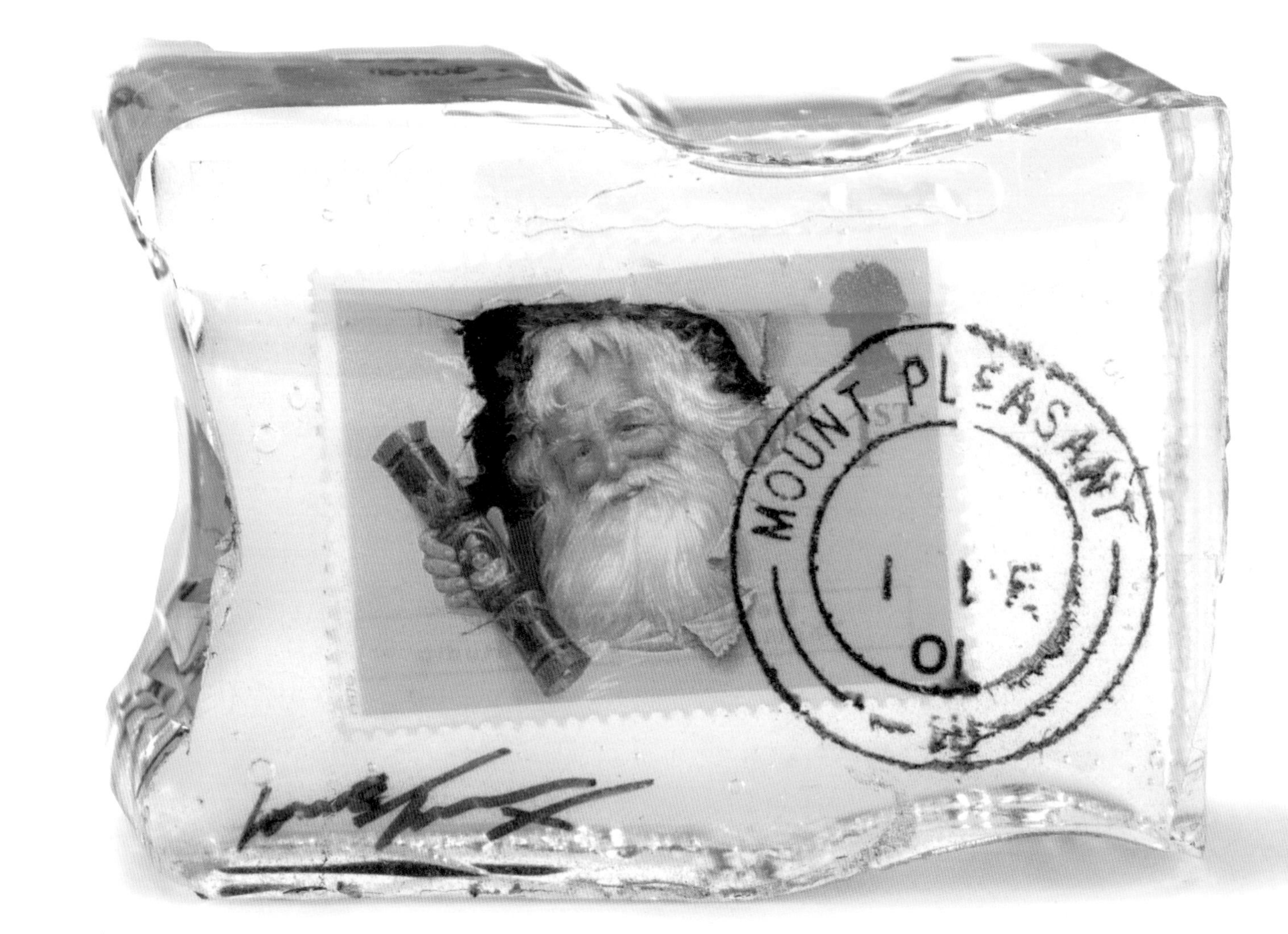

*I must immediately declare an interest in The Lawns…it's my house. Brilliantly designed as their first commission by Eldridge Smerin, it was nominated for the 2001 Stirling Prize and was the winner of RIBA's London Regional Award. The top floor glass studio was designed as thinking space and is where this book was conceived and developed.*

**Nick Eldridge:** "Glass transferring light is a key element of all our buildings. Modernity can almost be defined by that. Bringing light in, making things light: it's uplifting but hard to do; the building industry isn't geared up yet for this sort of construction on a domestic scale.

"Motorized blinds, moving walls… It's a large space but it's cosy, too. It can either be a massive party room or it can all be broken down into discrete areas. The technology works to create layers and veils that just don't appear in traditional housing.

"Clarity characterizes our work, showing how a building works. We never intend to compromise the basic honesty or you risk losing the quality of the overall scheme.

"Not very English? Well, I suppose it isn't typically English! But what is Englishness if it is not defined by the way we react to other cultures? Almost all the great architecture in Highgate has foreign influence: Dutch, French, German, Italian."

**Piers Smerin:** "The original house, designed by Leonard Manasseh in the 1950s, forms the core of the new house. But his design had been changed a lot over the years by previous owners. The idea was to open it up, to feel the full depth of the site when viewing from inside the building. That's a great, liberating feeling. This architecture is open, transparent. It embraces public context.

"Traditional architecture is very inward-looking, such as a nearby house, with its high, brick garden wall, and small windowss - it's all about cutting the public out. The Lawns is about opening up, showing the internal workings. The approach creates drama and excitement.

"The top floor, the studio, is the most overtly contemporary aspect of the scheme. It's as beautiful by night as it is by day, because of the wonderful interior glow.

"This architecture is not so different from product design. You're creating something that knits a number of different influences together, and, if you do it right, it endures over time.

"The skill lies in knitting it all together. It's all too easy for it to fall into a soggy mess. Here, with this building, we think the openness gives it a calmness. And of course, with the press of a button, the blinds can make it as private as you like.

"The point is to do things carefully, with forethought and intelligence, with the utmost care. To the highest quality."

THE LAWNS

TATU
GRILL

*It is of considerable political and social significance that a bar with a huge glass front feels safe enough to open on the Lisburn Road in Belfast. Colin Conn and his wife, Bronagh Crawley, of Box Architects have created an environment full of self-confidence.*

**Colin Conn:** "This involved the reorganization of several offices on a city block to clear a large space - quite a complicated exercise in itself. We've built a large, quadruple high, space at the front, and a one-storey-high back. This makes it cosy to the rear and 'cathedralesque' in the front area.

"This elevational treatment makes it stand out on the busy Lisburn Road. And it's stand-out is enhanced by the dramatic illuminated overhanging canopy. Yes, I think it makes a statement!

"We've tried to introduce as much natural daylight as possible: roof lights; long, concealed slots allowing light to trickle down... There's nowhere in the bar without natural light. And we've effectively taken the back off the building. So what was a dark and poky place is now infused with light.

"One of the main features is the floating ceiling, with its large, walnut, curved belly, like a cloud. There are light slots on either side of it, and the overall effect is that if feels like it's defying gravity - that it might fall at any moment.

"The main entrance is through a tight zinc box. This adds to the surprise, making the tall space behind it all the more dramatic. The floors are polished concrete. The bar looks very hard, but wherever you touch it, it feels soft.

"The toilets have been a talking point. The ladies and gents share a common, trough-like basin. You can't see each other, but you can easily reach under the barrier and touch each other. A sort of underhand contact... But it also means you can hear the gossip on either side.

"It's a statement of confidence that has come about precisely because of the peace process. Previously, design was a bit timid here. But now bars are opening up everywhere. Before, a typical pub was a place that you couldn't see into, as if it were shameful to be in it. Now we're celebrating."

# RSA WINE LABELS

*Every now and again the Royal Society of Arts asks an artist or designer to make a label for its house wine. Sir Hugh Casson and David Gentleman are recent celebrities honoured with the task. In 2001, it was Quentin Newark, founding member of Atelier Works.*

**Quentin Newark:** "I have always hated wine labels. Given how complex wine is and how many varieties there are, the labels are so unimaginative and so predictable. They'll have a picture of a château (though you can never be sure if it is the actual château), or, if the vineyard is feeling *nouveau*, it'll be a watercolour landscape. Yawn.

"When they asked me, I wanted to avoid any of the usual clichés. I wanted to make a label that in some way had a special relationship with the bottle, and was clever in a way that couldn't be bettered. Well, all designers dream of this!

"The first idea was an icon of a glass. After all, that's what you want out of a bottle: a glass of wine. And we combined the two labels into one bigger, asymmetric one. The details about the wine are still on the back, but part of a single label.

"We wanted simple, attractive typography. It's a sans serif, which, is almost never used on wine labels, perhaps because people want the type to appear old even though the wine is modern. And we've put the writing on its side, following the shape of the bottle. This is because, frankly, the information is going to be of no real help unless you are a complete expert, so it doesn't need to be prominent. Most bottles use their label to tell you that – er – you know nothing about this wine!

"Then I had the idea to cut the glass icon out of the label, and so show the colour of the wine. Then it got really exciting. The glass is full of wine! When the wine gets poured out, the wine level drops down through the glass, just as it does in your own glass. The label colours (cyan for the red, and pink for the white) are deliberately bright and celebratory. Open the wine and feel brighter...

"I suppose, really, this label is about *having* a glass of wine, rather than about some obscure vineyard."

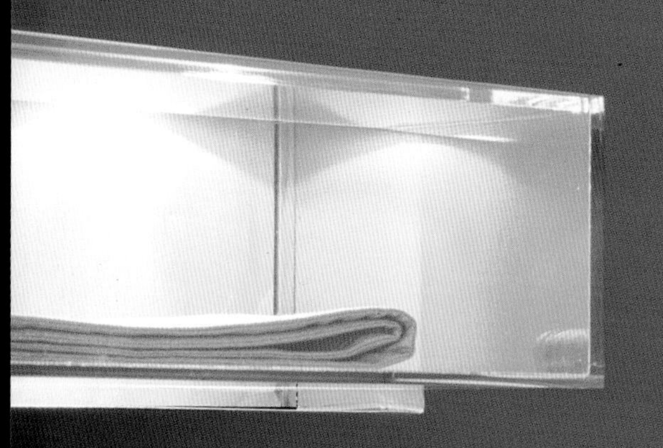

*When Farhan Azman and Joyce Owens of Azman Owens were asked to come up with ideas for the Alexander McQueen store in London, they couldn't think of a single good idea. Until they began to think about the man himself. The result of that decision to focus on personality is one of the most innovative and striking stores in the UK.*

**Farhan Azman:** "Alexander invited us personally to take part in a mini-competition. There were four at first, and then one architectural firm pulled out. It was a nervous time. We were looking for a concept, a big idea that would support and be the reason behind every design decision we made. Two days before the presentation, Joyce and I looked at each other. We still had no ideas at all! So we went back to his brief, and talked about his personality. We remember him talking of his love of theatre, and also the fact that he doesn't have a style. That there's no Alexander McQueen dress like there might be a Calvin Klein dress.

"Those two ideas came together: a theatre that can change its sets to suit the play or the seasons. So we designed a framework installation system, with steel beams and columns within the shop. It was designed to accept big panels of aluminium – themselves acting as frameworks for anything. They acted like stages, for displays, advertisements, products...

"And we motorized them, so the whole set-up of the shop could change. We made them programmable to any speed, so they can rotate or go up and down. They can move as slowly as the hands of a watch so the place is different when you leave to how it was when you came in.

"We had glass changing rooms, which caused a bit of interest in the press, and we had this spectacular window display. It's a massive glass box that projects through the shop-front window. It looks like it crashed through. It cost £30,000 and is fully waterproof. The idea is that you can create weather scenes in it to reflect the season – like windstorms, or rain, or bright light. Alexander did a scene from Kubrick's *The Shining* for the opening: all snow and UV light.

"We originally planned for the box to go up three storeys: basement, ground and first floor. And we told Alexander we were going to fill it with water. He was very excited about that. We had worked out it could take the weight of the water. But when we told the engineers what we wanted, they laughed at us. 'You can't do that, you silly girls! The pressure will be too much. The walls will have to be a metre thick!' Well, we felt pretty stupid. And we couldn't face telling Alexander. In the end we waited until we were sure he was in a good mood...

"We had this big, long, aluminium display and pay counter – which works well, but the wall opposite – well, we had no ideas. And then we thought: 'Let's extend this idea of dramatic pieces of glass and make displays for his new accessory range.' So we made these lovely jewel boxes. They glow in the dark and you can see them from the street when the shop lights are dim.

"Alexander suddenly decided he wanted to paint that wall pink – he'd just done a pink collection. I said to him: 'Alexander, you don't really want pink.' But he insisted. I had to insist back. 'It won't work.' 'It's my shop,' he said, 'I'll have it any colour I like!' 'Alexander,' I said, ' do you want me to do the Emperor's New Clothes routine and tell you pink is great when it definitely isn't?' He laughed, and we painted it green.

"We are very happy with this shop. It is rich and textured and layered and it serves its purpose and works well. But now Alexander has been bought by Gucci and they're going to scrap the shop. Well, that's a pity. But we're having fun building Alexander's house right now."

MONUMENTALITY

# HEART TUBE HAT & POINTED LACE MASK

*Geniunely new schools of fashion are rare. But Helen Storey has created a new genre – a genre that has only existed before in the science fiction of Iain M. Banks. She takes microscopic biological forms and makes clothes out of them. Here she's collaborated with Philip Treacy to create the Heart Tube hat.*

**Helen Storey:** "Biology and frocks don't seem to go together, but amazingly, they've worked as a perfect foil for one another. This was all part of a much bigger project which put an artist and a scientist together to create a project that explained areas of science in such a way as it might fire the public's imagination.

"My sister was doing a project at the time about the first 1,000 hours of human life, so I thought: 'Why not do a project describing the first thousand hours of human life in textiles and fashion?'

"We split the first 1,000 hours into 10 key events. One was the development of the heart. I allowed science to be the dictator of the design brief, and I got to the point where I was drawing loads of hideous-looking hoods. Part of the biology that I had to stick to was the fact that, in the foetus, your heart tubes grow over your developing brain before they fuse and turn into the main organ. And descending from them in an elegant crescent is your developing diaphragm. Well, I couldn't cheat on all that, so I thought the best way round it was to collaborate with one of the best British talents in terms of head gear: Philip Treacy.

"The negotiation in the project was always between something that was aesthetically pleasing and yet scientifically accurate. So I took that brief to Philip, and we sat on his shop floor, and he underwent a compressed version of the process I went through, and the upshot of it all was that I found out that fashion could communicate knowledge.

"It's a strange but illuminating experience to take your design brief from what you see down a microscope. Some of my friends told me to dye it black, cut it down and get it into Harvey Nics for Christmas. Somehow, I think they were missing the point."

*Perhaps the most famous hat-maker on the planet, Philip Treacy created the Pointed Lace Mask (opposite) for his 2001 haute couture collection. He believes you don't have to be crazy to wear his hats – just a bit conservative...*

**Philip Treacy:** "I like to make hats that defy gravity. I'm from an Irish Catholic background, and much of my work and colour palette is inspired by religion. The brocade wimple has its roots there.

"The scale is relative and designed in proportion to the customer's body. It's big, but I don't see any reason why not. There are no rules. Scale is a personal choice.

"Sometimes an individual hat is inspired by a personality or a face, or even a mood. This hat came from our *couture* show last season. The idea behind the show was 'extreme elegance'. I never worry about going too far. In my mind, you can never go far enough.

"The whole purpose of such an image is to inspire peoples' sense of what a hat is about. It's visual titillation.

"It used to be that hats were just something appropriate for ladies of a certain age. I find it interesting that the hat has changed its meaning; it is no longer associated with a conservative world where everyone wore hats. In fact, I treat them as an accessory of rebellion.

"The most exciting and technically difficult part is to transform a two-dimensional idea into three dimensions. Making the mould is the most fulfilling part of the exercise. All the lines have to work together in three dimensions from every angle. It must be aesthetically pleasing from all angles. It's the most difficult and exciting part, because you are bringing an idea to life.

"London is the best place for hat-makers. It's the home of the hat. And English customers are unlike any others. Our international customers might say: 'I like this hat because it's crazy.' English customers say: 'I like it because it's chic.' Most of my customers are actually quite conservative.

"I'm not trying to make crazy hats; I'm trying to make beautiful hats. The object of the exercise isn't to be avant garde so much as to say everything I can about beauty and elegance through a hat."

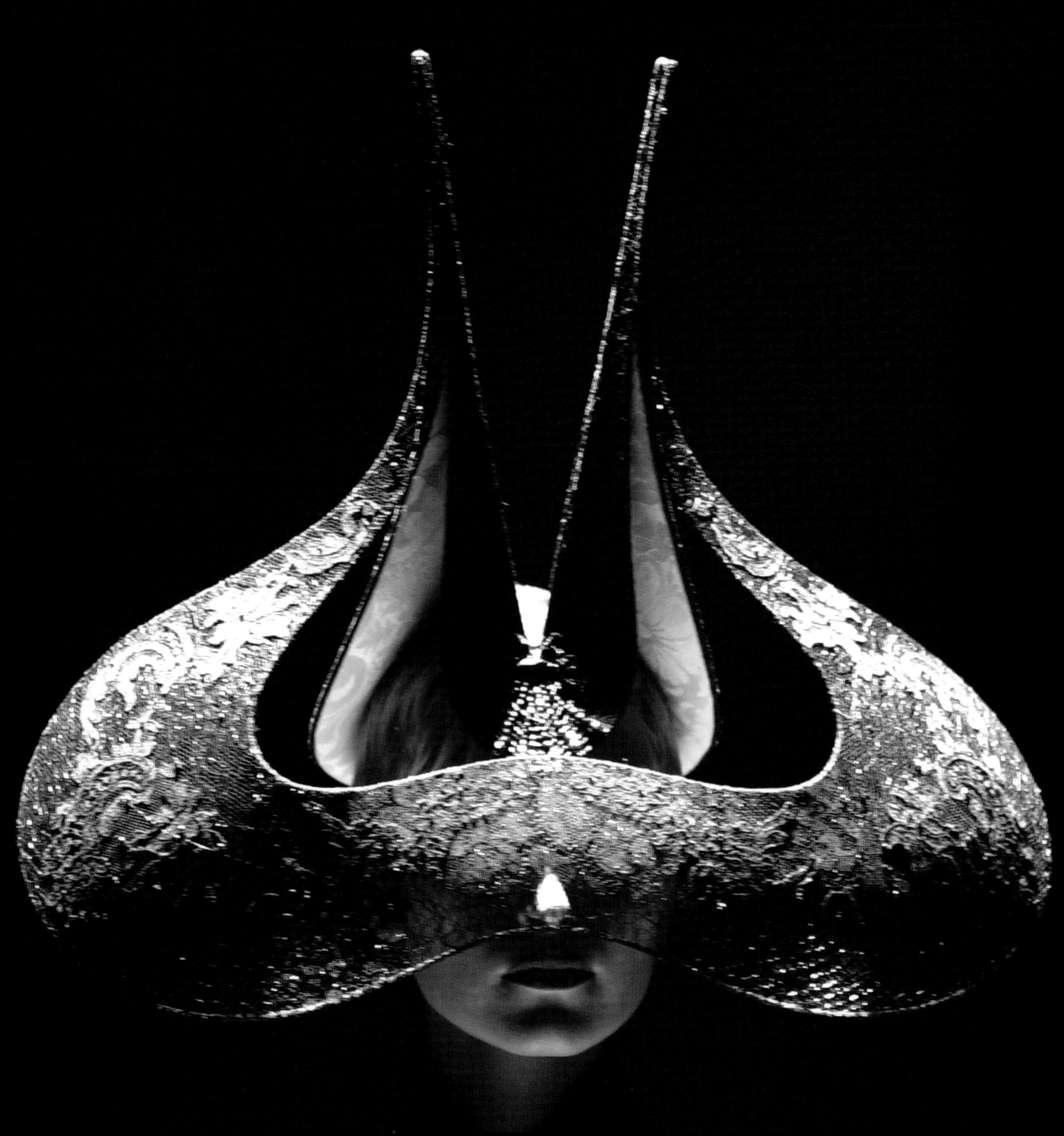

# STRASBOURG TRAM TERMINAL

*Zaha Hadid was born in Baghdad and educated at the American University of Beirut before she came to London to study at the Architectural Association. In 1980 she set up her own practice. She then went on to win some of the most prestigious architectural contracts in the world, and is still winning them, such as the new Tram Terminal in Strasbourg, France. The project has arisen from the city's determination to combat pollution and congestion. The idea is that people will 'park and ride' into the city centre. In her work, Zaha has reflected the 'clean sweep' that the city's initiative represents.*

**Zaha Hadid:** "To me, the whole design is about movement, dynamism and transition, a reflection of the idea of mass movement. This project can't be taken in isolation from our other work. We've recently been very interested in landscape and topography and how it intersects and interacts with humanity. We are exploring the concept of 'artificial nature'. This project is one large gesture. I see it as a land-art piece.

"It's also about the intersection of three fields. We've the car park field and the roof field, and where they meet falls the shadow stretching up into the car park: the third field, making the union seamless, an overlap.

"So often transport systems are segregated: 'Here is the bus station, over there is the car park, through there you can catch a train.' This piece is about effortless flow.

"In the car park, designed for 700 vehicles, we consciously avoided the standard rectilinear layout, going instead for this almost organic sweep defined by the parking lines, flowing in towards the terminal, almost like iron filings oriented along the lines of a magnetic field, or like logs flowing in a river.

"The trams in Strasbourg are wonderful. They are low - easy to climb onto. There's no step up so they can be used easily by young, old or disabled people.

"I reflect this idea in the tram-station design. The idea is that people can drive easily into the car park, park easily, and then move from there easily to the tram station. Ease of movement between different media.

"It's important to be able to move easily between the different modes of transportation. Three different types join here: the tram, the car and the bus. It's a point of exchange between pedestrians and cyclists and these other modes of travel.

"That union defines the dramatic shape of the massive roof. The cut-outs allow for the entry of the trams on one side and the buses on the other. The lines flow to the roof to create a unified whole.

"Movement fascinates me: moving through space, like cinematography.

"I enjoy the way the roof is made of one continuous surface of concrete. I think the way it moves up from the ground in that seamless way is very interesting.

"And there is further geometry in the lighting. There is a connection between the lampposts and the lighting strips in the roof. They all are on converging and directing trajectories, guiding people easily to their choice of destination. They work to create both horizontal and vertical fields of light.

"Is there a design revolution? Yes, but it's been going on for 20 years. There are wonderful ideas coming out of Britain now, but it's time for them to become the norm, to become more mainstream. Exciting architecture should be recognized not as some sort of folly, but as great thinking."

# WHAT GOES DOWN, MUST COME UP

*A beautifully simple idea: it's a laundry bag that lifts those difficult-to-reach socks up to you as you empty it. All the work of Rosario Hurtado and Roberto Feo at El Ultimo Grito.*

**Rosario Hurtado:** "Sometimes you work to a commission – and sometimes you just dream things up. Things bother you, get you going as a designer, and you do something about it. This arose from a common domestic irritant. The washing-powder box stipulates, say, 'one scoop for five kilos of clothing'. But how much is five kilos? Who's going to weigh their washing? So that was the starting point.

"And then we started thinking about big laundry bins, how you have to bend down and hunt around for that last sock. Or you have to reach into the bottom just to collect a few bits and pieces. We thought: 'There must be a better way of doing this!'

"So we came up with this. When it's empty, the bag is folded up at the top of the frame. The weight of the clothes pulls it down. If it's halfway down the frame you know you've got five kilos of clothes.

"If it's at the bottom you know you've got 10 kilos and it really is time you put that washing machine on!

"It's pretty simple: just four legs with springs attached to the rim and the base. The base slides down the legs under load. It reminds us of an inverted gasometer. This folds nicely as well.

"We started with Lycra, but that was too floppy. So in the end we used kite material. It doesn't stretch and it looks good."

*As one of the few 'household-name' designers in the UK and an inspiration to all innovators, James Dyson needs no introduction. But we'll give him one anyway. Famous for his vacuum cleaner, and even his ball-barrow, James is constantly creating new ideas and products. Now he's taken the front-loading washing machine, and made it better at its job and much better-looking.*

**James Dyson:** "It's no bigger externally. It's bigger inside, and so the outside expresses that. Also, of course, it's got a larger door so it's easier to get larger loads in and out.

"The fact that the whole front is inclined adds to its appearance of power. We wanted the controls at 45° to make them easier to use. Most washing machines require you to squat down in front of them to make the programming. I also didn't want a slab-fronted thing. This design also helps cut down on noise.

"We made this of polycarbonate, which allowed us to make it into interesting, strong shapes.

"Most washing machines rely on a long, hot soak in bleaches and biological detergents to get things really clean, but that's not good for energy consumption or the environment. And it's not very good for the clothes, because they don't like high temperatures or strong detergents.

"Hand washing gets clothes cleaner than even a hot soak. So it occurred to us to try and recreate hand washing. We built and tested all sorts of Heath Robinson devices. Then we discovered what it was that makes clothes clean - and it's not rubbing the clothes or squirting water through them. It's flexing the fabric. Essentially, that's what goes on when you hand-wash.

"We hit upon the right design quite by chance. We wanted to put a large paddle in the middle of a drum, and to do it required splitting the drum in two. As we were building the rig we said: 'Oh, let's forget the paddle. Let's try driving the drums going in opposite directions. We've never seen that before.' And when we did it, we got exactly the result we wanted.

"Well, that was pretty lucky. Serendipity is a vital part of the design process, but it seems to occur when you're trying hard."

DYSON CONTRAROTATOR

*This book is big. Very big. It was, as Alan Fletcher explains, almost too big to be a book. But, he insists, it's not really a book at all. It was a filing system for material he thought was great but had no immediate use for and nowhere to store it.*

**Alan Fletcher:** "This wasn't a book project; it was housekeeping. I didn't set out to do a book. I thought: 'My God, I must put this stuff in order because I can't find it anymore.'

"Big? It's not that big! It was once about twice as big. I think it's rather small. But I got to a point when it became a matter of physical property. I couldn't lift the bloody thing up. That's not a good idea for a book.

"It's more like a garden than a book. I did a bit of pruning there, added something new here, changed my mind. It's a changing scene. It's not like climbing mountains 10 times a day and sticking a flag on the top. It's not like that. It's a stroll through the country. That's why I think it's more of a journey than a destination. I decided: 'Right, on the first of January in the year 2000 I'm going to stop.' So I did.

"I found the writing very hard. I realize I don't have that mindset. Drawing's different. Doodles – no thinking required. But words... You have to check the dictionary! Foreign territory. And I have a terrible fear of sounding ponderous and pompous.

"The whole project was self-education. Trying to decide does this go under 'Brain', or under 'Mind'? Or maybe 'Intelligence'? I really had to think hard. And then I realized I could put it anywhere. I could have dropped the whole lot on the floor and shuffled it. It wouldn't have made any difference.

"I guess I am a perfectionist. But I like to make something look like it's just happened, like it was thrown together in a moment, even though it might have taken months. I like it to look effortless. Perfection can look so laboured.

"I have no idea what the book is about! About living, I suppose. We're surrounded by people who live their lives with a bag over their head. They don't see anything, except perhaps maybe a nice pair of lips, or something cheaper than something else. But other people's knowledge can enrich your life."

Words and pictures on how to make twinkles in the eye and colours agree in the dark. Thoughts on mindscaping, moonlighting and daydreams. Have you seen a purple cow? When less can be more than enough. *The art of looking sideways.* To gaze is to think. Are you left-eyed? Living out loud. Buy junk, sell antiques. The Golden Mean. Standing ideas on their heads. To look is to listen. Insights on the mind's eye. Every status has its symbol. 'Do androids dream of electric sheep?' Why feel blue? Triumphs of imagination such as the person you love is 72.8% water. Do not adjust your mind, there's a fault in reality. Teach yourself ignorance. The belly-button problem.

PHAIDON

# THE MAGNA PROJECT

*It was a dark day for Rotherham when the Templeborough steelworks closed. But no one could have envisaged the use to which the building was to be put. Wilkinson Eyre was given the task of turning it into the UK's first Science Adventure Centre. They took up the challenge and won the 2001 Stirling Prize for their brilliant solution. The vast space inside has been turned into an awesome and inspiring representation of the four elements that go into the steel-making process. The Magna Project tells the story of earth, air, fire and water.*

**Chris Wilkinson:** "This was a very challenging project. We had this huge, redundant steelworks to convert in Rotherham. A building half as big again as the Tate Modern. Seven storeys inside. No windows. In its time it would have been lit up by the blast furnaces, but when we arrived it was big and dark.

"Our task was to transform it into a science adventure centre. It was to be partly educational and partly entertainment - and, indeed, partly historical, since the steelworks represented an important part of the local culture. There had been 10,000 people working in there. It had been the most productive steelworks in the country, and its loss was a huge blow to the local population. Which partly explains, I guess, how the local council managed to secure millennium funding for the conversion.

"But the funding was limited, so to conserve funds we decided to leave the building more or less as it was. We did little to the structure apart from rendering it weatherproof again. And we created four pavilions, representing the four elements.

"The pavilions are accessed by high walkways and bridges. You can stand up there and look down on the steelworks below – and you can see visual representations of what the place was once like.

"The Air Pavilion was made to look like an airship hanging in space. It's very exciting to enter it. Inside, the science of the air (from aerodynamics and wind effects on bridge design to wind instruments) are all represented in interactive displays.

"It's actually a platform suspended in space on beams tied back into the main fabric of the building. The structure appears rather like the Eden Project – inflated fabric cushions, but shaped and floated into aluminium extrusions. Cables hold it in tension and create the cigar shape.

"The Water Pavilion is a stainless-steel lozenge like a submarine or a ship. The form is like an elliptical spiral – fascinating shape. The Earth Pavilion, down in the basement, is made out of steel plate which supports a roof that looks like the Earth's tectonic plates in partial eruption. Inside, it's all about minerals and mining. They've got JCB diggers in there! And the Fire Pavilion is a sort of firebox hanging at the end of the building. Flames shoot from the slots in the form of a fire tornado.

"You get a fantastic sense of power and size from the exhibits. Well, that's what the whole show is all about: something monumental, something vast. Something so much bigger than us. It was great fun to do: letting one's imagination run wild with modern materials. I think it's an experience that can be enjoyed by all ages."

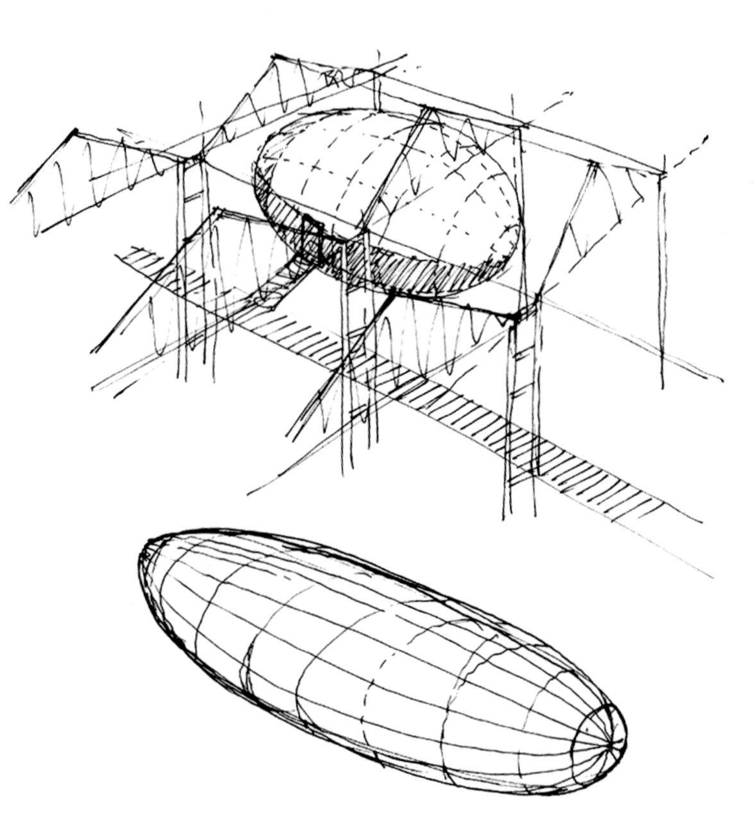


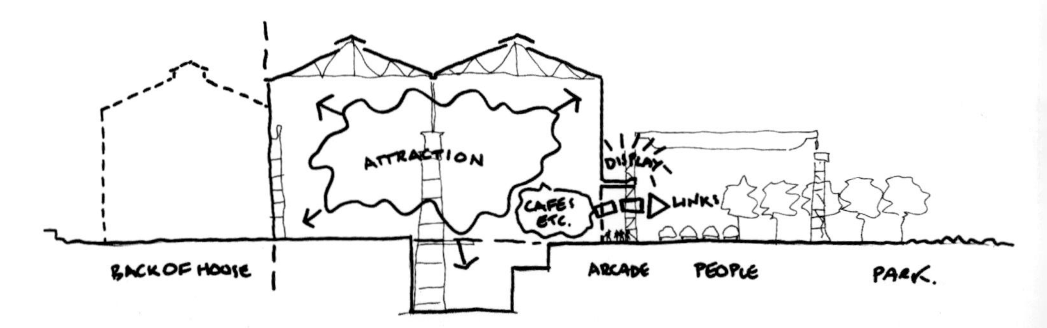

*When publishers Laurence King approached it's 25th birthday as a company and 10th as a publisher, the company felt it was time to update its image. Up to that point it had been known variously as Calmann & King, Calmann & King/Laurence King... It was time for some clarity. And if you want to be bold and clear, who better to turn to than Vince Frost.*

**Vince Frost:**
"I think the problem was people were buying Laurence King books but weren't really aware who had published them.It made sense to enhance the association of those quality books with a memorable name. Strengthening a brand often works to improve business.

"I tried at first to get them to change the name to 'King': 'King would be very strong,' I said. But they felt it would be too much of a departure and just cause further confusion. The word 'King' was quite a temptation to explore. We had all sorts of attempts to pun on the word. We made crowns out of three Ks. But it didn't work. I think I even suggested calling the company 'K' and dropping the 'ing' altogether.

"Meantime I was playing around with ideas for window displays and came up with the big, solid K on its back symbolizing (and indeed supporting) an open book. We created a bookstand for the 10th anniversary. The bookshops all loved it - which makes a pleasant change. Most promotional stuff gets chucked in the bin. I think it worked because it also looked like a universal symbol for bookshops.

"Then I started to play with the wooden K for the catalogue. We used it to illustrate the various sections. So, for example, we'd photograph the K in front of a collection of pictures to illustrate that this was the art section of the catalogue.

"For the book spines, we wanted a typeface that was bold and easy to spot. We didn't want to do anything too fancy or complicated. Spines vary in width. The logo had to work in different colours. It had to be able to work on the spine and stand alone. Usually we write 'Laurence King' under the K, though sometimes the full name has to be dropped for space.

"Laurence says he chose me for this because he likes the way that we do things: all rather simple and bold."

# RACHEL WHITEREAD DAYBED 1999

*Rachel Whiteread is internationally famous for her monumental sculptures, which include* Water Tower *(1998) in New York, the* Holocaust Memorial *(2000) in Vienna, the famous internal casting of a derelict East London house and her work for the empty plinth in London's Trafalgar Square. She's also made a daybed, which she doesn't think is monumental at all.*

**Rachel Whiteread:** "I thought it was interesting to stretch my wings a little bit and start thinking about furniture that can exist in people's homes and not only as sculpture. I was interested in this because it was being done through SCP in East London – a furniture shop I know very well.

"As I started to think about it, the idea that came through was all about space underneath a bed. It was a culmination of two past sculptures.

"I think I drove the company mad because I made six prototypes. I'm very exacting about what I do. It had to be right. I wanted these holes that ran right the way through it – they would originally have been the legs, the underside of the bed. I played with these few elements, aiming to make an aesthetic object.

"I decided to use this particular type of material. I remembered it from the '60s. My parents used to have it on a daybed. It had recently been put back into production. It was made by Bute. The original piece I made was about dust underneath a bed, and this material seemed to reflect that in its colour and its texture – the colour of house-dust.

"I made 10 original pieces which were almost like artworks. Now that it is in production, it has become something else.

"People like it and respond to it, because it is a cross between a sculpture and a piece of furniture. I think it's a place you can pause on. It's not so comfortable that you can lounge around on it for days on end; it's just for relaxing, and reading a newspaper, or having a rest on."

"Well, it doesn't appear monumental to me. I think monumentalism applies more to my other work. You can call *House* monumental, and the piece in Trafalgar Square monumental, but I think you'll be hard-pushed to call a piece of furniture monumental."

WALSALL BUS TERMINAL

*When the RIBA announced a competition to build a new bus terminal for Walsall, architects Alford Hall Monaghan Morris* (pictured below) *saw an opportunity to explore ideas for urban design. The designers took their inspiration from the traffic flow to create a vast roof that sat well with Walsall's townscape.*

**Peter Morris:** "Part of the brief was all about the circulation of buses, so the elliptical shape came naturally out of that. And that immediately showed potential as a powerful idea for creating the roof.

"Walsall has a very fragmented townscape: high buildings, low buildings, narrow, wide, empty, full. We needed a dramatic pure form that could hold its own against such a backdrop. The elliptical form was powerful enough to deal with that. In one sense it's a very alien form, but in fact, it sits there very comfortably.

"We didn't want to just think 'bus station'. We thought: 'There's a bigger idea here!' We believe public transport should be celebrated. So we made it more like an airport or a train station than a bus station. The buses actually drive into it.

"Early plans for the canopy were based around a steel grid. But this changed to a concrete ellipse with a smooth underside. We were actually inspired by the David Niven film *A Matter of Life and Death,* in which you see him staring down from Heaven to Earth through a circular opening in the clouds.

"So we perforated our canopy with such windows on the sky.

"It creates great drama when the light moves and changes through the day. The arrangement of the skylights looks random, but in fact it's all organized to follow the flow of the buses.

"The big roof is the story. The composition is better than I could have imagined. It does everything I hoped it would, and more. It's a big, urban room, framing the townscape. Wonderful, unexpected successes.

"I think we live in a much more fertile business community. People out there are more prepared to take a gamble. That's good news for creativity in this country."

# LONDON MARATHON POSTER

*Alan Kitching established the Typography Workshop in 1989, designing for publishing, advertising and industry. He is now widely regarded as one of the world's leading typographers, a pioneer in his field. He lectures at the Royal College of Art, where he recognizes something special is happening. Overseas students come and then decide to stay and work here. In his own words: "There's something in the air." He was commissioned to create a magazine pull-out for the London Marathon, and used his distinctive style and innovative approach to create a powerful, informative and highly praised graphic-art piece.*

**Alan Kitching:** "Originally, they wanted me to do a map, to show people exactly where the run was going. Maps of the route have been done so many times before, and maps of London are easy to come by. The route zig-zags and doubles back throughout London past a series of internationally famous landmarks. So I said to them: 'Let's do something different.'

"It was to be a four-page spread - over two double pages - like an extended advert. I saw it as a long strip. So I ran a strip of numbers down the side, representing the mileage, rather like a tape measure, which seemed fitting for athletics. The numbers worked to encourage you to turn over the page.

"And I used the landmarks to illustrate the run. It goes by Tower Bridge, Buckingham Palace, Canary Wharf, the Cutty Sark... It became more of a portrait of the run. It even included 'The Wall'. Not the London Wall – the wall you hit at 22 miles: the terrible pain barrier. It's not a conventional map, of course, but it does the same job. As with a map and the landscape it represents, you are guided by landmarks.

"I don't classify myself as a designer; I'm more a typographical artist. I guess my hallmark is the way I produce the image. It's ink on paper, using good old-fashioned metal and wood to print with. It's taken me 10 years to learn how to re-use this old-fashioned technology, but it's worth it. Using hand-pressing techniques makes the image so much more human. It's more akin to painting than modern printing. I often print by using a hand roller rather than a press. Hand, hand, hand in everything I do. As much by hand and eye as possible.

"I created five hand-printed copies as a limited edition. I used my hand press on this job because I had to register the colours exactly, to make them coincide with the image.

"It's a bit like the difference between digital and analogue. Analogue has that human quality that digital currently finds hard to reproduce."

**view from**
thirty five thousand
maniacs.

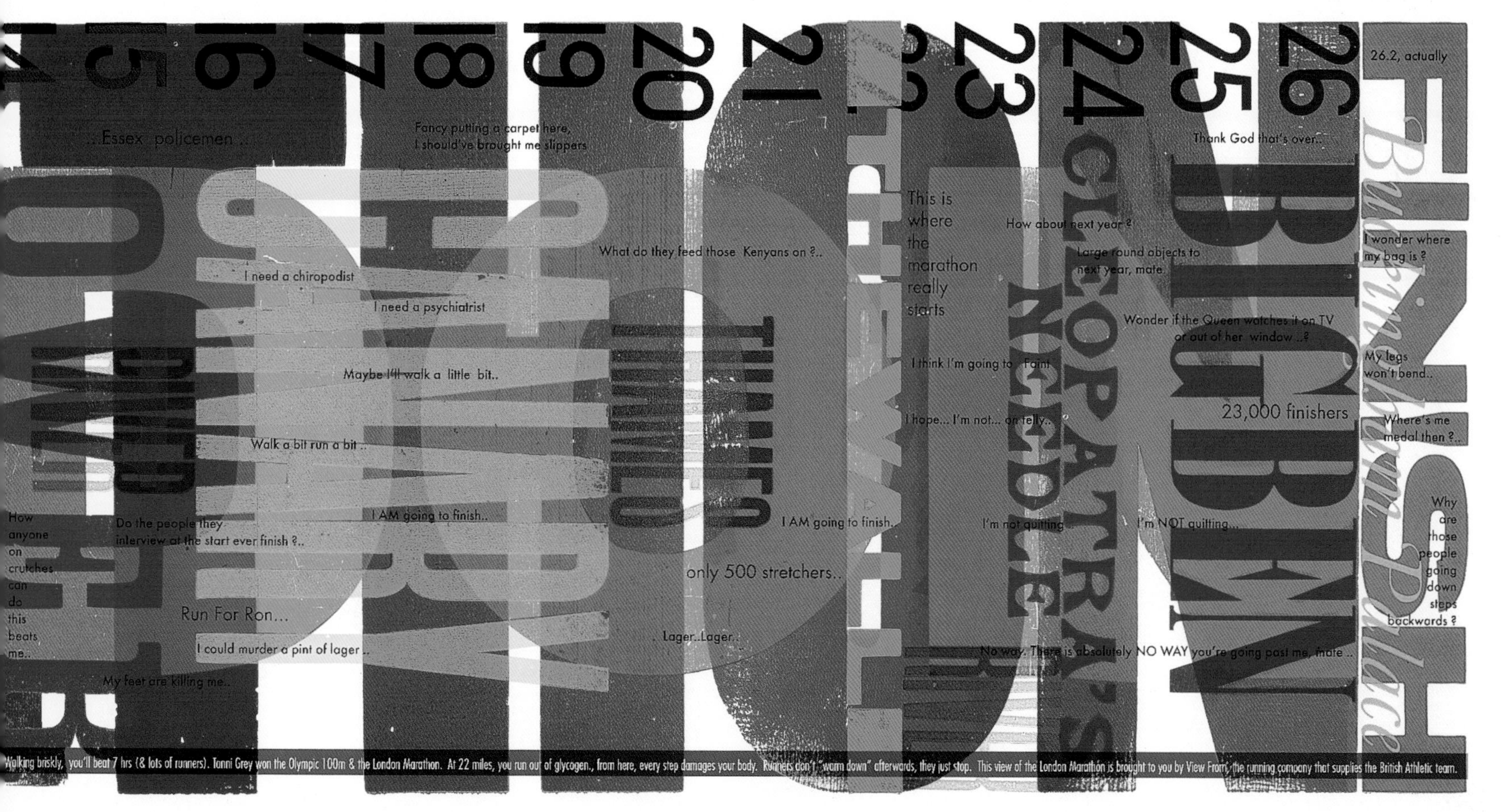


view from.
britain's no.1 running co.

PROJECTIONS

# MINIMAL CUTLERY & SKYHOUSE

*Projections: My final theme looks at work that hasn't happened yet. I asked people who are featured earlier in this book for ideas; dreams; unrealised and yet to be launched projects. The result is a fascinating glimpse of creativity across design disciplines – a look at what could be and, in some cases, what will be. Their response, shown on the following pages, is a gallery of visionary thinking and inspiration.*

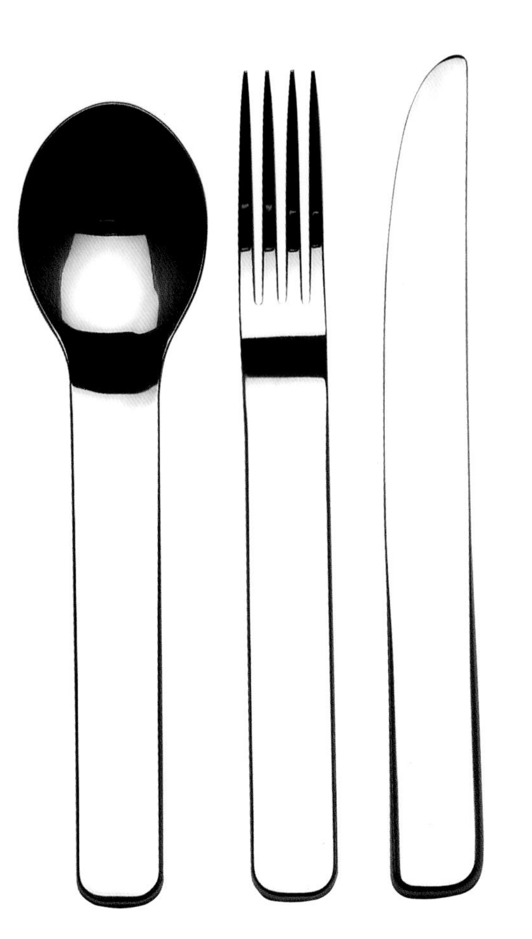

**David Mellor:** "In almost fifty years of cutlery design (yes, 'Pride' was first produced in 1953) I have been hoping one day to arrive at the absolute minimal set made to the finest possible standards – a sort of minimal deluxe.

"I took as the starting point the ultimate flat knife which I considered to be functionally viable. The flat form was then developed in the fork and three spoons, designed ergonomically to cover all requirements: a capacious soup/serving spoon, middle-size dessert spoon and smaller tea/coffee spoon.

"Though so basic in concept I wanted to get away from the idea of functional austerity with this design. The free flowing form in fact is almost sculptural while the weight of the satin polished stainless steel gives this cutlery a very sophisticated look.

"From the initial sketch wood prototypes were made, then metal pre-production prototypes. The project is now at tool-making stage and should be in production in mid 2002."

**Marks Barfield:** "Skyhouse is a proposal to provide well-designed, high-rise, high-density housing. The tenure will be mixed, including shops, crèches, restaurants, health clubs, gardens.
It will also feature community-use 'sky-lobbies'.

"Skyhouse is a cluster of three slender towers of different heights that are connected so they derive structural support from each other.

"A significant proportion will be set aside as affordable housing for people on lower incomes. Alongside these, in proportions that ensure a good social mix, market-value flats for sale and rent will make Skyhouse commercially viable. We are currently looking for a site where there's potential for urban regeneration."

# FREDA SANS & GOOD MORNING WESTMINSTER

**Freda Sack:**
"In type design we are continually searching for the perfect form: a sans serif face for the new age – in the way that Futura was the *zeitgeist* of the early 20th century – and has now become a classic; a typeface with its own life ahead – used to carry ideas and information, giving them new shape and form.

"Future fonts are always part of my thought process – and commissions, especially if they happen to be for a specific use, like the Yellow font, always bring new inspiration, becoming the catalyst for an embryonic idea. Tighter restraints often bring about different ways of thinking and functioning.

"The challenge is finding new relations between ideas and shapes, to create a typeface with a unique character from a seemingly limited number of elements, using creative skills and experience, and arriving at it through insight."

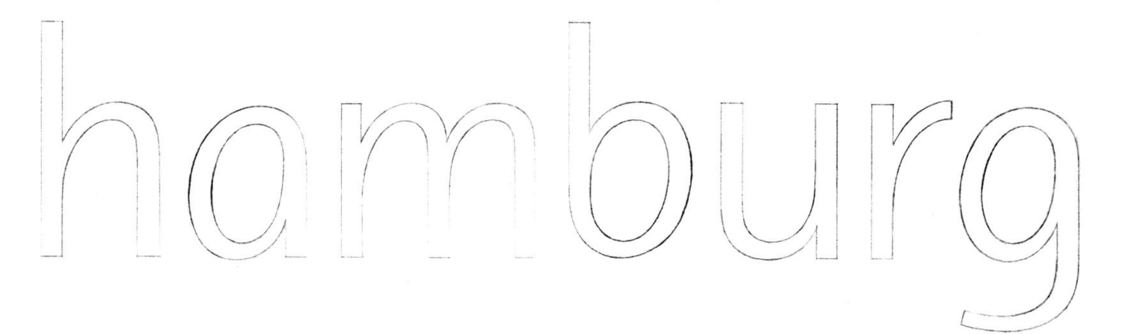

**Ron Arad:**
"This project is designed to sit in a public space in Soho, London, outside a distinctive new building. It is a tall spiral structure, comprising a stainless steel base and a twisted shape above made of pixelboard. The concept behind the sculpture is communication; the pixel board displays text or SMS (short message service) messages that spiral up and away from the base of the sculpture. Messages can be sent from any standard mobile phone and are displayed continually on the pixelboard. 'Good Morning Westminster' complements the building and the Soho location by being both something that is physical, a tall spiral structure, and invisible, the mobile phone network."

# GLASS BRIDGE & FORMULA ONE OF THE FUTURE

**Thomas Heatherwick:** "The world's first bridge made of just glass is an innovative idea that has been developed over the course of five years by the design team. It is a reaction against the fashion for structures claiming to be made from glass but actually constructed with the addition of mechanical fixings and strengthenings.

"The glass bridge consists of a composite beam, made up of forty five 7.2 metre lengths of 20mm glass, spanning the canal. It tapers from a depth of 500mm to just 100mm at its centre, enclosed by tilted glass sides. The surface of the bridge is treated to ensure that it is non-slip. At night the bridge is illuminated by an internal lighting system hidden in the abutments, removing the need for separate external fittings."

**Gordon Murray:** "I was lucky enough to be designing Grand Prix cars for 20 years during a period when the regulations allowed a great deal of lateral thinking and innovation. It was not uncommon to think of an idea, design the part, get it onto the car and go one second a lap faster – all in the matter of a week or so.

"During the eighties and the nineties the regulations put a stranglehold on such innovation and I eventually left the sport in 1989.

"When the publication *Motor Sport* asked me to 'design' the ultimate Formula One car for the new millennium – a vehicle designed with no rules – I was delighted to accept.

"The experience of free-thinking design is a very good exercise for the mind and in retrospect the process of drawing this vehicle helped me enormously in my daily design work."

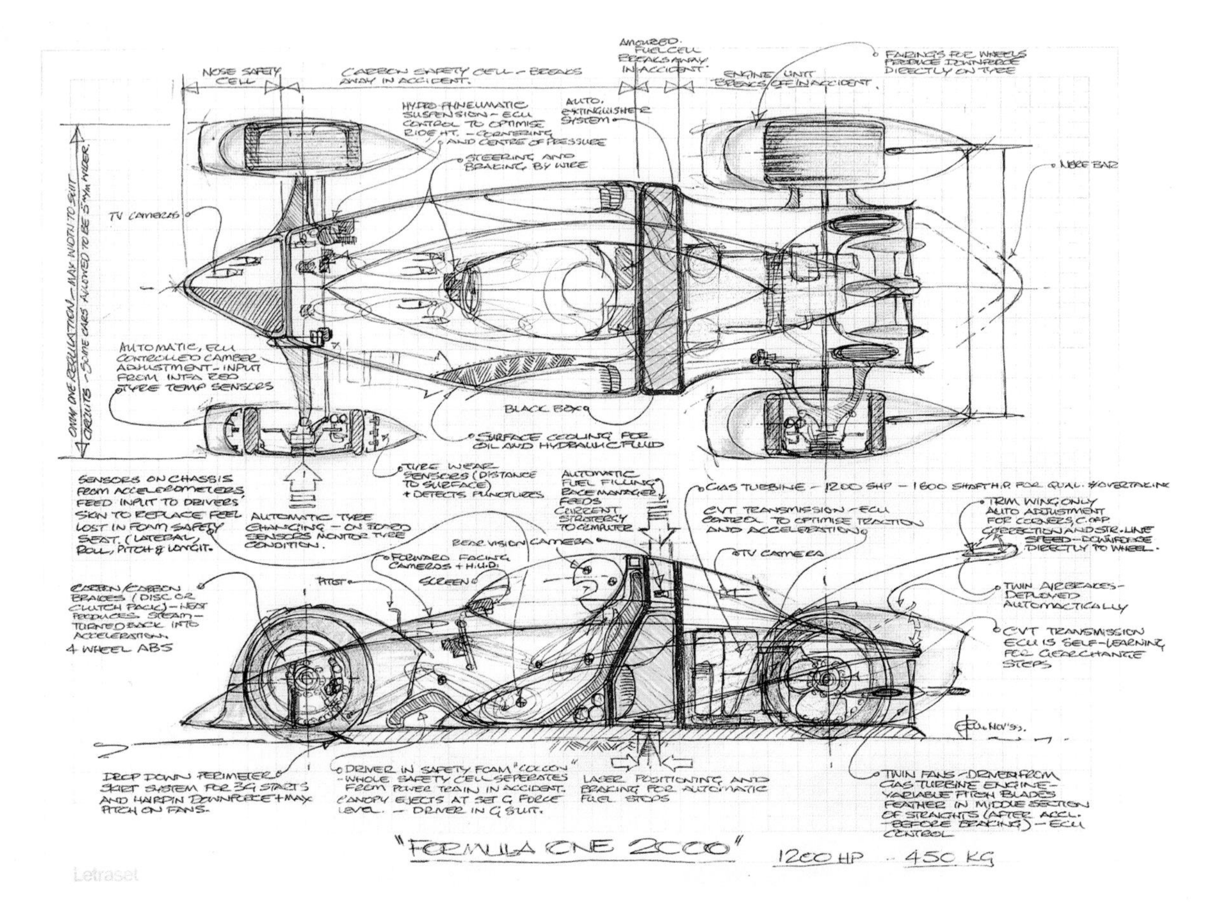

# OVERLAY SCREEN & BATTERSEA POWER STATION

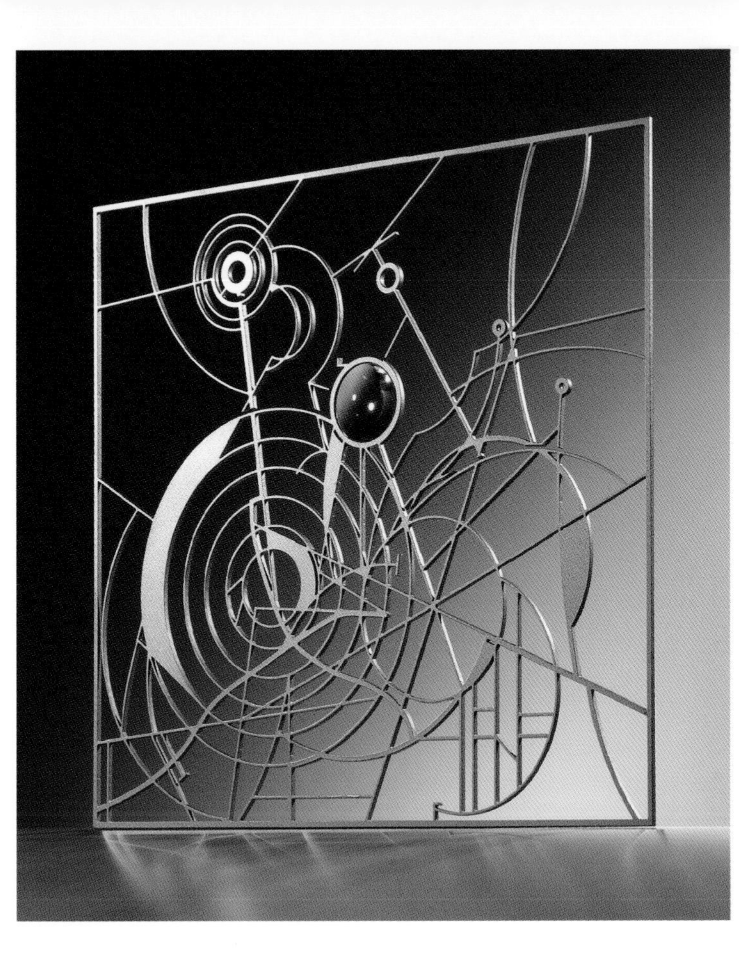

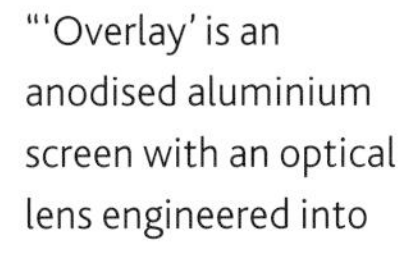

**Wendy Ramshaw:** "'Overlay' is an anodised aluminium screen with an optical lens engineered into its structure. The screen creates a decorative open wall at the edge of a mezzanine in a domestic interior in the Barbican complex, London. There were no restrictions on material or concept.

"The design presented itself in my studio via already existing works lying in a pile of overlapping, intertwined metal parts. A drawing inspired by the random chaos of these curved and formal lines was precisely transferred to computer. The small original pencil drawing was eventually transformed, becoming a huge metal drawing in space."

**Nicholas Grimshaw:** "NGP's design for Battersea Power Station forms part of one of the largest urban regeneration projects in Europe. It comprises the development of fourteen hectares of land on the Thames, with the iconic power station at its heart.

"NGP intends to highlight the landmark building's architectural virtuosity while providing viable proposals for its reuse, to include a mix of entertainment and retail, with a theatre as the principal attraction. In this way it will conclude the South Bank's 'cultural ribbon' made up of the Tate Modern, the South Bank Centre and the BA London Eye. A riverside Jetty, also designed by NGP, will offer Riverbus services to and from the development."

**Norman Foster:** "Designed for the insurance company Swiss Re, this new London building rises 41 storeys and includes offices and a shopping arcade accessed from a new public plaza.

"The diagonally-braced external structure allows column-free floor space and a fully glazed envelope which allows plenty of daylight.

"Each of the floors is rotated with respect to the one below. This allows the spaces between the radiating fingers of each floor to combine to form spiraling light wells. These act like the building's lungs, generating pressure differentials that assist the natural air-flow. The system offers a dramatic reduction in energy consumption."

**Charlie Thomas:** "This is a self-initiated project to create a micro 'homewares collection'. A continued investigation into the production of goods for consumption – a development (a brand-extension) from my foray into paper clothing.

"My consideration was to create objects for the home following the 'chuck out the chintz' campaign. It develops the use of paper into a range of self-assembly clocks and other home accessories made from Italian marbled papers. It also extends my range of materials to include ceramics in an antiquity-inspired collection of decorative and utility slip-cast pieces."

# IRONING BOARD/MIRROR & MEDIA VILLAGE, DUBAI

**Nina Tolstrop:**
"I have always found it a problem to find a suitable place to store an ironing board and a hassle to get it out just for ironing a shirt. So my idea was to create an ironing board that always was at hand and did not take up any extra space. The design that I came up with is an adjustable dressing mirror that in a single hand operation becomes an ironing board. The mirror is in hardened glass and the ironing board is covered with heat resistant silver textile. The base is made of 6mm stainless steel with aluminium castors."

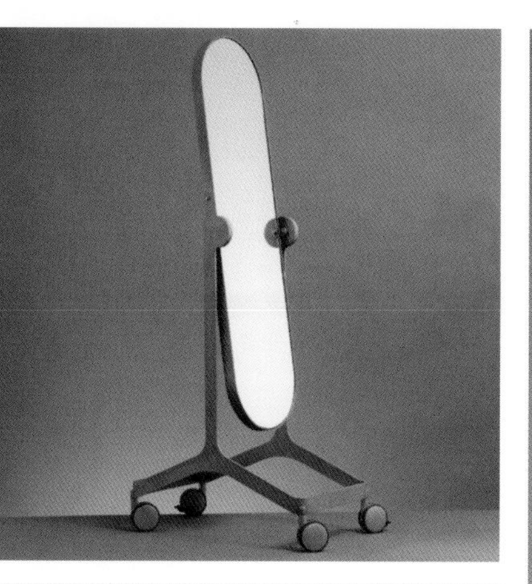

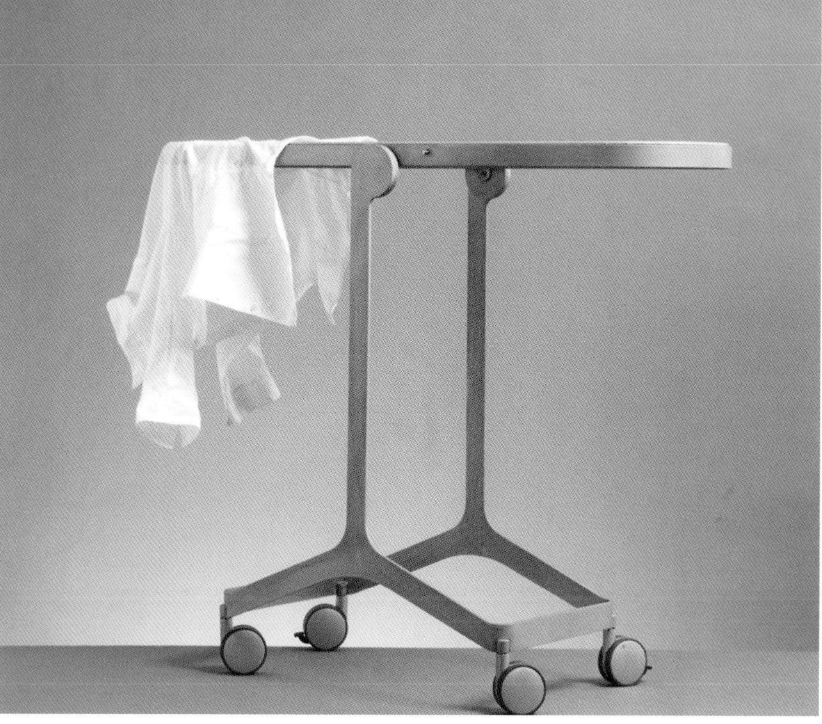

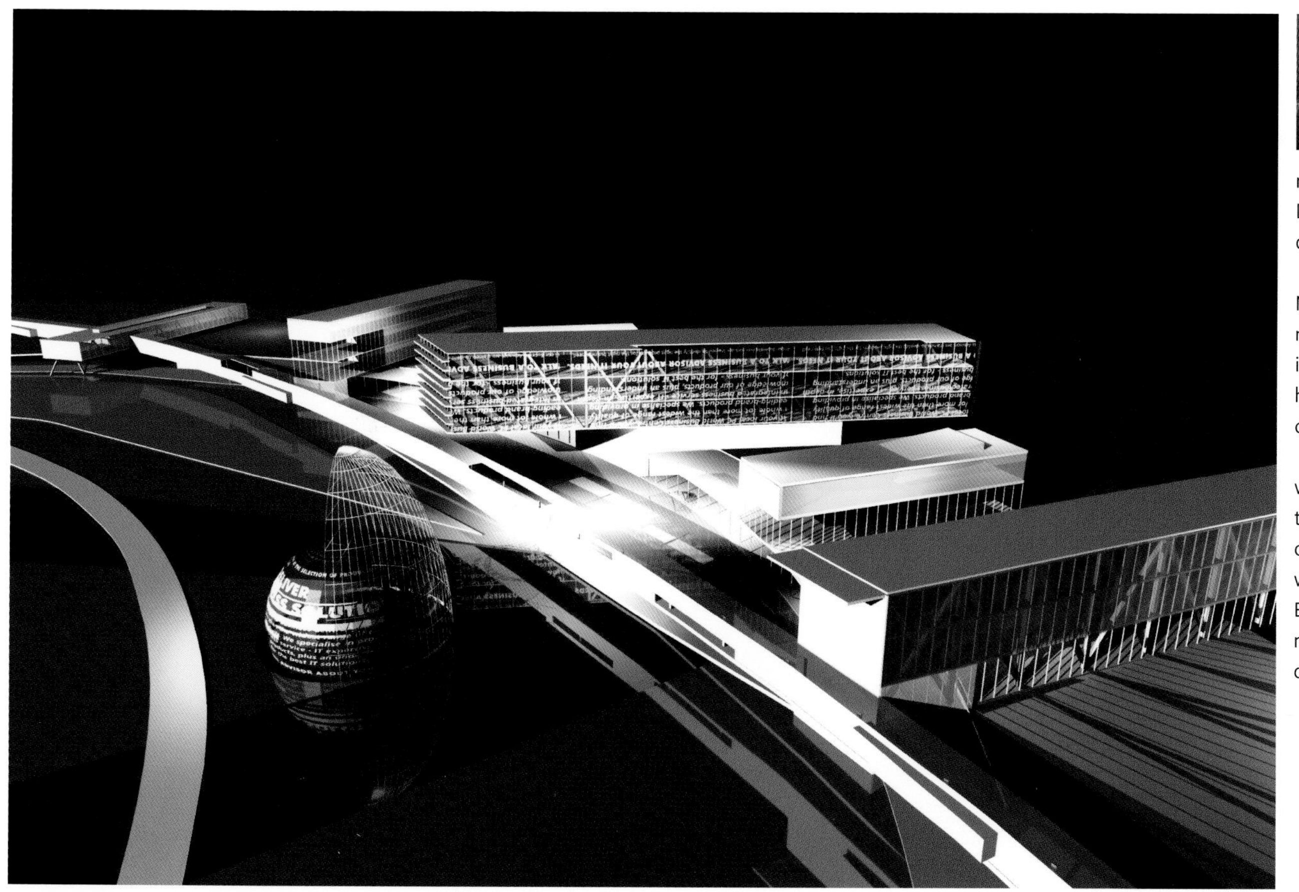

**Tony Kettle:**
"Dubai Internet City provides an infrastructure for the development of the new e-commerce business. Nearby is Dubai Media City catering for all forms of media.

"The link between the two cities is the Media Village, a media shop front and a melting pot for the expression of new ideas and concepts. The buildings are highly flexible, reflecting the transitional quality of new media.

"Buildings are connected via moving walkways. Users are transported through information galleries displaying continuously updated media in the walkways and on surrounding buildings. Each building is juxtaposed against the next at various angles, creating a complex composition."

**Danny Lane:** "*Against the Wall* is a gravity-based installation of scale and simplicity. The work is made from around 1,000 identical planks of glass, 12mm thick, 75mm wide and 4 metres long.

"A rigid stainless steel bar is fixed to the wall and floor, leaning into the wall and away from the composition. The glass planks are then packed face-to-face, forming the sculpture. An undulation/curb keeps the base end of each piece of glass from slipping away from the wall.

"A further development of this work will create a new passageway in Canary Wharf, London, later this year."

**Richard Rogers:** "Richard Rogers Partnership, working with Barcelona-based architect Alonso I. Balaguer, is designing a new urban park in L'Hospitalet, 10 km west of Barcelona. The centrepiece of the urban park is a 26-storey five-star hotel tower providing a striking entry point into Barcelona. There will also be conference centre for 1,800 people, a 400-seat auditorium, a headquarters building for Hespería and a large sports club.

"Construction is scheduled to be complete in spring 2002.The scheme is the latest in a line of urban regeneration projects that helped Barcelona become the first city to win the RIBA Gold Medal."

# IRENA & CENTRE FOR CONTEMPORARY ARTS

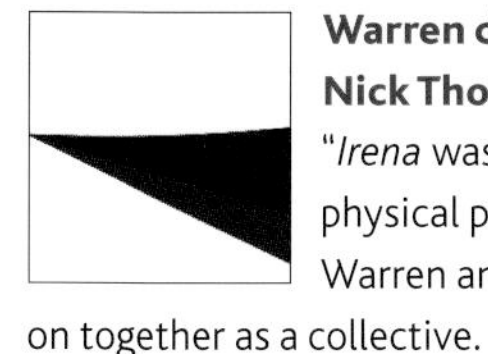

**Warren du Preez & Nick Thornton Jones:** "*Irena* was the first physical piece that Warren and I worked on together as a collective.

"The piece was born out of the need to challenge, deconstruct, discover and rebuild while merging the disciplines of photography and graphic art. *Irena* has an illusory 3D presence rendered on a traditional 2D plan.

"It's an image that needs to live with scale. It's built up of many graphic shapes that once scaled up become an interesting landscape of shape and form."

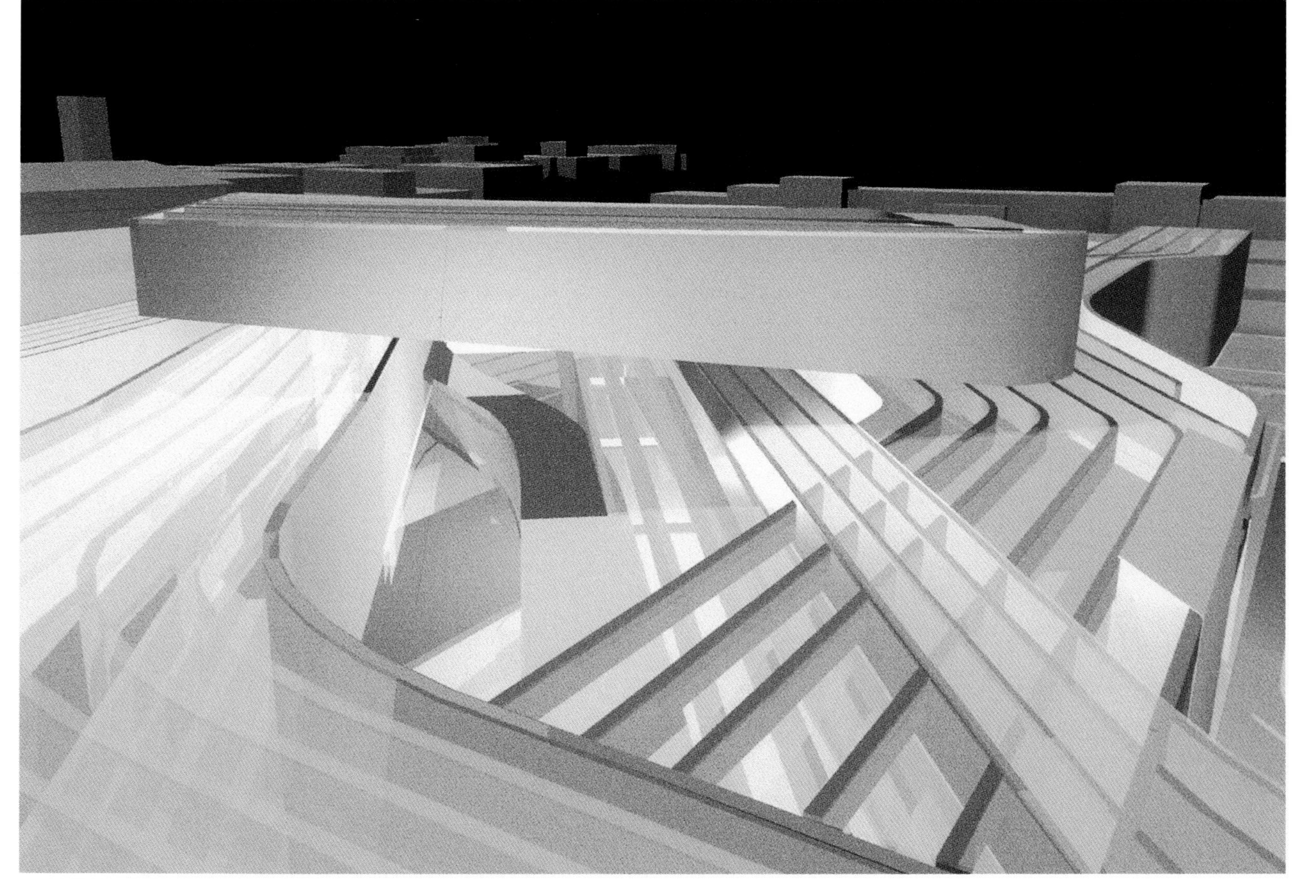

**Zaha Hadid:** The Rome Centre for Contemporary Arts addresses its urban context by recognising and reacting to the former army barracks, acting more like an 'urban graft', a second skin to the site. By intertwining the circulation with the urban context, the building shares a public dimension with the city, through its overlapping, tendril-like paths and open space.

The Centre is porous and immersive - a field space. It moves away from the object-oriented gallery, instead putting the notion of 'drift' into architectural form. Drifting thus emerges as both architectural motif and navigational aid. Constantly-changing geometry and wall space works to liberate the curator.

# INDEX

# CREDITS

**The author and publisher would like to thank the designers and manufacturers who submitted work for inclusion, and the following photographers and copyright holders for the use of their material:**

**7** ©Nancy Honey
**12-13** (below left and right) ©Aston Martin Lagonda
**16** all images ©Burberry Ltd
**17** (left) Mike Abrahams/Network
**20** (above left) ©Yukio Futagawa, (below left) ©Visium/Rudi Meisel, (below right) ©Copyright The British Museum
**21** Nigel Young/Foster and Partners
**22** (left) ©Keen Group and others, (below left) Archive of Robin and Lucienne Day
**24** (above left) ©Adrian Gatie/ Derek Birdsall 2001
**25** Alan Batham
**28** (left) Neil Wilder/IPG
**29** ©Philip Vile courtesy of Branson Coates, 1999
**32** (above left) Udo Hesse, (below left) ©Peter Cook/View
**32-33** (below) ©Peter Cook/View
**33** (above) ©NGP
**34** (above) Maxine Law (below) Ozwald Boateng/Showroom, design and artwork Kevin Allison
**35** Etienne Bol
**36-37** all images ©Keen Group and others
**39** (above left) Richard Davies, (below left) ©Dennis Gilbert/View, (below far right) ©Roderick Coyne
**40-41** ©Dennis Gilbert/View
**42-43** ©Roderick Coyne
**44** (above left) Grant Smith, (above right) ©Richard Rogers Partnership, (below) ©Mike Goldwater/Network PIctures
**45** (above left) Paul Constant, (above right) Bob Cramp, (below) Bob Cramp
**46** ©Dennis Gilbert/View
**47** (far left) ©Yukio Futagawa, (below left) ©Wolff Olins 2001
**50** (above left) Sandro Sodano
**51** Alan Batham
**55** (above left) ©Bernie Reid @ Creative Union, (far right) Nova Story: art illustration by Bernie Reid @ CreativeUnion.co.uk, photography by Andy Shaw, styling by Beca Lipscombe, Thanks to all involved
**58** Alan Batham
**59** (above left) ©Gautier Leblond, (below left) Alan Batham, (above right) Matthew Stuart
**63** (above right) 'Spiritualized, Ladies and gentleman we are floating in space', packaging shot ©Farrow Design, (below) 'Spiritualized, Ladies and gentlemen we are floating in space', album packaging ©Farrow Design/J Spaceman
**66-67** (main image) ©Richard Leeney
**68** (above left) Karen Hatch, (below left) Charlie Thomas
**70** (above right and left) James Clarke
**71** all images James Clarke
**74** (above left) Julian Hawkins, (below left) Julian Hawkins, (above far right) ©2001 Aardman Animations Ltd
**75** ©2001 Aardman/W&G Ltd
**76-77** (main image) Tim Douglas
**77** James Harris
**80** (above far left) ©Quentin Blake, (left and below) ©Crown copyright 2000, designed by Atelier Works, cartoon illustrations by Quentin Blake, the Children's Laureate
**88** (above right) Mathieu Pernot, (below right) Adam Broomberg & Oliver Chanarin
**89** (above left) Stefano Montesi, (middle left) Stephen Gill, (above right) Adam Broomberg & Oliver Chanarin, (middle right) Adam Broomberg & Oliver Chanarin
**93** Chris Moore
**96** (above left) James Cant, (right) ©Wilkinson Eyre Architects
**97** (above and below) ©Nick Guttridge/ View
**97-98** ©Wilkinson Eyre Architects
**100** (above) Charles Glover, (below) Steve Speller
**101** Steve Speller
**103** (right, above and below) ©Studiomama.com, photo Richard Davies
**104** (above left and above right) Dan Stevens, (below right) ©Katsushisa Kida
**105** ©Katsushisa Kida
**106** (below right and below far right) ©Christopher Moore Ltd.
**107** ©Christopher Moore Ltd.
**109** all images ©Wilfred Hösl Fotograf, David Auden (director)
**110-111** ©Wilfred Hösl Fotograf, David Auden (director)
**112** Eve Racine and Barbara Metz
**114** (below right) ©2001 Matt Laver Photography, all other images ©RMJM Scotland Ltd.
**115** ©RMJM Scotland Ltd.
**116-117** ©RMJM Scotland Ltd.
**126** (below far right) Colin Campbell
**127** Stuart Haygarth
**128** ©Rolls-Royce Plc
**130** ©Warren du Preez & Nick Thornton-Jones
**131** ©Warren du Preez & Nick Thornton-Jones
**132** ©Chris Gascgoine/View
**133** (above right) Fletcher Priest Architects, (below left) ©Chris Gascgoine/View, (above right) Charles Glover, (below right) Steve Speller
**134-135** Steve Speller
**137** (above) Perry Hagopian, (below) ©Ron Arad 1998, photo Wilhelm Moser
**141** ©Jim Henson Company
**142** ©Alexander McQueen 2001
**144** (above left) ©John Pawson 2001, (below left) ©John Pawson 2001, photo Richard Davies
**145** ©John Pawson 2001, photo Richard Davies
**146** (above left) Brigitte Bouillot
**147** ©Lyndon Douglas
**148** (right) ©Vitra Ltd., photo Hans Hansen
**150** (above) Ed Reeve, (below) Nick Gutteridge
**151** Jean Marc
**153** ©Richard Bryant
**154** (left and below right) *Paper Jewellery*, Thames and Hudson 2000, (above far right) Paul Constant
**155** Sara Morris
**160** (above left) Richard Holttum
**161** ©Mike Hoban Photography
**162** ©Victoria and Albert Museum 1994, image: Ken Jackson
**163** (left) Peter Wood, (above right) ©Marks Barfield Architects, (below right) The British Airways London Eye: conceived and designed by Marks Barfield Architects
**164-165** The British Airways London Eye: conceived and designed by Marks Barfield Architects, photo ©Nick Wood 2001
**168** (above left) Justin Chan, (below far right) ©Judith Burrows
**169** ©Judith Burrows
**170** (above left) Charles Glover, all other images Alan Batham
**171** (above) Andrew Putler, (below) ©Chris Gascgoine/View
**172-173** ©Chris Gascgoine/View
**174** ©Box Architects
**175** (centre) ©Atelier Works, photo Alan Batham (above right) Ben Kirchner
**176** Keith Collie
**177** (above and below) Keith Collie
**180** (right) Alan Reevell, (below left) ©Helen Storey, photo Jason Loewe
**180** Piero Baision
**182** (below far left) ©Hélène Binet Photographer, all other images ©Zaha Hadid Office
**183** ©Airdiasol/Roger Rothan
**186** (top right, right, below right) Alan Batham
**187** Alan Batham
**188** (left) James Cant, (right, above and below) ©Wilkinson Eyre Architects
**189** ©Wilkinson Eyre Architects, photo: Morley Von Sternberg
**190-191** ©Wilkinson Eyre Architects, photo: Benedict Luxmoore
**192-193** all images ©Frost Design, photography Dean Hollowood
**194** (above left) Chris Tubbs, image courtesy of Projects Art Consultancy
**194-195** Chris Tubbs, image courtesy of Projects Art Consultancy
**196** (above left) Matthew Chisnall
**197** Timothy Soar
**198** (above) Gillian Cargill
**198-199** (below) Client: View From...(Sportswear), Agency: Grey Advertising, 1996, image: Alan Kitching c/o Debut Art
**202** (below left and right) ©Marks Barfield Architects
**203** (below right) Perry Hagopian, (below left) ©Ron Arad Associates 2001
**204** (above right) Charles Glover
**205** (above left) Graham Pym, (above right) Paul Constant, (below left) Udo Hesse, (below right) ©www.smoothe.co.uk
**206** (above left) ©Richard Davies/ Foster Visualisation, (above right) Yukio Futagawa, (below left) Karen Hatch,
**207** (above right) ©STUDIOMAMA.COM, photo: Richard Davies, (below left and right) ©RMJM Scotland Ltd
**208** (above left) Peter Wood, (below right) Dan Stevens, (below left) ©Richard Rogers Partnership
**209** (above left and right) ©Warren du Preez & Nick Thornton-Jones, (below left and right) ©Zaha Hadid Office.
**back flap** ©Nancy Honey

**Costal Photographs around Great Britain:**

**1** Corfe Castle Estate, Dorset: the pinnacles glowing orange taken from near Old Harry Rocks, ©National Trust Photographic Library/Joe Cornish
**10-11** View of the foreshore at Formby Point, Merseyside, ©National Trust Photographic Library/Joe Cornish
**30-31** Brandcaster Harbour, Norfolk, ©National Trust Photographic Library/Paul Wakefield
**48-49** St David's Head, Dyfed, South Wales, ©National Trust Photographic Library/Geoff Morgan
**72-73** The Rumps, Cornwall, ©National Trust Photographic Library/Joe Cornish
**94-95** View of Countisbury Cove, Devon, ©National Trust Photographic Library/Paul Wakefield
**118-119** Eastern Shore of Strangford Lough near Killinchy, Northern Ireland, ©National Trust Photographic Library/ Joe Cornish
**138-139** The Gower Coast from Thurba Head, West Glamorgan, ©National Trust Photographic Library/Joe Cornish
**158-159** Lizard Peninsula, looking over Kynance Cove, ©National Trust Photographic Library/Mike Williams
**178-179** Staple Island on the Farne Islands, Northumberland, ©National Trust Photographic Library/Joe Cornish
**200-201** St. Abb's Head, Scotland, Reproduced by kind permission of the National Trust for Scotland/photo Glyn Satterley
**216** White Cliffs of Dover, Kent, ©National Trust Photographic Library/Stuart Chorley.

**Typeface**
The typeface used throughout this book is Bliss, designed by Jeremy Tankard.